# POSITIVE RELIGION
# IN A REVOLUTIONARY TIME

# POSITIVE RELIGION IN A REVOLUTIONARY TIME

BY

## Eric C. Rust

THE WESTMINSTER PRESS

PHILADELPHIA

STANDARD BOOK No. 664–24890–X

LIBRARY OF CONGRESS CATALOG CARD No. 78–90782


Acknowledgment is made to Harper & Row, Publishers, Inc., for permission to use quotations from the following:

Friedrich Schleiermacher, *On Religion: Speeches to Its Cultured Despisers*, tr. by John Oman. Copyright © 1958 by Harper & Row, Publishers, Inc. Ludwig Feuerbach, *The Essence of Christianity*, tr. by George Eliot. 1957.

Published by The Westminster Press ®
Philadelphia, Pennsylvania

PRINTED IN THE UNITED STATES OF AMERICA

TO

DAVID

MARGARET AND JOSEPH

CHRISTINE AND KENNETH

# *CONTENTS*

# PREFACE

THIS BOOK has arisen out of the present preoccupation with secularity and "religionless Christianity." That the age of secularity is on us, none of us would dispute. It is, however, a debatable issue whether this means the end of religion in the best sense of that much abused word. I have sought, therefore, to ask what Bonhoeffer meant in the enigmatic statements contained in his prison letters and to ask what formative forces lie behind the statements he made, especially the theological outlook of the nineteenth and early twentieth centuries. It has seemed to me for some time that the religious thinkers from Schleiermacher on were asking the right questions and not finding satisfactory answers. In the last century, the forces that make for secularity were well advanced and the issues were becoming clear. Theories of projection and relativism were matched by an increasing emphasis on immanentism and an attempt to safeguard mystery and transcendence. It was increasingly recognized that, if the Christian religion was to be meaningful, it must be concerned with the secular. At the end of this period stand the two figures of Barth and Tillich. Barth's "Nein" would put an end to all questioning and stand man under the divine Word, although his later thought began to open the door to a wider perspective. Tillich clung to the description "religion" for Christianity despite the clamor of Barthian disciples and, toward the end of his influential career as teacher, held that Christian theologizing needs to be set in the history of religions. In his method of correlation he sought to maintain the questioning of his nineteenth-century predecessors, to which Barth had given the quietus. Now, in the post-Barthian period, the same questions are facing us again. What does it mean

to be theonomous man in a secular age? Is religion outmoded?
Thus the issues are raised once more of the nature of the religious
consciousness, of the validity of describing Christianity as a religion, and of the relation of Christianity to other world religions.
It is in this setting that we must understand and answer the statements of Bonhoeffer.

I have sought in the two closing chapters to look at contemporary critics of "religious" Christianity and to define the kind of
transformation that the religious expression of Christianity needs
to undergo in meeting the challenge of a secular age. Thereby I
have endeavored to accept the criticisms but also to preserve the
values of the religious dimension of the Christian faith for our
time. It would seem that there are two live options before us—to
identify Christianity with secularity and to hope that secular man,
depersonalized and alienated, will meet God in his secular condition, *or* to see the church as a worshiping community that makes
people aware of the transcendent presence in the midst of life and
teaches them to see the secular as always the possibility of the
sacramental when faith opens their blind eyes. Personally, I am
opting for the second alternative.

In the preparation of this book I am indebted to my friends
and colleagues Dean Penrose St. Amant, Profs. Glenn Hinson and
David Mueller for help, criticism, and encouragement. This
would be a far inferior work but for them, although the imper-
fections that remain rest on my shoulders. Mrs. Glenn Hinson has
performed as skillfully as ever in deciphering and typing my
manuscript. Mr. Manfred Grellert, my graduate fellow, has helped
by critically reading the manuscript and preparing the index. To
my wife, as so often before, I express my appreciation for encouragement and fellowship as the book has taken shape. I have dedi-
cated the book to my son and my daughters and their husbands,
who have been a constant joy across the years.

E. C. R.

*Southern Baptist Theological Seminary*
*Louisville, Kentucky*

# I

## *Religion and the Secular Order*

THE PROPHETIC INSIGHTS of Bonhoeffer have often been taken out of their context and misapplied, yet the insights remain and the situation that he envisaged is now upon us. We find ourselves in a world that is increasingly becoming secularized and detached from any religious and specifically Christian reference. As modern science has increasingly taken over the areas of human life that at one time were the province of religion, the relevance of religion in general and of Christianity in particular to man's existence has correspondingly lessened.

It would seem as if Comte's analysis of human history is proving prophetic. This father of sociology declared that human history had passed through the theological and metaphysical stages and was about to enter the final and positivistic stage. In the two earlier stages, man had been concerned with questions about God and final causes. His answers had respectively taken the religious forms of myth and symbol and the philosophical structures of rational speculation. Now, with the advent of science, religion and metaphysics were superseded. No longer would man ask questions about the metempirical. He would be concerned with controlling his life by the methods that science provided and that would mean a positivistic preoccupation with the sensible, with what could be empirically observed and ordered. Abstract speculation and mythological creations that deal with what can not be empirically verified could have no place in a scientific society, and this meant the end of religion. Science could deal at its own level far more successfully with the issues that hitherto had turned men's eyes to their gods. It is significant, however, that despite all his protestations, Comte spent his last years promulgating a new religion of humanity, of which the scientists would be the priests and of which the cultic rituals were shaped on those of the Catholic Church. For man is such that religion springs eternal in the human breast!

But there are, today, many who would dispute this last statement in the light of the contemporary scene. They take certain *obiter dicta* of Bonhoeffer and apply them to their own condition. In his last letters, the German theologian and church leader wrote:

Our whole nineteen-hundred-year-old Christian preaching and theology rest on the "religious *a priori*" of mankind. "Christianity" has always been a form—perhaps the true form—of "religion." But if one day it becomes clear that this *a priori* does not exist at all, but was a historically conditioned and transient form of human self-expression, and if therefore man becomes radically religionless—and I think that that is already more or less the case. . . . What does that mean for "Christianity"? [1]

And again:

Man has learnt to deal with himself in all questions of importance without recourse to the "working hypothesis" called "God." In questions of science, art, and ethics this has become an understood thing at which one now hardly dares to tilt. But for the last hundred years or so it has also become increasingly true of religious questions; it is becoming evident that everything gets along without "God"—and, in fact, just as well as before. As in the scientific field, so in human affairs generally, "God" is being pushed more and more out of life, losing more and more ground.[2]

In these statements we find two affirmations—that religion is not a universal and constituent element in man's nature and that this fact is becoming increasingly evident as secularization of life proceeds at every level. There is the further implication that "Christianity" has been mistakenly identified as a form of religion and that we shall need to free "Christianity" from this involvement if we are to speak to secularized society. Hence we find Bonhoeffer calling for a "non-religious interpretation" of Christianity and speaking about "religionless Christianity." [3]

Immediately certain questions are raised. The first is how Bonhoeffer is employing the word "religion." The second is the issue of the universality of the religious response. The third is how he applies his understanding of religion to Christianity. When we have considered these issues we shall endeavor, in the following chapters, to examine the views of religion to which Bonhoeffer was heir in the Protestant tradition since and including Schleiermacher. Thereby we shall endeavor to formulate some understanding of the nature of religion and of the Christian faith. This will lead to a discussion of the place of Christianity in relation to world religions and finally to an examination of the significance of Christianity in a secular age and of the truth in Bonhoeffer's statements.

## Bonhoeffer on "Religion" and the "Religious A Priori"

Bonhoeffer, as a student, was under the influence of teachers such as Seeberg who accepted the reality of a religious *a priori*. It was a common idea among certain Protestant thinkers of the nineteenth century that, constituent in man, was a capacity to be directly aware of and comprehend the divine. It was held that there must be that in man which made it possible for him to grasp the divine disclosure. Bonhoeffer defines such an *a priori* as a mold into which the divine disclosure could be poured.[4] There has to be in man an organ that makes it possible for God to enter the human consciousness. This capacity is provided by the religious *a priori*. Seeberg had been careful to emphasize that such a religious *a priori* had no content of its own. He regarded it as an intrinsic capacity, whereby man could become aware of the transcendent Presence and receive the content of the divine revelation.[5]

Bonhoeffer rejected this idea as inconsonant with his own understanding of the theology of the Word. He argued that it made revelation identical with religion. For him, faith was the work of God. The *a priori* might hold of natural religiosity, but it certainly did not hold of faith. God created faith in the believer, and there was no ability to "hear" the Word before the actual hearing. He therefore put a complete hiatus between Christian faith and natural religion which he regarded as belonging to the flesh. The personal appropriation of the Christ has no *a priori* rootage but arises out of the absolute freedom of the divine activity in disclosure.[6] On Bonhoeffer's view, any suggestion of idealistic-transcendentalism must be rejected, and he acknowledges at this point his dependence on Barth, as well as maintaining that he stands in the Lutheran heritage.[7]

It is evident from this that Bonhoeffer would regard religion, however and wherever expressed, as of the flesh, as belonging to the human sphere and, of itself, bearing no marks of divine revelation. Here he once for all rejects the position of his mentor, Seeberg. How, then, does he define religion? This question is so central to Bonhoeffer's thought, especially in his prison letters, that we must endeavor to answer it. Yet it is very difficult to arrive at an exact statement. We must remember that Bonhoeffer so often is concerned with the form that Christianity has assumed because, as he thinks, it has been given a religious dress. Hence an understanding of what he means by religion is bound up with the "religious" expression of Christianity in the past nineteen centuries. He can even suggest, as we have already seen, that Christian preaching and theology have so far rested upon the "religious premise" of man and that the pattern of religion, possibly the true pattern, has been Christianity in this form.[8]

Allowing for his view that Christianity, as so often expressed hitherto, is a paradigm of "religion," we can understand Bonhoeffer's indication of the characteristics of religion in his prison letters. Two of these to which he refers several times are the individualistic and the metaphysical aspects of religion. By individualistic (and remember his Christian reference!) he means a preoccupation with personal salvation. As Bethge has put it, "the religious man is preoccupied with himself and his interior states in such a way as to forget his neighbour, even though this individualism may take ascetic and apparently self-sacrificial forms." [9] Man concentrates in religion upon his own personal problems—the issues of guilt, personal frustration, spiritual well-being, death.[10]

By the metaphysical aspect of religion, Bonhoeffer seems to be implying that religion is a structure in which, as in metaphysics, man centers his system in himself and brings in God and the supernatural to complete his picture of reality.[11] God is the answer to man's questionings, the solution of his insoluble problems. He is the *deus ex machina*, a working hypothesis at the boundaries where human weakness and human ignorance become evident, a "stop-gap for the incompleteness of our knowledge." [12] Religious people are always anxiously seeking to make room for God as human ingenuity overcomes some human weakness or human intelligence fills up the gaps which our ignorance has left. Thus Bonhoeffer declares that speech about God so often arises where available human knowledge and resources are inadequate to meet the situation. He adds: "It always seems to me that we are trying anxiously in this way to reserve some space for God." [13]

In this sense it is clear that for Bonhoeffer "religionless Christianity" is bound up with the issue of the divine transcendence. God's transcendence is not a "beyondness" to our cognitive faculties. He is not the God at the boundaries of our ignorance and weakness but the "beyond" in the midst of our knowledge and strength. Bethge suggests, indeed, that a third characteristic of "religion" is that the deity is envisaged as a being who periodically invades the "world" from "beyond" in order to help his children surmount their difficulties. Hence we have Bonhoeffer's description of religion's God as a *deus ex machina*.

At this point, we need to note the kind of definition of "religion" that seems to emerge. Evidently Bonhoeffer thinks of religion in terms of what he calls a "working hypothesis" or a "stop-gap." We have already quoted [14] the passage in which he notes that the process of secularization has freed science, ethics, and art from the idea of God as a "working hypothesis" and that it may well be that the questions with which religion deals may also not need such a hypothesis. He suggests that, in the case of death, suffering, and guilt, "it is now possible to find, even for these questions, human answers that take no account whatever of God." He continues: "In point of fact, people deal with these questions without God (it has always been so), and it is simply not true to say that only Christianity has the answers to them." [15] He attacks the theologian's use of existentialist philosophy and the techniques of psychotherapy and their employment by secular enthusiasts to demonstrate to apparently happy, healthy, and vigorous man that he is actually evil, sick, and in despair. He believes that the ordinary man is not affected by such an attempt to penetrate his "bourgeois complacency." Satisfied with his own modicum of happiness he has no inclination to indulge in existential despair and to look for trial and calamity where they are, at least superficially, absent.[16]

It would appear that Bonhoeffer is prepared to define "religion" as the attempt to supplement reality with God.[17] We shall see, in the course of our study, that this idea goes back to Feuerbach. At this point it will suffice to note certain deficiencies in such an approach. First of all, let us note that Bonhoeffer pays little, if any, attention to the religious experience of humanity as a whole. In confining himself to Christianity, he has undoubtedly put his finger upon some weaknesses in historical expressions of the Christian faith. It is true that Christians have made use of God, dragged him in to fill up the deficiencies in their own control of their lives and of the world. Still more would this be true of other religions. But to make this an all-embracing characteristic of religion is to ignore the testmony of the religious consciousness at all levels. There seems little doubt that Bonhoeffer has been strongly influenced by Barth and is prepared to write off the word "religion" as describing a purely man-made structure having nothing to do with revelation.

In the second place, all religions lay claim to some degree of revelation. In other words they have a relational structure. However much the human imagination and creativity may contribute to the patterned expressions of the world's religions, they all have a basic sense of being related to an ultimate reality "beyond" man himself, a reality that has laid hold of man and disclosed something of itself to him—in a legal or moral code, a prophetic teaching, a mystic experience, a personal presence. Christianity too lays claim to revelation, and the nature of this revelation is its distinctive feature. On such a basis, we have no right to uphold its uniqueness by postulating a complete dichotomy between it and other faiths, so that the word "religion" is not in reality applicable to it. It may be remembered that in Fielding's *Tom Jones*, the Rev. Mr. Thwackum is made to say: "When I mention religion, I mean the Christian religion; and not only the Christian religion, but the Protestant religion; and not only the Protestant religion, but the Church of England." [18] One has the feeling that theology is guilty of similar arrogance, the more so when, with Karl Barth and those whom he has influenced, it even refuses the description "religion" as applicable to the Christian faith. We must return to this discussion later.

In the third place, Bonhoeffer's description of religion would seem to be overly intellectual. It is often reduced to a mode of thinking, a deceased mode because it is a human effort at the boundary of man's unsolved problems. We catch little acknowledgment of the emotional and volitional aspects that are present in all religious experience. The very relational nature of religion is indicated by the elements of gratitude, awe and adoration, the sense of the presence of mystery and of reality that transcends normal sense experience. Again we must develop this later, but it needs to be remembered that religion in its manifold expressions is not an attempt of man to project deity as a "working hypothesis" at the intellectual and moral boundaries of his existence. Man's religious *response* (and note my italics!) is generally much more than regarding God as a "working hypothesis" and indulging in the solution of our intellectual and moral problems on such a basis.

In the fourth place, Bonhoeffer's description of religion as individualistic is only partially true. His criticism actually centers in Protestant pietism with its concern for personal salvation, its emphasis on conscience and its reduction of life to a moral battlefield with a strict Puritan ethic. Hence he attacks the interior-centered man whose life is torn apart by moral conflicts and calls for a whole man in whom the action and intention are bound together. He notes that the Biblical viewpoint regards the "heart" as the whole man in relation to God and not to just the inward life.[19] What he says specifically of Protestant pietism, he applies to "religion" in general. Now it is true that the world's religions fall into groups that are often defined as world-affirming and world-denying. Bonhoeffer's defining characteristic is applicable to the latter, but it does not apply totally to the former, especially the historical religions—Judaism, Zoroastrianism, and Islam. These religions place a marked emphasis upon the moral aspect of life and show a concern for other persons. It is true that they, with all other religions, are concerned with some form of individual salvation and place an emphasis on individual piety, the relation of the individual to the deity, yet they also have a concern with the life of man in this world. Furthermore, while in all religions there has been overmuch concern with the boundary situation of death and with the attainment of some otherworldly status, be it in terms of heaven or nirvana, it also needs to be remembered that, in their best moments, the world's faiths have been creative centers in the formation of man's cultural life and have profoundly affected his social structure. The last influence has not always been to man's betterment, as, for example, the caste system of India, yet it would be false to class all religions under the rubric of individualism with a corresponding lack of personal and social concern. Many instances could be cited of the revolutionary impact of Christianity upon the social order, but then we could hardly use these since Bonhoeffer would presumably have contended that these demonstrate that the Christian faith never has been essentially "religion."

## Religion in the Light of the Human Sciences

It needs to be noted, in Bonhoeffer's favor, that his view of religion would find support at the level of a positivistic and sociological attempt to define religion. For religious behavior from this viewpoint might well seem to be the attempt to supplement reality by bringing in some form of deity. There is little doubt that religion arises, humanly speaking, through man's awareness of his "thrown-ness," what in Heidegger's terminology, might be termed his *Dasein*-ness. Heidegger, it will be remembered, sees man's existence as a "being unto death." Man's basic insecurity, his felt insufficiency, his awareness of encompassing mystery have provided the soil in which religion came to birth. Here Bonhoeffer is correct—religion is concerned with the boundary situations where man's insufficiency and incapacity become evident. It arises in man's dire struggle for existence, his need for self-realization, his search for meaning. This much our social and anthropological studies have made evident in the last century.

From the anthropological point of view, the most viable understanding would seem to be that both religion and magic (the forerunner of science) began together and were closely intertwined in man's early behavior. Man found himself in an often hostile environment, subjected to forces he did not understand and beset by mysterious powers. Undoubtedly the conditioning factors for the religious response to the mysterious background of the universe were man's needs to cope with his seemingly alien surroundings. In the process of time, magic emerged as the attempt to control man's environment by compulsion, while religion emerged as the effort to meet man's need by the persuasion of the mysterious powers that man felt to be present in the depths of his world. So science and religion were set upon their separate and yet supplementary ways.

It would seem ironical that science should claim to investigate the sphere of religion, and, indeed, this might be taken as an indication that ultimately science will supersede religion, so that the latter's area of concern will be explicable in purely scientific terms. At this point, Bonhoeffer has made a fruitful contribution in his idea of the ultimate and the penultimate. He identifies the "ultimate" with the eschatological, God's last word of grace, "justification." The "penultimate" are the things before the last, the human setting for the reception of the Word, the preparing of the way. He can speak of feeding the hungry man, removing injustice, befriending the lonely as acts of alleviation that prepare the way for the "ultimate." [20] Thus the penultimate can be identified with the natural—with humanity, goodness, reason—for "the natural is that which, after the Fall, is directed towards the coming of Christ." [21] Within the natural, which is so in the light of Christ, Bonhoeffer includes the biological organization and legal ordering of the world. It is with this area of the penultimate and the natural that the natural sciences and the human sciences are concerned. They can study religious behavior and the structure of the religious consciousness but they cannot deal with the ultimate, the eschatological. This is the sphere of grace and faith. Now the weakness of Bonhoeffer lies in his indictment of the religious consciousness and his failure to acknowledge that even man's religiousness, though it be in the natural and the penultimate, may also be lifted up into the ultimate and eschatological.

At the scientific level, religion might be defined as man's attempt to deal with the exigencies of his situation by behavior that might relate him to some more permanent and sufficient controlling power or powers behind his world. We cannot expect the human sciences to move beyond such an expression, but we need to remember that man has an inner and private dimension with which science cannot deal. His characteristic religious behavior might be accounted for in terms of the gods or god as a "working hypothesis." Yet this would be to ignore those aspects of man's inner life which are also characteristic of religion, viz., his belief in, fear of, attraction to, and loyalty to such powers, his sense of being related to the mysterious depths of his world. We might suggest psychologically that the religious object was a man-made figment of the human imagination, a postulation arising out of the human condition, a projection of man's needs and hopes on the backdrop of a seemingly alien world, an escape fantasy. But we should be denying the validity of certain aspects of man's religious life at all levels of development, in particular, the sense of being related to and of encountering a power beyond himself. Rather than man's thrown-ness causing and creating the gods, it may well have provided the conditions under which such an awareness was awakened. Man's potential kinship with the divine moved into actual awareness and received content as his sense of need was awakened. The Christian could see here the divine initiative, the power behind the universe evoking a responsive awareness, as man faces the exigencies of his condition.

It is significant that in higher manifestations of man's religious experience what began as a means to meeting the exigencies of the human situation has become an end in itself. Man's response to the mysterious depths of the universe has been transformed from major concern with the boundary situations of death, natural calamity, and human guilt to the adoration of and communion with the deity. What Bonhoeffer has called the natural or the penultimate opens up to the ultimate. The vision of God as an end in itself has been a mark of all the world's great religions at their highest level. Man has become increasingly aware of the disclosure situations out of which his religious response takes its rise. Religion is a relative experience and revelation is its concomitant.

Of course, Bonhoeffer, influenced by both Heim and Barth, would deny the latter as a religious premise. Undoubtedly here we see the working presupposition that there is nothing in man by which he may grasp the infinite or claim kinship with the trans-

cendent depths of the universe. Once more we return to Bonhoeffer's denial of a religious *a priori*. Man is *incapax infinitum*.[22]
He has no point in which God can gain space. Religion may express man's natural curiosity, but faith is the work of God. Only
the Word makes possible a direct contact between man and God.
We cannot posit any immediacy or any mental form within man
himself by which reception of the Word is possible.[23] The Word is
opposed to human experience of value and of good. Outside of
Christ no man is a real man.

Bonhoeffer would hold that only as Christ forms himself again
in the believer does authentic existence, existence in relation to
God, become a reality. The real man is he who has been conformed to the Incarnate. Man's quest for the superman and the
cult of the demigod are not man's proper concern. His right and
duty is to be man, and Christ transforms a man, not into a form
alien to him, the form of God, but into that man's proper form.[24]
"Religion" may express man's quest for some "working hypothesis" by which he may deal with the realities of his situation, but
it is not revelation. Bonhoeffer does not even discuss any possibility of some measure of revealed truth in religion. Man only
becomes true man in Christ, but then we must ask ourselves
whether we are to limit the activity of Christ to that focalized in
his incarnate presence or to accept his cosmic presence manifested in the creative and enlightening Word. It is worthy of note
that, in his *Ethics*, Bonhoeffer frequently quotes the passage of
Col., ch. 1, in which the cosmic Christ theme appears. His emphasis on Christ's Lordship over the world might also have led
him to a different view of the relation of revelation to religion.

## Christianity and Religion

So far our consideration of Bonhoeffer's description of "religion" shows it to be a somewhat restricted definition, yet one in
keeping with his theological premise. His restriction of revelatory
activity to the incarnation and its historical consequences pre-
cludes any positive assessment of the world's religions as revela-

tory. At the same time, there are aspects of his indictment that
are prophetic as we face the new era of world history which would
seem to be emerging at the present time. We would want religion
to have a broader and much more positive base than Bonhoeffer
and his disciples would allow. We would allow for revelatory content and refuse to acknowledge such a sharp dichotomy as one
that sets Christianity apart and seeks for a religionless Christianity. Yet there is little doubt that man-made patterns and
metaphysical structures distort man's religious life, that often
religious man has been more concerned with the boundary situations of his unsolved theoretical and practical problems than with
the issue of living out his faith in the midst of life, that the man
of faith (whatever be his faith) has tended to concentrate on his
own salvation in some form or other, and that Christianity also
manifests such blemishes in the nineteen hundred years of history. Does this, however, mean that those nineteen hundred
years have been permeated by a mistaken association of the
Christian faith with the religious dimension of man's life? Furthermore, if we attempt to speak about a religionless Christianity
in a secular world, there are other religious faiths that might call
for a similar disentanglement, especially those of the world-affirming type.

W. Cantwell Smith makes a pointed comment on the view represented by contemporary advocates of religionless Christianity:

> To hold that other men are "religious," and to disdain them for it,
> while one's own group is superior (because it has, rather, "faith"; or
> because it is world-affirming; or whatever) is not merely much too
> simple a way of dealing with the beam in one's own eye. More im-
> portant is that, in calling attention to the motes in other people's, it is
> in danger of almost denying that they have eyes, or at least that they
> can see.[25]

Comte prophesied that the religious and metaphysical eras must
be succeeded by a scientific one. But, as we have pointed out,
even he had to seek to express the religious dimension of his nature by creating a new religion of humanity. The issue of the re-

ligionless nature of the present age is emphasized by Bonhoeffer
and his many disciples (who often misrepresent him), and, in
this sense, Comte was prophetic. Because of the increasing secularity of the present century, Bonhoeffer took comfort in his
theological premise. He saw "religion," as he defined it, continually losing its hold upon the areas of man's life, until his own
denial of a religious *a priori* would seem justified. Mankind was
no longer religious, and if Christianity was to survive, it must take
a religionless form. It is at just this point that real difficulties begin to arise, for he does not seem himself to be too clear about
what this implies.

Remembering the Lutheranism of the Germany in which Bonhoeffer was reared, we can understand his attack upon a piety
that concerned itself so much with the boundary issues of bourgeois ethics and death and devoted itself so greatly to the cultivation of otherworldliness that it allowed Nazism to rise to
power. Such otherworldliness belied the true nature of the Christian faith with its emphasis on creation, on the incarnation, and
on the Lordship of Christ in this present life. Men's eyes were
turned within and not outward toward the world. But does this
mean that religious inwardness is to be completely rejected and
that the authentic Christian faith must be so this-worldly that it
must reject the inward aspect which characterizes all religions?
Does it not still remain true that men need to be forgiven and
reconciled to God? Granted that we need the outreach of a faith
that is concerned with man's life in this world and its social
structures, granted that man's Christian hope needs to be related
to this contemporary world and not transformed into an otherworldly preoccupation with heaven, but is this possible without
some degree of inwardness, of communion with God, which so
often Bonhoeffer's disciples seem to dismiss as a part of the outmoded religious garb in which Christianity has hitherto been
clothed?

Strangely even Bonhoeffer himself would not agree at this
point. Some of what he seems to dismiss as "religion" still remains
as an integral part of his own "Christian faith." It is certainly evi-

dent that disciples like John A. T. Robinson have misunderstood the martyred theologian. Bonhoeffer's earlier writings *The Cost of Discipleship* and *Life Together* manifest a deep concern for that inward communion with Christ and genuine piety which some would regard as a part of out-moded religiosity. Evidently Bonhoeffer did not. Although he speaks in his letters of the need for rewriting both these books in the light of his increasing concern with secularity, the letters also disclose the depths of his own devotional life—for example, his diligent Bible study, the regularity of prayer, and the resources he found in the psalms. He finds consolation in Ps. 50 when the bombs are falling, and writes that it takes trouble to drive men to prayer.[26] He does, however, hint that this is something to be ashamed of. Furthermore, it is clear that he did not discard the traditional forms of the Christian liturgy and evidently derived much help and inspiration from the observance of the Christian year. His life is measured, not by secular time, but by the Christian calendar, while separation from home and family became especially poignant at the time of religious festivals. Isolation from hearing the preached Word and from the fellowship of the Christian community make his imprisonment harder. The picture that emerges is one of deep inwardness and piety.

Bonhoeffer does, moreover, make much of what he terms the "secret discipline." By this he meant that the traditional expressions of doctrine and liturgical forms with their myth and symbol should not be discarded, even though they had no significance for secular man. Rather, the man of faith should treasure them and seek always their abiding meaning, endeavoring to conserve the latter until such time as the secular world might again be able to listen. Such a secret discipline requires the absence of self-display. The Christian should not parade before men that inward life by which his outward behavior is made possible. Phillips suggests that the secrets are the church, cult, prayer, dogmas, the life in Christ, and that these secrets "are not circulated in public in their uninterpreted form." [27] They include preaching, baptism, communion. To quote Phillips again:

The discipline consists in the refusal to betray the secret by profaning it or to disregard it by confusing it with or substituting for it inappropriate secular elements in the process of non-religious interpretation or this-sided existence.[28]

Thus even the church should expose itself by its very existence and not by exposing the secrets of faith cheaply.[29] In a revealing letter, Bonhoeffer seems to hint at what he means by the "secret discipline." He writes:

What I mean is that God wants us to love him eternally with our whole hearts—not in such a way as to injure or weaken our earthly love, but to provide a kind of *cantus firmus* on which the other melodies of life provide the counterpoint.[30]

What the secret discipline indicates is a secret reliance on and communion with God that is not outwardly asserted but that is yet the inner resource without which love for the world would be impossible. Men see our good works, but they do not see us.

What emerges is the picture of a man whose churchly loyalty stands clear and whose deep inwardness is very evident, but who at the same time despises all cant, hypocrisy, and outward parading of piety. In other words, we have a picture of a truly religious man, pious in the true sense of that much misused word. The only trouble is that Bonhoeffer, because of the sad mishandling of such words in the life of the church, has associated religion and piety with man-centered structures, with escape mechanisms, and with "a stop-gap for our embarrassments."[31] He himself, in one of his letters, suggests that " 'Christianity' has always been a form—perhaps the true form—of 'religion,' "[32] but goes on to argue that such a form is historically conditioned and transient. Yet, as we see it, he still wants to retain the true essence of religion without calling it by that name because of his own preempted definition of the word.

It should be emphasized that the Biblical approach to religion is ambivalent, although the word itself, as used in modern speech, has no true equivalent in the Biblical languages. So far as the Old Testament is concerned, the fanatical zeal of the Hebrew religious leaders for Yahweh prohibited any recognition of surrounding faiths. The exclusive claim of the Decalogue is echoed time and again by the Hebrew prophets who denounce the religions of the surrounding peoples with severe condemnation. For one thing, the Hebrew faith derived many of its religious symbols and practices from its neighbors. It was particularly indebted to Zoroastrianism for some of its later angelology and demonology. Its vision of God does stand out uniquely, and yet some of the symbolic structure in which that vision is expressed is derived from its neighboring cultures. In the second place, there are passages in the prophets that suggest a much more universal dimension of the divine saving activity. There is the passage in Amos that speaks of God calling the Syrians from Kir and the Philistines from Caphtor (Amos 9:7). There is the declaration in Malachi that the living God has those who call upon his name among all peoples (Mal. 1:11). Even of Cyrus the Persian conqueror whose religion was that of Zoroaster, it can be said that Yahweh has girded him, called him, anointed him, though he has not known the living God (Isa. 45:1-7).

It is to the New Testament and the disclosure of the incarnation that we must look for a wider vision. There is one word in Greek, *deisidaimonia*, that in Latin is rendered *religio* and that does carry something of the significance of our word "religion." Yet is is not clearly defined in its New Testament usage. In one passage it is used positively—Acts 17:22—where Paul commends the men of Athens as being "very religious" (RSV). In the other passage it is used negatively and contemptuously—Acts 25:19— where Festus refers to the charges brought against Paul by the Jews as questions arising out of "their own superstition" (RSV). In the latter case we have a typical Roman attitude, namely, to tolerate people's religions as keeping them happy under the Roman yoke and therefore annoyance when such a state of affairs does not arise. As far as the early Christians themselves were concerned, their environment abounded in religions from the official Roman "imperial cult" with its Caesar worship and state liturgy to the mystery religions and other Oriental cults. The latter offered that personal consolation and salvation to the individual for which the cold official cult with its political motives had no place. In this sense they would fit into Bonhoeffer's definition of religion. We can understand, therefore, both the negative reaction of the Christians to their pagan surroundings and the fact that they could be described by their contemporaries as atheists, for did they not reject the gods and lords of many of their neighbors?

Yet, at the same time, we can see other forces at work in the Christian consciousness that ultimately would lead to a new attitude toward the religious experience of man. For one thing, even the pagan religions, in the course of time, made their contributions to the structures of thought and patterns of liturgy in which Christianity was expressed. For a second thing, in the New Testament itself, we find indications of a wider view in which the divine activity in Jesus Christ is given a broader background of revelation. In The Acts, Paul can identify the "unknown God" of the Athenians with the God and Father of the Lord Jesus Christ (Acts 17:23), while, to the men of Lystra, he can speak of the living God as not having left himself without witness in the order of nature (Acts 14:17). Again, in the epistle to the Romans, Paul can speak of God's eternal power and deity as being clearly perceived through his created works so that men know God and yet become blind and senseless, even in their religious thought and behavior (Rom. 1:21 ff.). Perhaps the most remarkable insight in the New Testament comes from the Prologue of the Fourth Gospel. Here the cosmic Christ who ultimately becomes flesh and pitches his tent among men is also the Logos who lightens the minds of all men and prevails in spite of the presence of the darkness (John 1:4-5, 9).

It is not surprising, therefore, to see a process in which "religion" was Christianized and became a typical description of Christianity itself. Early in its history, the Christian church began to take over the pagan religious festivals and transform them into feasts associated with the divine disclosure in Jesus Christ. So the

Roman festival of Sol Invicta, which celebrated at the winter solstice the unconquerable sun-god, was transformed into Christmas, which celebrated the birth of the Sun of Righteousness. Easter, too, was fixed by history in association with the Jewish Passover, and celebrated the resurrection of Jesus Christ, yet quite early it took over and Christianized practices associated with the spring equinox. Indeed our word "Easter" is derived from *Eastre*, the name of the spring-goddess. The fact that such associations should be made is at least a reminder that the Christian faith had some affinity with the religious hopes and aspirations of the human race. As we have suggested above, it would seem that man's need for deliverance from the exigencies of his situation and the religious attempts to meet that need were not outside the divine activity, but rather pointers to that final moment when the desire of all nations should be made manifest. Once Christianity could be described as a religion in which faith was man's response to the presence of God in Jesus, the word "religion" was filled with new insight.

The Christianizing of "religion" led to a new attitude toward other religions, and this became especially evident in the liberal Protestant thought of the nineteenth century until the First World War and the emergence of Karl Barth. The opening up of the world in the fifteenth and sixteenth centuries had already brought to the Christian church an awareness of the varied religious life of the human race. Until then, its sole contact among the world's great religions had been Islam. The Christianized West had long left behind the crop of esoteric mystery cults and gnosticisms of the Roman period. If such lingered on, they usually took a Christian dress as heresies within the body of Christendom. During the medieval period, with its scholastic rationalism, the sole revelation was that available to the Christian believer. All other knowledge of God was relegated to the level of natural theology, with its rational argumentation from natural order to the existence and attributes of deity. This engendered an intolerance which claimed Christianity as solely the true religion.

This intolerance persisted until, in the seventeenth century, at least the Protestant churches became aware of the many forms in which the religious experience of the human race had been expressed. In this period, when Christian missionary activity came to birth and began to flourish, questions began to be raised about the status of the non-Christian religions. The old natural theology with its rationalism slowly found itself superseded by a study of the world's religions. Christians began to realize their solidarity with other religious men.

From the time of David Hume to that of Karl Barth, the Christianizing of "religion" led men to realize that the divine initiative might be present in all religions, evoking the human religious response. Religions contained very evident elements of human imagination and creativity, but the presence in them of some aspects of divine self-disclosure could not be discounted, however distorted and misrepresented it might have become in passing through the alembic of the human mind. The Christianization of religion had meant the recognition that man's religion was born out of the divine-human relationship as a response to the divine self-disclosure. If this was true of the Christian religion with its affirmation of the initiative of the divine grace in Jesus Christ evoking the responsive commitment of faith, why should it not hold in some measure of other religions also?

Bonhoeffer was the heir of all this, which reached its final expressions in thinkers as diverse as Rudolf Otto and Ernst Troeltsch. But another attitude toward religion is to be seen in Feuerbach, Marx, Freud, and, strangely inverted, in Karl Barth. This also was in the atmosphere that Dietrich Bonhoeffer breathed. Add to these the growing secularization of the common life and the indirect influence of thinkers like Auguste Comte, and we have a picture of the complex of forces that played upon the martyred theologian and which are still present in our own theological atmosphere. If we are to understand Bonhoeffer's challenge aright and our own response to it, we shall need to examine these component influences in more detail.

Today the Christian is assailed on two sides. On the one side is the growing secularization of the world. Men seem to deal with their situation quite adequately at the level of science, ethics, and art without any reference to God or recourse to religion. Christianity seems irrelevant, and the seemingly prophetic voice of Comte reminds us that, in this new era, religion is *passé*. Here Bonhoeffer's challenge is emphatic. Christianity is not a religion. Its religious garb must be dropped and it must be given a nonreligious interpretation to communicate with modern man.

Certain things need to be remembered at this point. The first is Bonhoeffer's exceedingly narrow definition of religion. Here we must take account of his peculiar position in a concentration camp where he was led to a somewhat exaggerated appreciation for the secular men with whom he found fellowship and to a loss of appreciation for those religious Germans and pious Lutherans who reconciled their "religion" with Nazi tyranny. A second point is Bonhoeffer's own practice of the "secret discipline" in which the finer elements of true religion were still expressed. A third point is that Bonhoeffer was himself by no means clear how "religionless" Christianity was to be expressed or even what a "nonreligious interpretation" of Christianity meant. It is true that his last thoughts, if committed to paper, are not extant, and also that he was only at the beginning of his thinking on this issue. Yet the secular society, which he foresaw with no religious *a priori*, is hardly a good description of the secularized and affluent America of the first two decades after the war. Here religion in Bonhoeffer's sense was very evident, and the Christian churches enjoyed a surge of piety that often was far from Christian in motivation but yet very "religious." What we seem to need is not the abolition of religion in the best sense, but an expression of it that is relevant to a society that justifiably regards many of the current expressions of Christianity as highly irrelevant. Our attempt at the justification of religious Christianity must seek further light here later.

On the other side, we find ourselves in a world where the new techniques of communication and the population explosion have made us more than ever aware of the world's religions. This raises the issue of the relation of Christianity to other faiths. If

Christianity can shed its religious garb and express itself in a secular way, either it must arrogantly regard all such religions as irrelevant or else ask whether these other religions may also adopt a secular interpretation. On the other hand, if Christianity is true religion in its highest expression, its relation to the other religions becomes an important matter, and the whole issue of religious truth is raised. Our answer to the issues raised in the preceding paragraph will determine the way we face up to the question just posed.

# II

## From Absolute Dependence to Ultimate Concern

### PART 1: SCHLEIERMACHER AND THE CULTURED DESPISERS

THE EIGHTEENTH CENTURY saw science in its first heyday of success. The deterministic structure of Newtonian physics had raised difficulties for men of faith. Rather than ceasing to believe in God, man had moved from Christian theism to a deistic stance in which God was regarded as the transcendent creator who had endowed his creation with the fixed and immanent laws of nature and morality. The universe was regarded as a self-running mechanism in which all activity at the subhuman and human levels was structured within the laws set by the Creator. Generally such thinkers did not consider divine providence as implying a direct relationship of God to his world but rather as evidenced in the ordered and legal structure of the universe. They either discounted or completely rejected revelation and the miraculous. They took refuge in a rational theology in which they emphasized the ordered and teleological nature of the universe. Furthermore, they sought to justify the Christian faith by eliminating every element that could not be established by such rational procedures and thus to show that "the Gospel was as old as creation." [1] Their approach began at the empirical level and accepted the causative structure of the science of their day. Yet they still remained religious, except that their religion was deistic and not Christian. They reduced religion to three basic principles —God, freedom, and immortality. Their century saw the rise of Unitarianism in England and New England. In many senses their time is comparable with our own although there are differences. Our scientific premises are different, with determinism giving place to contingency and randomness, and their deism is now replaced by the rejection of religion and, at the best, agnosticism.

Upon such a scene of religious deadness, Hume broke in with still more disastrous effect. He demonstrated that a purely empiricist approach gave no rational justification of the ideas of causation and substance, the existence of the soul or the existence and nature of God. Man might have such as natural beliefs, but he must not seek to justify them on the basis of the scientific picture of the world. Science basically was required to adopt a positivistic stance and accept its causative and deterministic structures as imposed because of the beliefs of the knowing mind. As for God and religion, Hume made it quite clear that, on his premises, these had no rational validity. If science called human freedom in question, Hume now called immortality and God in question. More than ever a place had to be found for religion and God.

Three thinkers, in diverse ways, sought to carve the way out of the impasse. Kant sought the justification of the religious postulates through the practical reason and man's moral experience. What the theoretical reason or pure reason was unable to arrive at, the practical reason, grounded in man's sense of moral rightness, confirmed as postulates—God, freedom, immortality. He defined religion as, subjectively regarded, the "recognition of all our duties as divine commands." [2] Hegel went beyond the critical idealism of Kant to a monistic idealism in which the Christian revelation was transformed into a universalistic form and Christianity became an imaginative expression of the process by which the Absolute Idea moved to self-realization.[3] Thus Hegel returned to the rationalistic emphasis in a new way. Kant had sought the roots of religion in the categorical imperative. Hegel sought to make religion an imaginative, concrete, and particularistic presentation that needed to be superseded by the rational, abstract, and universal concepts of his philosophical system. Hegel saw religion as an intermediate stage in the grasping of absolute truth. Philosophy surpassed religion, transforming the concrete images of the latter into the abstract concepts of the former and satisfying the philosopher's soul as religion could not. At its best, religion is the knowledge possessed by the finite mind of its nature an absolute mind, but this knowledge needs to be classified and "demythologized" at the level of philosophical thought.

These emphases respectively on the moral and the rational were matched by a third attempt which placed its emphasis on the emotional side of man's nature. Schleiermacher, in seeking to define religion, sought at the same time to criticize the approaches of both Kant and Hegel. He found a place for God in man's religious feeling.

## Schleiermacher and Religion as the Feeling of Absolute Dependence

Schleiermacher was one of the great religious philosophers and systematic theologians of the modern era. His influence is still with us, and, despite criticisms leveled at him by theologians like Barth and Brunner, his significance for our own situation should not be underestimated. There is currently a revival of interest in his thought, for, as with us, he was facing a period when many of his contemporaries were contemptuous of Christianity and convinced of its irrelevance. As preacher and university professor in Berlin he set himself to meet and convince the "cultured despisers" of faith.

Schleiermacher's approach was grounded in an analysis of the human self-consciousness. He recognizes that man's conscious life has three aspects—perception, feeling, and activity. Perception leads to knowledge and is emphasized in rationalism. Activity results in conduct and is emphasized in morality. Now Schleiermacher was strongly opposed to both Hegel and Kant. Seeking a ground for religion that did not reduce it to either rationalistic natural theology or man's ethical life, he turned to feeling as the basic element in religion. The religious man, he contended, is not concerned with the nature of the first cause nor is his religion derived by passing from moral laws to a universal law giver.[4] Equally, religion is not to be explained by a mixture of philosophy or science and morals—it is not an "instinct craving for a mess of metaphysical and ethical crumbs."[5] It is grounded in the feeling aspects of the human consciousness. It is here that Schleiermacher analyzes man's self-consciousness.

It should be noted that Schleiermacher's thought becomes more crystallized over this matter as we move from his first work, *Speeches on Religion to Its Cultured Despisers*, to his influential study of systematic theology, *The Christian Faith*. It is in the latter work that the emphasis on man's self-consciousness becomes focal. In the first work, Schleiermacher draws upon his own pietistic background and upon the Romanticist ideas current in his time. In his famous second lecture on "The Nature of Religion," he declares that true piety does not have God by knowledge and science. True religion is contemplation, but not the contemplation that issues in a rational knowledge of God, based on relations between finite things. "The contemplation of the pious is the *immediate* consciousness of the universal existence of all finite things, in and through the Infinite, and of all temporal things in and through the Eternal."[6] Again, the contemplation of human action by the pious man does not give rise to a system of ethics. Rather, he seeks God's activity among men. Piety is "a submission to be moved by the Whole that stands over against man,"[7] while morality is manipulative and self-controlling. So true religion is a sense and taste for the infinite. It is grounded in feeling, and Schleiermacher's emphasis falls on the immediacy of this feeling.

We have, however, to examine what Schleiermacher means by feeling. The fact that he associates religion with immediate consciousness suggests that he is not thinking of a purely emotional state. He evidently associates some degree of awareness with this affective aspect of the consciousness. It is noteworthy that in the first edition of his *Speeches on Religion,* he associates the word "intuition" (*Anschauung*) with "feeling" (*Gefühl*). Although he drops this usage in the second edition, it would seem evident that the idea of feeling has now absorbed the idea associated with intuition. Thus feeling is not purely subjective for Schleiermacher. It is relative in the sense that it involves immediate awareness of what is other than the feeling subject. It would have been better, as Tillich [8] points out, if he had used "intuition" instead, although he does use "divination," by which he means immediate awareness of the divine. Actually the ambiguity involved in Schleiermacher's use of "feeling" serves his purpose. It enables him to differentiate religion from science and morality according to his faculty psychology and yet, at the same time, to employ feeling differently to describe an emotional awareness. We need, however, to remember that he is not indulging in pure psychologism.

In describing religion as an immediate pious feeling, Schleiermacher is seeking, in actual fact, to transcend the subject/object dichotomy. Both rationalism or science and morality imply the over-againstness of subject and object. Motivated by his background of piety and by the persuasive romanticism of his age with its pantheistic tendencies, Schleiermacher seeks for identity and holds that in religion the subject/object relationship is transcended. There is little doubt that in this early stage of his thinking, he himself had strong pantheistic leanings, partly because of the deism against which he was rebelling. It is significant that he does not speak of the "other" of whom the pious man is immediately aware as "God" so much as the "Whole," the "Infinite," the "Eternal," the "Universe," the "World-Spirit," the "Eternal Being." Furthermore, he thinks of man as an individual, concrete embodiment of the Whole. It seems clear that his is not pantheism but a form of panentheism in which the divine spirit is present

all pervasively in the universe and in the deeps of man himself.
He can write of religious feeling:

It is immediate, raised above all error and misunderstanding. You lie
directly on the bosom of the infinite world. In that moment, you are its
soul. Through one part of your nature you feel, as your own, all its
powers and endless life. In that moment it is your body, you pervade,
as your own, its muscles and members and your thinking and forecast-
ing set its inmost nerves in motion.[9]

Thus man lives in the Whole, feeling its surging life and creative
power flowing through himself, for its presence is all-pervasive.
In the depths of his own being he feels the presence of the Universe. In this feeling the polarity of subject and object is transcended. Schleiermacher sees "the universal existence of all finite
things in the Infinite," [10] and feeling is "the first contact of the
universal life with an individual," "the holy wedlock of the Universe with the incarnated Reason for a creative, productive embrace." [11] Hence there is a divine in us, and this "is immediately
affected and called forth by the feeling." [12] Indeed, we can claim
to have God in our feeling.[13]

    This basic feeling for the Universe is the ground of religion.
Indeed, all feeling is to some degree piety! We are told:

Your feeling is piety, in so far as it expresses, in the manner described,
the being and life common to you and to the All. Your feeling is piety
in so far as it is the result of the operation of God in you by means of
the operation of the world upon you.[14]

We note the panentheist emphasis in the phrase "the being and
life common to you and to the All." It is understandable why
Schleiermacher finds difficulty with the idea of personal immortality as commonly understood. In his *Speeches on Religion* he
clearly does reject immortality as personal survival of death.
His approach is to emphasize eternal life as a present experience,
the realization of oneness with, identity with, the Whole. What
is individual and fleeting disappears as we attach ourselves to
God. In religion the outlines of personality are expanded until

they are lost in the Infinite. As we become conscious of the Universe, we become one with it.[15] The true immortality can be had now in this mortal life. "In the midst of finitude to be one with the Infinite and in every moment to be eternal is the immortality of religion." [16] In this way, Schleiermacher endeavors to interpret "Whosoever loses his life for my sake, the same shall keep it, and whosoever keeps it, the same shall lose it." False immortality as individual survival is no immortality. Those who desire it lose it. Surrender of life out of love for God means annihilating the personality and living in the One and the All.

In the same way, in this early stage of his thought, Schleiermacher avoids the word "God" (how contemporary!), since he finds it difficult to speak of a personal God. We have already listed the abstract and panentheistic descriptions that he prefers. It is true that he speaks of "God" in the third edition of his *Speeches*, from which we are quoting in Oman's translation, and that the Spinozaistic flavor of the first edition has been replaced by a more Christian emphasis. Yet he still balks at the idea of a personal God outside and beyond the world, for this "is only one manner of expressing God, seldom entirely pure and always inadequate." [17] True religion is the immediate consciousness of God "as He is found in ourselves and in the world."

Schleiermacher's immanentism is evident, although it is unfair to attribute to him a rejection of transcendence. He is so anxious to emphasize the immediacy of pious feeling that he undervalues any objective contemplation of God. The Whole is all-pervasive, even in the deeps of man's own soul, and true piety may be expressed even if that Whole is envisaged as impersonal. Conception of the deity oscillates between a narrow anthropomorphism and an exaltation above all personality as the universal and necessary ground of all thought and existence. But, Schleiermacher adds:

It matters not what conceptions a man adheres to, he can still be pious. His piety, the divine in his feeling, may be better than his conception, and his desire to place the essence of piety in conception, only makes him misunderstand himself.[18]

What matters is the cultivation of the "religious sense."

So far Schleiermacher has not specifically defined religious feeling. As we have seen, he seems to regard all feeling as religious, remembering that, for him, feeling is that primary basis of apprehension to which the subject/object dichotomy is secondary. Feeling is immediacy, almost, if not actually, identity. A man's feeling is pious insofar as it is the operation of God upon him through the operation of the world upon him,[19] and so there is no sensation that is not pious, unless the subject himself be diseased or impaired in some way.[20] In his notes on the chapter "The Nature of Religion" in the *Speeches,* Schleiermacher tells us that "all healthy feelings are pious, or at least that, in order not to be diseased, they should be pious." [21] Indeed, the Universe is ceaselessly active, continually revealing itself to us,[22] and the pious man "can detect the operation of the World-Spirit in all that belongs to human activity, in play and earnest, in smallest things and in greatest." [23] He knows God in the divine operations upon him within and without. Deep calls to deep as, most of all, he recognizes the infinite within him.

In *The Christian Faith,* Schleiermacher departs from this generalized description and becomes more specific. (His position is amplified also in his *Dialectic,* his basic philosophical work even though it is fragmentary.[24]) He more carefully associates feeling with human self-consciousness. Let us begin with this, since out of it emerges a more definite statement about the pious feeling. Schleiermacher identifies feeling with immediate self-consciousness. The description "immediate" is employed to differentiate such self-consciousness from that which arises out of the relationships to society and the world into which man is "thrown." Schleiermacher calls the latter "mediate self-consciousness," because it is the result of a reflective synthesis of the differing moments of life. It is grounded in man's participation in the world. In it man is aware of himself as an ego shaped within the intramundane and intrapersonal relationships of his environment. Such mediate self-consciousness posits the individual personality by the aid of memory of past moments and the interrelationships of the present. A man knows himself to coexist with the world. His world provides the raw material that is shaped from within man and gives rise to that selfhood of which he is aware in his self-reflection. Such self-consciousness is thus mediated through the world and human society.[25]

Schleiermacher contends that the Ego which is grasped in such a process of reflection is only one factor in full self-consciousness. The other factor is the source of the particular determination represented in the Ego. This is not objectively represented in the reflective or mediate self-consciousness. At this level, Schleiermacher sees two elements. Man both acts and is acted upon. He is both a doer and a sufferer or a receiver. Thus he recognizes in himself both a relative freedom and a relative dependence. He knows himself to have shaped something of what he is. He also knows himself to be dependent upon his social, natural, and cultural environments. The kind of self he is reflects his world in greater or lesser degree. But this relative dependence, of which he is aware in reflective self-consciousness, points to a deeper factor. Man has not determined his time and place, however much he may shape them with his relative freedom. The fact of his freedom means that there is a relative dependence on society and the world. But there is radical dependence beneath both his relative freedom and his relative dependence. He is a posited being, but not a self-posited being. His happened-ness, his thrownness, is something he has to receive and to suffer. It is this not-self-caused factor, the Other, which is not objectively expressed in mediate self-consciousness. This Other is the source of his happened-ness, of the particular forces that have together shaped and molded his Ego. Man has been posited in a certain way and with such positing he has had nothing to do. In relation to it man has no freedom but only dependence. There is for man no such thing as absolute freedom, but there is absolute dependence.[26]

Schleiermacher finds the awareness or feeling of absolute dependence in the immediate self-consciousness. This primordial feeling of thrown-ness enters consciousness with our primary awareness of our own innermost selfhood. As immediate, such self-consciousness is to be differentiated from that reflective self-consciousness which is mediated by our intramundane relations. Indeed, it is prior to our subject/object and self/society relations and thus to our knowing and our doing. It is immediate awareness of that inner underived self which thinks and wills, which shapes the raw material supplied by a man's natural heritage and his social and natural environment. It is consciousness of the inner unity of self. Niebuhr points out that, at this level, self means "the underived self . . . the self that is not qualified by or determined by specific objects and energies located in this world. It is the self in its original identity, in its being-in-such-and-such-a-way (*Sosein*)." [27] Schleiermacher's immediate self-consciousness refers, then, to that basic unity of selfhood which is not derived from the world and its relations.

As feeling, this immediate self-consciousness underlies all our thinking and doing. It is a "feeling" of the presence of the total undivided personal and "thrown" existence, and necessarily accompanies every moment of that existence, even when complete absorption in some immediate condition might seem to obliterate it.[28] Commenting on Schleiermacher's position in the *Dialectic*, Spiegler writes:

This self-possession of the ultimate wholeness of life, if considered by itself can be designated as an "immediate self-consciousness" or "feeling." It is the sustaining ground in the structure of consciousness.[29]

My "happened-ness," "thrown-ness," within the polarity of human existence with its patterns of relationships, its thinking and its willing, expresses a unity of selfhood that I immediately possess and of which I have immediate consciousness. But this feeling is also a feeling of absolute dependence. As such it is prior to all our mediated feelings of relative freedom and relative dependence in our relationships with the world and society. It is in no way derivative from our participation in the world or "our co-existence with the world" to which such relative relations apply.[30]

It is at this level of the immediate self-consciousness that Schleiermacher finds the roots of man's religious life, for he identifies the feeling of absolute dependence with the pious, or religious, feeling. It is God-consciousness as well as self-consciousness. My feeling of my selfhood involves a feeling of the Other, the "Whence" of my absolute dependence. The "feeling" as religious points to the transcendental ground, to God. Furthermore, this is no mediated feeling arising out of the polarities of human existence. It is immediate, constituting an identity that transcends all the polarities; it is an immediate intuition of a man's participation in the Other.

We need to remember the definition's emphasis on absolute dependence and Schleiermacher's careful rejection of any such thing as absolute freedom (cf. Sartre). Man is an utterly dependent being. His unity of selfhood is something that he possesses in immediate self-consciousness but which, in that same primary feeling, is intuited as a totally derived being. He is posited. Religion arises in this self-consciousness. It is the felt fundamental relationship, absolute because it stands behind all intramundane relationships and makes them possible. The latter, in their relative freedom and relative dependence, are present in the mediate self-consciousness, but man's self-consciousness has a deeper and religious level where he "feels" his relationship to the Other, to God. As H. R. Mackintosh puts it:

Pious feeling . . . can emerge only as we are face to face with a cause which conditions our freedom equally with our dependence, and which evokes the consciousness that the whole even of our spontaneous activity comes from a source beyond ourselves.[31]

Schleiermacher tells us that the original signification of the word "God" is "the *Whence* of our receptive and active existence, as implied in this self-consciousness." [32] Such feeling of dependence is not conditioned by any previous knowledge of God. It is, indeed, prior to conceptual knowing. If "God" be a concept or idea at all at this level, Schleiermacher argues, it "signifies for us simply that which is the co-determinant in this feeling and to which we trace our being in such a state; and any further content of the idea must be evolved out of this fundamental import assigned to it." [88] Otto holds that, on this basis, "God" is an inference. Yet what Schleiermacher is trying to say is that we have an immediate consciousness of the "Whence" of our "thrown" existence, that on which we have absolute and unconditioned dependence. Furthermore, he is suggesting that God transcends all our polarities. He is no object alongside all objects, but is the transcendent ground of all objects and all polarities.

We must not accuse Schleiermacher of psychologism. As we have seen, although he seems to use "feeling" subjectively at times, he means by it something more at the level of consciousness. The ambiguity of the word protects him in some of his statements, but here his position is evident. God-consciousness and self-consciousness are the two sides of the same coin. They come together within the fundamental relation of absolute dependence. Man's immediate self-consciousness is consciousness of a relatedness that transcends the intramundane polarities and points to man's unconditioned dependence upon the transcendent ground that is "God." Such feeling is thus "a laying hold by the soul of a trans-subjective Reality." [34] To quote Schleiermacher:

In this sense it can indeed be said that God is given to us in feeling in an original way; and if we speak of an original revelation of God to man or in man, the meaning will always be just this, that, along with the absolute dependence which characterizes not only man but all temporal existence, there is given to man also the immediate self-consciousness of it, which becomes a consciousness of God. [35]

Tillich remarks that God "is present in our immediate consciousness and all that we can say about him are expressions of the immediacy." [36] Our primary self-consciousness is also "immediate consciousness of the Other." The First Cause that rationalistic natural theology arrived at by logical inference was declared by Schleiermacher to be immediate to man's self-consciousness in its most fundamental form.

Although ontologically prior to man's mediate self-consciousness, this God-consciousness is always manifest in and with man's specific intramundane relationships. Spiegler, interpreting Schleiermacher's thought, reminds us that "piety as an emergent form of the ontological presupposition of knowing and doing has its own integrity, though it is not separated from knowing and doing." [37] The "feeling of absolute dependence," although underlying all man's polarities, can never appear by itself. It always appears within the human consciousness along with man's consciousness of involvement in his world and its network of intramundane relationships.

Schleiermacher sees three levels of man's self-consciousness. The highest or primary is the immediate self-consciousness with its religious or pious "feeling." The lowest level and the middle level belong to what we have termed the mediate self-consciousness. They constitute man's consciousness of coexistence with the world. The lowest level is that of animal consciousness. The middle level is that of sensible self-consciousness. It is really here that man becomes fully world-conscious. To this level belong the feelings of relative freedom and relative dependence in relation to the world. These two lower levels are never, however, without the background of the highest level with its God-consciousness. This immediate self-consciousness "remains self-identical while all other states are changing." [38] Yet it can never be without these other states or levels of consciousness. On its own, it would "lack the definiteness and clearness which spring from its being related to the determination of the sensible self-consciousness." [39] Hence Schleiermacher sees a reciprocity between these levels of self-consciousness in any moment if the integrity of the Ego is to be maintained. He recognizes, moreover, that piety attains specific definition only through the sensible self-consciousness, so that suffering and doing impart qualifying characteristics to the feeling of absolute dependence.

The God-consciousness, when it attains explicit definition, does so in relation to the world-consciousness. Conceptual expression and clarity arise as the God-consciousness is "combined with, and related to, a sensible self-consciousness." [40] Thus the God-consciousness or piety in its historical expressions will reflect the determinations within which the world-consciousness or sensible self-consciousness moves. This means that our theological formulations will reflect and be expressed in terms of our cultural involvement. God's relation to the world means, furthermore, that man's God-consciousness and world-consciousness can never finally be in conflict. The two levels of self-consciousness cannot be contradictory.

## Christ and the Religions

From what we have just said, it is evident that Schleiermacher emphasizes that religion at the observable level is a historical and cultural phenomenon, marked by the characteristics of its time. In its universal aspect as the feeling of absolute dependence, man's immediate self-consciousness, it attains specificity through man's thrown-ness or happened-ness, his sensible or mediate self-consciousness with its active doing and its passive suffering. Schleiermacher sees religion as including, not excluding, man's intramundane relationships. This means that the pious feeling will have many specific historical formulations. And so, in Western thought for the first time in any depth, Schleiermacher confronts the issue of the world's religions.

The contemporary contrast between revelation and religion represents a different cast of mind from that in which Schleiermacher's thought was set. He was concerned with man's felt awareness of the nexus relationships into which he was "thrown," including the most fundamental of those relationships which related him to the *Whence* of his thrown condition. The latter was the constitutive center of man's whole self-consciousness, and thus was a universal factor in every man. This universal integrative center of man's selfhood has been expressed in many ways in the course of human history, and Christianity is, historically considered, one such manifestation. In this relationship of man to God, the primary emphasis of Schleiermacher fell upon man and his feeling, not upon God and his self-disclosure. It is easy to understand why he should be accused of turning theology into anthropology and majoring upon subjectivity. His emphasis certainly does not fall on the eternal gospel or the Word of God, and yet, when he turns his attention to Christianity, he is Christocentric in his thinking.

The accusation of subjectivity is unfair, because he is concerned with the relatedness of man—absolute dependence, relative dependence, and relative freedom. Yet "feeling" is so central that it becomes the vehicle of revelation and significantly Schleiermacher mentions revelation far too infrequently. He tells us in the *Speeches* that "any feeling is not an emotion of piety because a single object as such affects us, but only in so far as in it and along with it, it affects us as a revelation of God." [41] We need to remind ourselves once more that he is not a psychologist when he speaks of feeling and that religion is not ecstatic subjectivity. There is an intuitive element in feeling at the level of piety. Schleiermacher's anxiety to cut out rationalism has led him to seek cover under a word that he uses ambiguously. Again, because of his emphasis on man's relatedness, Schleiermacher quite clearly holds that no actual religion can arise in a human soul without the divine activity. Revelation is the divine operation on the soul that is expressed in the feeling of absolute dependence. God has chosen to approach men through their feelings. In the *Speeches,* Schleiermacher writes: "What is revelation? Every original and new communication of the Universe to man is a revelation. . . . Every intuition and every original feeling proceeds from revelation." [42] So the religious man must "be conscious of his feelings as the immediate product of the Universe." [43] Revelation comes in the religious feeling for Schleiermacher, not through the Word. Feeling, not hearing, is what matters.

The emphasis on the Universe indicates a position that remained throughout Schleiermacher's thought—the pious feeling is always present with world-consciousness. Thus nature and grace are coterminous for him. God is present and active everywhere, always exerting his pressure on the world. Spinozaistic influence with its pantheistic tendencies underlies all of Schleiermacher's theological work. As we have suggested, he is not himself pantheistic, and he is careful to deny this, stating that he admired but did not follow Spinoza. Hence he carefully differentiates between world-consciousness and God-consciousness and emphasizes that the superior type of religion is that which shows a high degree of discrimination between the two, making everything finite depend upon the Infinite.[44] Yet he still thinks of God as the absolute and unchanging, one reason for his evasion of the description "personal." God is unvarying and undiscriminating in his operation. There is no special revelation. All is general, common to the pious feeling of men everywhere, and all religion is natural. H. R. Mackintosh remarks that "the Divine causality is like a vast undiscriminating pressure upon the world, diffused with virtual uniformity over the whole," and suggests that, in Schleiermacher's thought, there is nowhere "any action of God which we are justified in calling *special*." [45] Thus we may think of God and the world as operating *pari-passu* upon our consciousness, so that the religious feeling is evoked. This is revelation.

When, therefore, Schleiermacher differentiates between the religions, he falls back upon the world-consciousness that always accompanies man's God-consciousness or pious feeling. He carefully, as we have seen, differentiates religion from knowledge, even though, confusedly or intentionally, he is including a cognitive element in his "pious feeling." Specific religions do embody ideas. But such theological ideas are secondary, arising out of reflection upon the pious feeling and thus reflecting the culture in which they are formulated. Man's world-consciousness interacts with his God-consciousness to produce the variety of religions. Having declared that ideas and principles are all foreign to religion, Schleiermacher is prepared to admit that ideas are both connected with religion and necessary for the communication of the religious feeling to other minds.[46] Thus all religions have the pious feeling in common, but they are differentiated from one another by the intuited principle or idea in which their expression of that feeling is focalized and in the light of which the feeling is interpreted. They are thus different ways of reacting to the concomitant presence of world-consciousness and God-consciousness in the human soul. This implies that every specific religion is a culture-religion and that what is significant in any one of them is its God-consciousness.

Schleiermacher holds that this God-consciousness, which is universally present in all religions, is not to be understood by an analytical conspectus of all religions, but through the specific embodiment it has received in one's own religious consciousness. Niebuhr points out that Schleiermacher has an organic standpoint, as also had Hegel. The universal manifests itself in many forms, flowering, as it were, in many individual determinations. Schleiermacher tells us that religion

is infinite, not merely because any single religious organization has a limited horizon, and, not being able to embrace all, cannot believe that there is nothing beyond; but more particularly, because everyone is a person by himself, and is only to be moved in his own way, so that for everyone the elements of religion have most characteristic differences.[47]

In each specific embodiment it is present fully and in a unique way, and "knowledge of the general emerges through and is conditioned by intensive understanding of the particular."[48]

An inquirer must start with the distinctive historical embodiment in which his own religious self-consciousness is expressed. Within that awareness he must examine the relations of other religious embodiments to his own, seeking thereby to grasp the kernel of all religious experience. As Neibuhr puts it:

Inquiry into the religions cannot proceed by stripping away the layers of individualization in search of the generic, for, however much a specific religious self-consciousness may approach the proportions of piety as it is recognizable everywhere, the identity of the former is always stamped with the particular character of the mediator of its appearance.[49]

It is not a case of stripping off successive skins as one does with an onion, until the kernel is exposed. For every religion is an organic whole, not a mechanical structure of successive layers with the lowest layer that which the religion shares with all others. Religion *per se* can be understood only from within those historical wholes within which it has embodied itself. Within his own particular historical embodiment, a man can examine the relationship of his historical whole to other embodiments and seek that which all embody.

Schleiermacher does, however, seek a differentiation between the religions. Emphasizing the feeling of relative freedom in man's world-consciousness, he avoids the accusation of pantheism for himself, and, at the same time, suggests that, where there is not a real differentiation of world-consciousness from God-consciousness, we have a lower type of religion. A religious embodiment that differentiates the world from God, distinguishing the two types of consciousness, recognizing the reality of man's feeling of relative freedom and yet seeing the dependence of all things upon God, stands higher than one which merges the two types of consciousness and sees no distinction between God and his creatures. On such a basis, Schleiermacher sees the religions falling into two main groups—the mystical or aesthetical and the ethical or teleological.[50] The first group covers the religions of Asia. It fails to make a real distinction between God and the world or to recognize man's relative freedom. The second is concerned with man's relative freedom as this is expressed in his feeling of the moral imperative. It distinguishes God from his creatures and sees man fulfilling the divine purpose in human history. To this group belong religions such as Islam, Judaism, and Christianity. Clearly this scale of valuation reflects Schleiermacher's own Christian convictions, the higher embodiments of the pious feeling being those which come nearest to the Christian religion itself.

It will be noted that, in the concrete religions, knowing and doing became a significant part of the religious consciousness. This is because the pious feeling can only receive embodiment at the level of the world-consciousness with its knowing and doing. Hence mystical vision and the moral imperative fill the God-consciousness with concrete content, giving it cognitive and conative dimensions. The two types of religion—the aesthetical and the teleological—give the primary pious feeling of absolute dependence a cognitive, rational, and moral garb. But primarily religion is not the latter. Against the rationalism of Hegel and the moralism of Kant, Schleiermacher affirmed the "feeling" nature of religion. Religion must not be prostituted to either rationalism or moral legalism. Yet he was not happy with the mysticism of identity either, where feeling did have a larger place. He sought here, as we have seen, to protect himself against pantheism.

It is at this point that Schleiermacher finds himself in difficulty. As a convinced Christian, he holds to the finality and absoluteness of his Christian faith. But his presuppositions do not help him to maintain this. The Spinozaistic influences led him to think of God as the absolute and unvarying background in such a way that God's pressure on his creatures was so uniform and undiscriminating that special revelation had no place. Man's immediate religious self-consciousness was the same everywhere. All religions were distinctive organic flowerings of the God-consciousness, conditioned by the historical milieu in which they emerged. Some particular intuition or principle became central, and all religions were differing aspects of the primary God-consciousness. The religious man, says Schleiermacher,

must be conscious that his religion is only part of the whole; that about the same circumstances there may be views and sentiments quite different from his, yet just as pious; and that there may be perceptions and feelings belonging to other modifications of religion, for which the sense may entirely fail him.[51]

Thus at the philosophical level, in his *Speeches*, Schleiermacher sees continuity. The Absolute cannot absolutize itself in any historical embodiment, and no concrete expression can exhaust the infinite possibilities of the religious self-consciousness. Yet Christianity is superior to the others and, he suggests, may ultimately take them up into itself.

In *The Christian Faith*, Schleiermacher endeavors to move to a more absolute standpoint. Yet even there he balks at a real break in the continuity. No religion can claim the complete truth. No religion can lay exclusive claim to its own particular application of the idea of divine revelation and declare all others to be false. The complete truth would mean that God had disclosed himself as he is in and for himself. But such a truth could not come through finite fact or be comprehended by any human soul or even become operative in a finite world. God can disclose himself only in his relation to us with its human limitations. Even the most imperfect form of religion may yet, however, possess revelation.[52]

In both books, Schleiermacher sees the Christ as the most perfect embodiment of the God-consciousness and the one who most perfectly evokes such a consciousness in others. Hence he believes that Jesus of Nazareth and the Christian religion have given concrete expression to the very essence of the religious self-consciousness, whereas other religions have distorted it. In the *Speeches* we are told that

the truly divine element is the glorious clearness to which the great idea He (Christ) came to exhibit attained in His soul. This idea was, that all that is finite requires a higher mediation to be in accord with the Deity, and that for man under the power of the finite and particular, and too ready to imagine the divine itself in this form, salvation is only to be found in redemption.[53]

The Christian religion is like other religions in being the embodiment of the pious feeling around a particular intuition. It differs from them in that here the intuition has grasped the essence of the immediate religious self-consciousness.

Schleiermacher develops this in *The Christian Faith*. Christ is the mediator of a redemption in which man is delivered from forces in his world-consciousness that prevent the true expression of his higher God-consciousness. In other religions, these forces prevent the vitality of the immediate religious self-consciousness from coming to full flower. Such religions show little real union between the sensible self-consciousness or world-consciousness and the higher self-consciousness or God-consciousness. In them the latter is overlaid by rites and dogmas that inhibit its expression. Redemption is not central, and the rites and dogmas offer but an incomplete release of the vitality of the religious self-consciousness into men's lives.[54] This redemption and release Christ brought. He needed no redemption himself but was the perfect embodiment of the consciousness of God, and he has infinite power to communicate this to others. He is distinguished from all other religious founders "as Redeemer alone and for all." [55] Thus in *The Christian Faith*, Schleiermacher goes far toward declaring the finality of Christianity.

Yet, once more, Schleiermacher never escapes his presuppositions. The revelation in Christ is not supernatural, but natural. Christ only brings to full embodiment in himself that seed of piety which has been planted in all men. Here is no "Word from beyond," but a revealing development from within man himself. Since Christ was a man, the possibility of taking up the divine into himself must have been always present in man. Potentially the capacity for God-consciousness in Jesus was the same as for all men. Further, argues Schleiermacher, even if only the possibility is present and if the actual implanting of the divine element is a divine and eternal act,

the temporal appearance of this act in one particular Person must at the same time be regarded as an action of human nature, grounded in its original constitution and prepared for by all its past history, and accordingly as the highest development of its spiritual power.[56]

Once more we fall back upon the fact that revelation is natural and is fundamentally the same everywhere, the evoking of the God-consciousness planted in every man. Hence, in one respect, the Christ is not absolutely apart from the continuity that history manifests. Others may approach the level of his God-consciousness. Schleiermacher tries to retain the absoluteness by suggesting that what was unique was the complete control of every aspect of the life of Jesus by his God-consciousness. He does suggest, in the passage just quoted, that the implanting of such a God-consciousness in Jesus is "a divine and eternal act." Once more his Christian conviction is triumphing over his basic view of God as absolute and thus beyond all relations, especially special operations.

## The Significance of Schleiermacher

The problem faced by Schleiermacher is still with us. Having admitted a degree of revelation in all religions, namely, the pious feeling of absolute dependence, he logically could only think of continuity between all religions, including Christianity. They might be higher or lower on his scale of values according to the degree with which they disclosed the essence of the religious consciousness, but there was no difference of kind, only of degree. On the other hand, he faced his own Christian conviction that the Christian religion was final and absolute, alone offering real redemption. He sought to meet this by declaring Jesus of Nazareth to be the unique and pure embodiment of the God-consciousness that was at the root of all religions. The Christ was thereby the redeemer of all men from the misrepresentations and distortions from which man's God-consciousness suffered because of his world-consciousness. Yet, as we have seen, the revelation here is still natural revelation, akin to that in all other religions. Illogicality arises directly after Schleiermacher speaks of a special divine act in relation to the God-consciousness of Jesus. Then he implies a uniqueness that contradicts his contention that all men have the same seed of piety, the same pious feeling, and that Jesus has embodied this wholly and in purity. If Christianity is only one among other religions as this implies, then it differs from the others only in accidents and not in essence.

In our own time the issue has been expressed differently. It lies at the root of Bonhoeffer's declarations. He solves it by dismissing all religion as a man-made phenomenon and by declaring that Christianity is not a religion but the absolute disclosure. He sets faith over against religion. It is not our intention at this stage of the discussion to do more than point to the dilemma that Schleiermacher faced but did not resolve.

We can see some of his difficulty. It was bound up with his

presuppositions. He had adopted a philosophical stance under the influence of Spinozaism. Although he justifiably denied being a pantheist, he was panentheistic. This is quite evident in his attempts to deal with creation, where he shows little real understanding of *creatio ex nihilo*. It is evident also in his treatment of providence, for he grants to nature little independence and gives no attention to the presence in it of a random element. Man's conditioning by nature is identical with his being conditioned by God. This is in keeping with his tendency to understand God philosophically in the light of Spinoza's "substance." It accounts for his difficulties when he comes to speak of God as personal. God is absolute and unvarying power, whose activity is marked by regularity and who has no reserves of power. Schleiermacher tells us that "what does not become actual, is also, as far as God is concerned, not potential." [57] Presumably what God wills to do is all that he can do. Yet Schleiermacher's Christian convictions make him sure of the divine love that is manifest in the consciousness of redemption through Christ the Mediator. Hence grace becomes, as we have seen, coterminous with nature. As Mackintosh remarks: "All that is possible for God is real; there are in Him no reserves of power. . . . The whole of God is fact." [58] When, in consequence, Schleiermacher deals with "sin" it is regarded more negatively than positively. It is more the absence of full God-consciousness than the presence of active rebellion, at the philosophical level. Christ as full embodiment of the God-consciousness removes the barriers supplied by world-consciousness that inhibit the full realization of the God-consciousness in other men. Schleiermacher faces the same problem that Augustine did centuries before when he adopted a Neoplatonic philosophical scheme for his expression of the Christian faith.

The problem would seem to be the clash between a basic panentheistic monism and a warm and very real commitment to the Christian disclosure. In his able study of Schleiermacher, which concentrates on the *Dialectic*, Spiegler supports this. He points out that Schleiermacher, on the one hand, thinks of God in terms of the absoluteness of the transcendental formula and, on the

other hand, seeks to express his Christian convictions by filling
such an empty unity as an absolute beyond all relations with a
"living conception of God." His theology has, in consequence, no
objective reference. His predications concerning God are never
properly objective but reflect "the changing situation of the world
of relativity," having no anchorage in God as such. God is beyond our predication in the light of Schleiermacher's philosophical presupposition. "The dialectical-philosophical absolute cannot be treated as being simply identical with the 'living God' of
religion." [59] This means that Schleiermacher has real difficulty in
expressing any divine relativity to the world, including special
revelation. It explains why he falls back on "feeling" and a universal seed of piety, and yet even this raises difficulties from his
philosophical viewpoint. Schleiermacher is violating the divine
covenant "at its foundational level in the relationship between
God and the world" [60] when he remains true to his philosophical
presupposition about the absoluteness of deity.

Schleiermacher could have chosen a more viable alternative to
this absolutist interpretation of God. The divine relativity to the
world would have been safeguarded and the dilemma to some
degree avoided, had he thought of God as the living God, personal
being acting creatively and redemptively in his Word. Religiously
and theologically he is Christocentric, and yet his presupposition
leads him to an inadequate view of revelation, a weak Christology, and an emphasis on "feeling" with all its inherent ambiguity. His tendency to immanentism is inevitable once one
sees Schleiermacher's commitment to a monism that carries with
it the thought of an absolute beyond all relations. Schleiermacher
had, because of his theological piety, to accept some degree of
divine relativity, but he accepted as little as possible, striving to
hold together divine revelation and divine absoluteness. This explains his difficulty when he faces the issue of the absoluteness
and finality of Jesus Christ. The involvement of God with his
world is central in the Biblical understanding of creation, revelation, and incarnation, and yet Schleiermacher does not want more
involvement than his presupposition can safely carry, if it can
carry any at all! As Spiegler rightly suggests:

Barring God's involvement in relativity, no matter how difficult that thought might be to entertain otherwise, religion and theology must remain suspended over the abyss of absolute cleavage, in constant fear of plunging into the nothingness of their own actuality or into the nothingness of the non-being of God.[61]

We must return later to discuss how far God must be pictured as dipolar, as being/becoming!

Yet, with such criticism, we have much to learn from Schleiermacher positively as well as negatively. He is thoroughly Biblical in regarding man's piety as grounded in his selfhood and in emphasizing that such selfhood is constituted by man's relatedness. It is as a related being, world-conscious and God-conscious, that man is aware of himself. Thus, although at the highest or religious level of this self-consciousness, Schleiermacher emphasizes feeling and specifically excludes knowing and doing, he yet makes religion a response of the self to the all-embracing whole. Furthermore, "feeling" implies "intuition," while, in his thought, the *full* religious consciousness brings in the world-consciousness and involves both knowing and doing. Part of the fallacy in Schleiermacher's position lies in a failure to see that because religion is not science or metaphysics, this does not logically imply that it cannot include any knowledge at all. The presence of a common stock of symbols and dynamic images in the religious consciousness might suggest a cognitive aspect in man's religious response to reality. The religious consciousness is not just knowledge at the highest level but it does involve it. What Schleiermacher has done, however, is to make us see that religion is not reducible to metaphysics, rational theology, or morality. It is *sui generis* and represents man's fundamental *response* to reality, however much Schleiermacher himself failed to emphasize this element of response. In his own way he believes religion to be both universal and the basic aspect of human experience.

Tillich argues that Schleiermacher's mistake was to seek absoluteness for the Christian religion instead of seeking absoluteness in the Christ himself. The Christ stands in judgment on all religions, including the varieties of the Christ faith itself, and yet to varying degrees all religions contain a measure of his living truth. Tillich writes: "The superiority of Christianity lies in its witnessing against itself and all other religions in the name of the Christ." [62] So we turn our attention to this thinker who stands in many ways in Schleiermacher's situation, however much his approach may differ.

# III

## *From Absolute Dependence to Ultimate Concern*

### PART 2: TILLICH ON THE BOUNDARY LINE

TILLICH'S THOUGHT has been studied so frequently that we might deal with him in shorter compass. Yet his impact on contemporary theological thought, certainly in the States but latterly also in Britain and Germany, is significant, especially so in the area of the nature of religion and the concomitant issue of revelation. In many senses, Tillich is a twentieth-century counterpart to Schleiermacher. He himself has written: "Schleiermacher's 'feeling of absolute dependence' was rather near to what is called in the present system 'ultimate concern about the ground and meaning of our being.'" [1] It is significant that both have an idealistic leaning in their thought and that both combine this with a romanticist strain. Tillich was strongly influenced by the thought of Schelling, and many suggest that his existentialist emphasis leans much upon this thinker, rather than owing anything to Kierkegaard. Both Schleiermacher and Tillich are panentheistic in their presuppositions, but Tillich is not bound by the transcendental and absolutist viewpoint that so crippled Schleiermacher. Furthermore, as we shall see, Tillich has a much more positive and radical view of sin because of his emphasis on the demonic, which leans back through Schelling on the understanding of God in the thought of Jakob Böhme. Again, Tillich, like Schleiermacher, is not prepared to speak of God as ultimately personal. Rather, for him, God is ultimately the unconditioned ground of being, and the description is at best a symbol. There is a God beyond God, i.e., a depth of being which the symbol "personal" cannot adequately contain. Yet again, Tillich, like Schleiermacher, has difficulty with the idea of *creatio ex nihilo*. Finally, we find an immanentist emphasis in both thinkers, though it is differently slanted and Tillich has a far deeper understanding of transcendence.

Yet this is in no way to underestimate Tillich's contribution. His system has often made him a captive until, like Hegel, there is a deceptive omniscience about his thinking. But his understanding of revelation, his categories for the understanding of history, his comprehension of the relation of faith to reason, his understanding of the place of symbolism are, to name only a few, insights for which contemporary thought can be grateful.

### Religion as Ultimate Concern

Like Schleiermacher and Augustine, in whose tradition both Schleiermacher and he stand, Tillich would have us begin with man's self-consciousness. As we have seen, Schleiermacher's "feeling" is not mere subjective ecstasy, a psychological state, but it involves "intuition" and thus has a cognitive or noetic dimension. Schleiermacher's study of religion begins with the basic "feeling" of absolute dependence in man's immediate self-consciousness, and he is quite clear that this means direct and unmediated awareness of the Universe or God-consciousness. Tillich cites Schleiermacher along with Spinoza, James, Schelling, Hocking, Whitehead, and Hegel as, in various ways, presupposing "an immediate experience of something ultimate in value and being of which one can become intuitively aware." [2] He sees both religious naturalists and religious idealists rooting their theological concepts in "a 'mystical *a priori*,' an awareness of something that transcends the cleavage between subject and object." [3] In both empirical and metaphysical approaches no religious philosopher can escape such a presupposition, and the theologian differs only by adding to this "mystical *a priori*" the criterion of the Christian message. Tillich himself wants to stand in this position, and he interprets Schleiermacher as meaning by "feeling" "the immediate awareness of something unconditional in the sense of the Augustinian-Franciscan tradition." [4] Thus we have again what has been termed an "identity ontology," as would be expected of a panentheistic approach. Johnson, commenting on Tillich and Schleiermacher, notes that

each builds upon the initial assumption of an "inside knowledge," an immediate, pre-reflective knowledge of an immanent ground of unity that is both logically and ontologically prior to the separation involved in all human cognition and existence. [5]

Tillich carefully differentiates between two types of philosophy of religion—the ontological approach of Augustine and the cosmological approach of Aquinas. [6] He distinguishes them on the basis of their understanding of God. The ontological approach sees man estranged from God in his existence, yet he is not and never can be separated from God. Hence he can overcome his estrangement, for he discovers in God "something that is identical with himself although it transcends him infinitely." [7] The cosmological approach sees a real separation. Man meets a stranger when he meets God. He and God do not essentially belong to each another, as in the ontological type. Man can therefore possess no certainty about God and his separation from God can be real. Tillich would place himself in the first approach, and this enables us to understand better what he means by the "mystical *a priori*." He tells us the ontological principle means that *"man is immediately aware of something unconditional which is the prius of the separation and interaction of subject and object, theoretically as well as practically."* [8]

This is elucidated when we examine Tillich's understanding of personal being. He sees the ontological question, "the question of being as being," as arising in a kind of metaphysical shock—the shock of possible non-being. This shock raises the issue "Why is there something; why not nothing?" and a man then has to investigate "the character of everything that is in so far as it is." [9] Man's awareness of his finitude brings with it the awareness of the unconditioned and the infinite. So man is driven beyond the level of finite being to seek for that which is the ultimate ground of all finite being, the power of being. In his analysis of being, Tillich postulates *a priori* a basic ontological structure in which are three ontological elements or pairs of polarities. The basic structure is that of the self and the world. In his experience, man knows himself "as a 'self' having a 'world' to which he belongs." From this basic ontological structure there arises the subject/object structure of reason. Tillich sees self-consciousness and world-consciousness as necessary for each other.[10] Without world-consciousness, psychic as well as somatic, self-consciousness would have no content. "The self without a world is empty; the world without a self is dead." [11] Within this basic structure and in keeping with his dynamic view of selfhood, Tillich sees three pairs of polarities—individualization and participation, dynamics and form, freedom and destiny.[12] In these pairs, the first member corresponds to the self and the second member to the world. Thomas has summarized the position succinctly:

Obviously it is because the basic structure of being is "self" confronted by "world" that being can be interpreted as containing *individuals* which are self-centered but also *participate* in their environment, are *dynamic* or active but have *form*, and are *free* but are limited by *destiny* as parts of the world.[13]

The most characteristic aspect of such structured being is finitude. Everywhere being is limited by non-being. Indeed, for Tillich, "being, limited by non-being, is finitude." [14] We have to understand his use of "non-being," for he does not mean undialectical negation of being, a "nothing" which has no relation at all to being. For him "non-being" is a dialectical concept; like

Hegel's "antithesis." It has a dialectical relation to being. It is not the Greek *ouk on* but the Greek *me on,* so emphasized by Platonists. It is that which resists being and even perverts being, and it is literally nothing except in relation to being. Tillich is speaking here not logically but ontologically. We might describe non-being as that which has the potentiality of being but is meaninglessness. As such, it continually threatens being. For finite beings, this concept enables Tillich to stress the dynamic nature of selves. Everything that is finite both participates in the power of being and is "mixed" with non-being. "It is being in process of coming from and going toward non-being." [15] This constitutes both its finitude and its becoming. As Thomas puts it: "Dialectical non-being is that which both provides the potentiality of being and, in the case of finite being, resists or threatens being." [16]

At the human level, this finitude is experienced as anxiety. Anxiety describes man's self-awareness of his finitude. It is to be distinguished from fear of a specific object, for it is ontological, not psychological. "Psychotherapy cannot remove ontological anxiety, because it cannot change the structure of finitude." [17] As the inner side of finitude, such anxiety is omnipresent. It is the fear of the threat of non-being, and ultimately of the threat of death. This anxious awareness of finitude brings with it an awareness of the unconditioned and the infinite. Disrupted by space and time, subject to the transience and flux that continually condition human existence, aware of the threat of non-being, man yet finds himself able to look at his finitude in a way that transcends it. David Roberts writes that "in grasping his life as a whole as moving towards death, he [man] transcends temporal immediacy. He sees his world in the setting of the potential infinity, his participation in the setting of potential universality, his destiny in the setting of potential all-inclusiveness." [18] In other words, man is able to some degree to transcend the polarities of his being. In thus looking at his finitude in a way that transcends it, man is aware both of his finitude and of his belonging to the ground of being. Man, aware that his polarities will tend to separate and break up the unity of his being, is anxious about the loss of his essential being. The polarity of individualization and participation may so fall apart that one member assumes dominance, and the result is either loneliness and self-seclusion or mergence of the individual in the collective.[19] The disruption of freedom and destiny in their ontological polarity may lead either to a loss of freedom, with destiny being transformed into determinism, or to a loss of destiny by the freedom becoming completely arbitrary. As Tillich puts it, man "is continuously in danger of trying to preserve his freedom by arbitrarily defying his destiny and of trying to save his destiny by surrendering his freedom." [20] The traditional tension between determinism and indeterminism is an objective form of this ontological disruption.

So finitude becomes the possibility of the disruption of a man's ontological structure and of losing his self, of losing the meaning of his being. This threat as a possibility is always present, but the metaphysical "shock" also brings awareness of the unconditioned and infinite, of the power of being which even enables us to some degree to transcend our polarities and become aware of the threat. Man is aware of his potential infinity while being aware of his actual finitude. "Man knows that he is finite, that he is excluded from an infinity which nevertheless belongs to him." [21] Our human condition means self-estrangement and self-contradiction, but even in our finitude we are aware also of that which is infinite and yet identical with us, the ground and power of being. To quote David Kelsey:

A man realizes in shock that he is persistently threatened by biological extinction, cognitive skepticism, and moral nihilism. At the same time, he finds he has the power to engage in acts of self-affirmation by which he wards off threats to the biological, intellectual, and moral aspects of his personal life. This is the experience of the presence of the power of being in human life.[22]

Here is man's mystical *a priori*.

This awareness of the infinite and unconditioned as the ground and power of being is an awareness of that which transcends all our structured polarities and our estrangement and of that by the power of which we also are able to affirm ourselves. Because it transcends the subject/object polarity, it can be no object to us as subjects. "The *prius* of subject and object cannot become an object to which man as a subject is theoretically and practically related." [23] Hence Tillich refuses to identify this awareness with "intuition," for the unconditioned is no *Gestalt* to be intuited. It comes as a power and a demand. The awareness is itself unconditional, and an activity of the whole self in which it is impossible to divide up the psychological functions. The cognitive and voluntary functions are involved as much as the emotive. Schleiermacher's mistake was to cut off the "feeling" from the will and from the intellect. In his anxiety to separate religion from the cosmological approach of his time, with its rationalism and its moralism, he made religion less than an activity of the whole man. For it is out of this basic awareness that religion takes its rise.[24]

Tillich is quite clear that man cannot philosophize his way to the absolute, the Unconditioned, and he dismisses the arguments for the divine existence. For one thing, it is impossible to attain the infinite from the structure of finite being. In such arguments God is derived from the world and then he cannot be that which transcends the world infinitely. Rather he is "a missing part of that from which he is derived in terms of conclusions." [25] Furthermore, to speak of the "existence" of God is a contradiction, since he is beyond the estrangement of existence from essence which marks finite existence. "God does not exist. He is being-itself, beyond essence and existence." [26]

What the metaphysical shock and its awareness of the ground of being do is to raise the ontological question. As Tillich puts it: "The question of God is possible because an awareness of God is present in the question of God." [27] The question is not answered by human reason but by revelation. It is revelation which gives content to the primary awareness. How like Schleiermacher, except that Tillich has a much richer understanding of revelation! In revelation the mystery of being-itself discloses itself through the objective medium of a miracle or sign-event. Tillich strongly emphasizes that all revelation is mediated through the world, but that such revelation is only meaningful because of man's prior awareness of identity with the ground of being.

We shall defer till a little later a further discussion of revelation, but we need to note that the basis of Tillich's methodology at this point lies in his concept of correlation. Revelation's answer to finite man's ontological question means that theology must be an answering theology. "Questions implied in the human situation [are] placed in a position of correlation with revelatory answers." [28] Thus "God" is the answer to man's finitude, but all that can be derived from the latter is man's "participation in being and the threat of non-being; man asks about the ground of his own being and a power which can overcome non-being. If these questions are correlated with the notion of 'God' derived from revelation, then God must be called the ground of being and the infinite power of being which resists non-being." [29] Tillich himself has succinctly stated his point of view: "Philosophy deals with the structure of being in itself; theology deals with the meaning of being for us." [30] Reason may thus undertake a phenomenological analysis of the structure of being, but it has not the power to grasp being itself.

It is at this level of revelation that man's ultimate concern takes its rise, and here Tillich finds the roots of the religious consciousness. He regards religious faith as the state of being ultimately concerned. Its roots lie in the awareness of the threat of non-being and the power of being, in man's sense of estrangement and awareness of the unconditioned. Men have both vital and spiritual concerns, and Tillich includes in the latter category social, political, and aesthetic concerns. Yet such preliminary concerns lean back upon a basic concern, in which the total self is so involved that a man is completely captured by it. Such a basic concern involves the whole of man's being, "the structure, the meaning, and the aim of human existence." [31] A man's ultimate concern is that which has the power to threaten and to save his being in its totality. He is ultimately concerned about his being and his meaning. " 'To be or not to be' in this sense," writes Tillich, "is a matter of ultimate, unconditional, total and infinite concern." [32] Encompassed by non-being and estranged from being, man in his finitude is concerned for that which gives his existence ultimate meaning, the ultimate ground of all being, "God." Deep down in all men there is the ultimate concern, rooted in their primary awareness and fundamental anxiety.

Because man is conditioned by finite existence, he can easily be preoccupied and captured by transient and relative concerns. In consequence, he tends to erect false ultimates, making the nation his "god" or adopting the American "gods" of success and social status. Such false ultimates belong to the level of idolatry. They can be categorized as "demonic," for Tillich defines the demonic as the raising of something finite to infinite value, "the elevation of one element of finitude to infinite power and meaning." [33] Yet they do illustrate and point to that which ultimate concern involves. Any claim to ultimacy involves a demand for total surrender and a promise of total fulfillment, so that the unconditional demand is matched by the promise of ultimate fulfillment.[34] When man demonizes his nation, it demands his total involvement and promises his fulfillment in the nation's future, even though he falls a victim to war. When a man adopts social or economic success as his ultimate concern, there is demanded of him complete subjugation to the social and economic laws of his community and a promise of the fulfillment of his own being— here Tillich comments that "when fulfilled, the promise of this faith proves to be empty." [35]

How, then, is a false ultimate concern to be differentiated from man's true ultimate concern? Tillich's answer is to point to the ontological depth of genuine ultimate concern, its rootage in man's awareness of his finitude and of the power of being. His principal criterion is that "ultimate concern" unites the subjective and objective and transcends such a relationship. What is genuinely ultimate and unconditioned can never be turned into an object, for it rises infinitely above all objects that can be grounded in it. "God" as ultimate concern is not an object alongside other objects, an entity within what Schleiermacher called man's

"world-consciousness." "God" is "being itself." So we find ourselves back with our previous examination of man's basic anxiety
and awareness.

Tillich sees in man a capacity to transcend the relative and
conditioned experiences by which he is beset and unite himself
with the ground of his being. In doing this, he becomes theonomous man, genuinely self-conscious being. This occurs through
the act of faith, the religious act in the state of ultimate concern.
Faith is evoked as revelation creates a state of shock and makes
man aware of his condition. In faith the subjective and the objective are transcended. Man knows himself to be lifted out of his
condition of estrangement into union with "being itself," "God."
Tillich can speak of religious faith as "ecstasy," not in any subjectively emotional sense, but on the basis of the philological
roots of the word. In the act of faith a man "stands outside" or
beyond himself, and yet remains himself. The measure of self-
transcendence he has is lifted by the power of being into union
with the infinite. He becomes a truly unified person. As theonomous man he becomes a real self.[36]

The transcendence of the subject/object cleavage in the act of
faith is interpreted as a union with the ground of being akin to
Paul's suggestion that successful praying requires that God as
Spirit intercede within us. "God never can be object," Tillich
writes, "without being at the same time subject." [37] As subjective,
faith is ultimate concern; as objective, it is that which is believed. Faith has a content to which it is directed, but the act of
faith does not possess this content, the ultimate. That with which
we are ultimately concerned grasps us, so that faith is both directed on "God" and also God's act within us. To quote Tillich:
"In the act of faith that which is the source of this act is present
beyond the cleavage of subject and object. It is present as both
and beyond both." [38] Here Tillich stands in the line of Augustine
and the Reformed tradition.

Tillich is thus able to extend the criterion by which any concern
that is claimed to be ultimate may be judged. When any finite
entity is regarded as infinite and made the ultimate concern, it

will fail to transcend the subject/object cleavage. It will remain an object which the believer looks at as subject. Tillich suggests that "the more idolatrous a faith the less it is able to overcome the cleavage between subject and object." [39]

Faith as ultimate concern is an act of the whole self. It involves the cognitive, emotional, and volitional dimensions of human personality and reaches down into the unconscious. At the latter level, Tillich rejects any thought of projection, such as Freud postulates when he identifies the symbols of faith with expressions of the superego or father image. He does, however, suggest that faith inverts any process of projection. "Real faith, even if it uses the father image for its expression, transforms this image into a principle of truth and justice to be defended even against the 'father.'" [40] Faith is a conscious act, and unconscious elements are present only insofar as they are integrated into a healthy unity around that act. Faith is indeed an act of the self that transcends all dimensions of personal being. It springs out of man's essential freedom as he is grasped by ultimate concern, and it is a centered personal act. As such, it involves knowing and willing. It is no product of a will-to-believe, for it springs out of an actual awareness of the Other who is also working within. It does not spring out of emotion, even though emotion is constituent. It is indeed *sui generis* and cannot be explained in terms of any more basic element. "Faith precedes all attempts to derive it from something else, because these attempts are themselves based on faith." [41]

Tillich is careful to differentiate faith from the mystical *a priori,* even though the latter, with its awareness of kinship with the infinite, gives faith a base in man. He argues that the immediate awareness of the Unconditioned is of the nature of self-evidence, whereas faith is accompanied by uncertainty and requires a risk. Faith combines "the ontological certainty of the Unconditioned with the uncertainty about everything conditioned and concrete." [42]

The reason for this is that in revelation, the Unconditioned discloses itself to man in the concrete embodiment that the medium of revelation makes possible. Thus the language of religion is that of myth and symbol. It is true that these myths and symbols pass through a process of refining as we move from the lower to the higher manifestations of the religious consciousness. Yet even in its highest expressions, religion is still bound up with the representation of the Unconditioned in symbolic form. Such symbols and myths are adopted from the spatiotemporal framework of human existence and employed as analogies or models for the understanding of the Unconditioned. They are related to the media through which revelation comes to a particular faith. Furthermore, since they are adopted from finite being and since all being participates in being itself, the symbols do, to various degrees, participate in that to which they point. Thus the symbolic language of faith fills the primary awareness of the Unconditioned with concrete content. Yet although finite things can in this way point to God and become integral to his mediate disclosure, they always fall short of reality.

The Unconditioned always transcends the myths and symbols in which it is represented. In the process of refinement of such symbols two dangers have to be avoided. The first is the danger of identifying the symbols with the Unconditioned and thereby demonizing the finite—this happens especially in the lower forms of polytheism, but it also may happen in monotheism. Thus language about God as personal or loving or living is symbolic. He always transcends symbols taken from finite being, and yet they participate in him. Symbolic language is both affirmed and denied. The second is the danger of failing to strip transient elements from the permanent in any myth. Those aspects which scientific and empirical observation invalidate need to be eliminated, but complete demythologization is not possible. The language of myth remains, even though some symbols become outdated and new ones have to be formed. Hence Tillich speaks about the "broken myth," which separates "the creations of symbolic imagination from the facts which can be verified through observation and experiment." [43]

Because of this, faith involves both the unconditional element of ontological certainty and the risk that arises from the existential aspect of faith, the element of decision involved in a particular revelation. Faith is based on a foundation that is not risk —the self-evident certainty of the Unconditioned. But it contains the element of risk and existential doubt because it is an existential act. Thus the dynamics of faith include courage and doubt. There is in faith a dimension of courage that takes the risk that is involved. It accepts the insecurity present in every existential truth and takes it into itself by an act of courage. Tillich regards existential doubt and existential faith as the two poles of a state of ultimate concern, and holds that "serious doubt is confirmation of faith. It indicates the seriousness of concern, its unconditional character." [44]

Tillich presents a much more dynamic understanding of religion than does Schleiermacher. He recognizes the dynamic nature of personal being. Ultimate concern is very different from the "feeling" of absolute dependence. As we have seen, the act of faith is that of the whole self. Its uniqueness does not depend upon its being derived from one dimension of the conscious response of man, but in the fact that it involves and yet transcends all functions of the consciousness. Ultimate concern demands total surrender and it offers a promise of final deliverance from anxiety and estrangement. The whole man is thus engaged in the religious response.

Equally, Tillich has moved beyond Schleiermacher's preoccupation with an absolute beyond all relations. For him the source of faith, the ground of being, the Unconditioned, is dynamic— the living God. Because of this, he is prepared to see a dimension of non-being in God himself. The dialectic of being and non-being present in all finite existence is lifted up into the transcendent and unconditioned ground of all life's creative processes. If God be Creator and if history has meaning for him, a dialectical negativity must be posited of being-itself. Thus Tillich, in his own characteristic way, is saying something akin to the dipolar view of God in contemporary process thought, although he rejects the idea of a God as simply becoming because this subjects God to a process that is completely open to the future and has the character of an absolute accident.[44] He is influenced here by Böhme's concept of the *Ungrund* and Schelling's "first potency." [46] God both goes out from himself and rests in himself; he is both possibility and fulfillment. The dynamic element of becoming is balanced by the static aspect of rest, and such movement is possible in God because of the dimension of non-being, the form-destructive element that is present in his transcendent wholeness. Thereby God is the living God, whose acts make revelation possible in Tillich's thought, where Schleiermacher has real difficulty and falls back on subjectivity because of his transcendental formula for God.

This dynamic aspect of God is expressed in the description "the Holy." Here Tillich employs Otto's concept to stress that in revelation God, the Unconditioned, approaches men as a mystery that both repels and attracts, shakes and fascinates. Even though the Unconditioned transcends all our finite polarities, the duality in his nature of being/non-being means that the presence of God is both form-creative and form-destructive and further that both aspects of deity will be present in the divine disclosure. What is demonic in finite things is also a reality in God, for he is divine/demonic, creative/destructive. Hence the holy transcends even moral perfection. In men's expressions of ultimate concern they may so stress moral perfection in God that the terrifying aspect recedes. The Hebrew prophets grasped the moral element in the divine revelation, but, apart from the emphasis on judgment, tended to leave the form-destructive aspect on one side. God is both the puller and the shaker, the one who attracts and the one who strikes fear. Even in an idolatrous faith that so often is both demonic and destructive, the holy may be present. "This is the point," writes Tillich, "where the ambiguous character of religion is most visible and the dangers of faith are most obvious: the danger of faith is idolatry and the ambiguity of the holy is its demonic possibility. Our ultimate concern can destroy us as it can heal us." [47]

This dynamic aspect of deity is the objective pole over against the subjective pole of ultimate concern. In religion men meet their ultimate concern in revelation and become themselves ultimately concerned. This experience of being ultimately concerned matches the dual aspect of the holy God who is man's ultimate concern. In the act of faith both unconditional demand and a promise of final fulfillment are present. In the "shock" of revelation, man realizes his finitude and estrangement before the transcendence of God, feels the pressure of the unconditioned and the holy as demand, and yet knows also that through surrender to that demand he will be brought to personal fulfillment and return to that full unity with the infinite of which he is vaguely aware.

Just as in the divine infinitude, the form-creative submerges the form-destructive aspect, so man's redemption lifts him above his polarities and makes it possible for the demonic element to be submerged in full creative selfhood. This is redemption. Man becomes a real person. Tillich defines "courage" as "the self-affirmation of being in spite of non-being," [48] and declares that such "courage to be" must have a religious root. It leans back upon faith in the power of being-itself. Thus the courage in moral affirmation lies in the presence in a man's life of "the unconditional element in the moral imperative," [49] the unconditional demand of a man's ultimate concern.

## Revelation and the Religions

We have talked much of "revelation." We must now look at Tillich's valuable insights at this point. As we have seen, he regards the objective side of religion as revelation which takes place through the medium of nature or society or individual persons. The media of revelation are miracles or sign events that become "transparent," symbolic of the mystery of being-itself. Tillich holds that there is no reality, thing, person, or group of persons, which may not thus become transparent of the ground of being, since all participate in the ground of being. He tells us that "there is no difference between a stone and a person in their potentiality of becoming bearers of revelation." [50] Yet the things of nature do represent a lower aggregate of qualities that can thus point to the ground of being, so that revelation through nature is more limited in respect to the truth and significance of what is thus mediated.

We must not however, talk about natural revelation. Natural knowledge is man's reason operating upon nature and seeking to establish God by argument. Revelation is never natural, for it makes nature miraculous so that certain aspects of nature become "transparent," are transformed into symbols of some aspect of God himself. Nature in revelation is not a basis for inference. It is a medium through which man is grasped by the Unconditioned and becomes aware symbolically of some quality of the divine ground of being.

In the same way, history and personality may become revelatory. What makes history revelatory is not the social or personal greatness of those who participate in the revelatory events, but the fact that the occurrence "stands under the 'directing creativity' of the divine life." [51] Revelation takes place when individuals or groups of persons become transparent to the ground of being. What is important is not their historical significance or social importance or personal eminence, but the revelatory constellation into which they have entered under special conditions. The revelatory nature of the occurrence cannot be foreseen or denied from the qualities of the persons or groups. It depends wholly upon the activity of the ground of being in which all participate.

Historical revelation does not take place *in* history but *through* history. History always possesses the dimension of interpretation. Some group sees a pattern of events as interpretative of its historical destiny. So the Christian church becomes a medium of revelation as it associates itself with the historical happenings of its origination. The prophets interpret revelatory happening and thereby become media of revelatory interpretation. Hence historical happenings are revelatory in conjunction with interpretative groups or personalities. The total constellation constitutes a revelatory situation for other men and groups.

Revelation can take place through the medium of persons apart from their being interpreters of historical events. Others besides prophets may become personal mediums of revelation. The priest may become personally transparent, but this may be so, not because of his status and function or by the practice of his rites, but under special conditions of divine activity. Again, the saint is not revelatory because of religious or moral perfection but because he is transparent to the ground of being and able to enter as a medium into some revelatory constellation. So prophets, priests, and saints may all be gathered up into the divine activity as media of revelation.[52]

In his long and insightful discussion of revelation, Tillich does not specifically mention Christ or the Christian tradition except by way of illustrating his general theme. He sees a continuity in revelation at every level, so that any reality, thing, or event may become bearer of the mystery of being, since all participate in the ground of being. There is, for him, no reality that in some sense may not become "transparent," and revelation must not be limited to Christianity. "A seer, a religious founder, a priest, a mystic —these are the individuals from whom original revelation is derived by groups which enter into the same correlation of revelation in a dependent way." [53]

Tillich emphasizes that the mediums of revelation do not possess revelatory power in themselves. When men think that they do, the mediums are transformed into idols. The end of the power of a revelatory medium does not mean that God was not behind it, but it does mean that its idolatrous aspect is destroyed. Thus Tillich clearly believes that the "ground of being" has many mediums that are transparent to it, and that the priests, seers, and mystics of paganism have their places among these. We have already noted one aspect of this in our discussion of Tillich's understanding of the concept of the holy. Indeed, for him, all the religions of the world are in various ways preparations enabling men to comprehend the "new being" that comes in Christ. The revelation through the Christ would be meaningless were there not this prior revelation.

Tillich regards Jesus Christ as the final revelation, by which he means more than that he is the last genuine and original revelation. "It means the decisive, fulfilling, unsurpassable revelation, that which is the criterion of all the others." [54] It is not that Jesus Christ is the only revelation, but rather that no revelation can surpass him, and therefore that he is the criterion for all others. How is Jesus Christ final? Tillich answers that a revelation is final when it has the power of negating itself without losing itself. Every revelation is conditioned by the medium that it employs and therefore is subject to the limitations imposed by the degree of finitude of that medium. If, however, that medium is able to overcome its own finitude, then it becomes wholly "transparent" and the ground of being appears clearly in and through it. Now the highest possible creaturely medium with the least limitations is the personal. When such a personal medium appears that can completely sacrifice itself to and lose itself in that which it reveals, revelation has become final. "The bearer of a final revelation must surrender his finitude—not only his life, but also his finite power and knowledge and perfection. In doing so . . . he becomes completely transparent to the mystery he reveals." [55] Yet no person can completely surrender himself without completely possessing himself. This means that he must be theonomous man, a real personal being because he is united with the ground of being.

In Jesus Christ we find such a man. In him the estrangement from the ground of being has vanished, for in his humanity, he is completely united with God. Thus he is not existential man, estranged and separated, but essential man, able to triumph over life's vicissitudes and temptations, able to transcend its polarities. This is possible because he is so surrendered to God that the power of being operates fully within him. He is what he is as man because God's grace works fully through him. And because God is thus present in him, he becomes transparent to the divine mystery. Always he points, not to himself, but to the Father who works in and through him. This is the miracle of his humanity and it makes his revelation final in the eschatological sense.

Tillich carefully identifies Christianity as the possessor of the final revelation but *not* as the absolute religion. This differentiation allows for the many varieties of religion in which Christian ultimate concern finds expression. Its content is always the Christ, and yet the subjective pole of the Christian believer means that Christian religion can take many forms. Tillich points out that Paul did not elevate the Christian religion; rather he attacked some of its contemporary forms, especially those which were distorted by Jewish legalistic influences and by Gnostic speculation. Indeed he attacked all religions, not excluding Christianity, and elevated the Christ. "The superiority of Christianity lies in its witnessing against itself and all other religions in the name of the Christ." [56] The approach of Schleiermacher fails at this point—he defines Christianity as a religion and then declares it to be the highest or absolute religion. Yet equally we must not, with Barth and Bonhoeffer, declare that Christianity is not a religion, that all religions are human attempts to come to God, that they possess no revelation and that Christianity alone is constituted by revelation.

One other criticism of Schleiermacher by Tillich needs to be noted. As we have seen, Schleiermacher's approach made the Christian religious consciousness or experience, "feeling," the source of the contents of the Christian faith. Tillich, on the other hand, would regard experience as the medium through which such contents are existentially appropriated. He writes:

The event on which Christianity is based . . . is not derived from experience; it is *given* in history. Experience is not the source from which the contents of systematic theology are taken but the medium through which they are existentially received.[57]

This judgment manifests again the much more sensitive concern with revelation and the nature of the divine transcendence that we have found in Tillich. He does not fall into the trap of complete immanentism which Schleiermacher tends to do when he almost identifies God with the pious feeling and yet also presupposes the philosophical Absolute of idealistic monism.

In emphasizing that Christianity possesses the final revelation and that all other religions possess revelation to varying degrees, Tillich proceeds to differentiate the types of religion or of the state of absolute concern. His differentiation is very close to that of Schleiermacher, although he necessarily expresses the nature of his types in a different way. He finds two basic types of religion—religions either fall into the ontological type (cf. Schleiermacher's mystical or aesthetic religion) or they fall into the moral type (cf. Schleiermacher's teleological religion).[58]

The ontological type of religion emphasizes the presence of God to be enjoyed at the present moment. It may assume either of two forms—the sacramental or the mystical. In the sacramental form, the divine presence is mediated through a special medium whose sacred character is significant only for those who share this particular faith. The danger here is that the medium itself should be regarded as identified with the holy, instead of being that through which the worshiper is grasped by the holy and ecstasy is evoked. Tillich sees this to be the error in transubstantiation.

In the mystic form, the worshiper rises above all media, transcending even reality as a whole and claiming union with the ultimate.[59] Now since the divine mystery transcends all experience and all media, even sacramental media, through which faith attains expression, it would be difficult for faith to be based on such a mystical claim. But the mystic claims that there is a point of contact between the infinite and the finite in the finite world, in the depth of the human soul. Furthermore, Tillich reminds us that "the mystic is aware of the infinite distance between the infinite and the finite, and accepts a life of preliminary stages of union with the infinite interrupted only rarely, and perhaps never, in this life by final ecstasy." [60]

Yet such a mystical element is present for Tillich in all religions. For the sense of God's presence in Tillich's thought has a dual form. There is the mediated immediacy of the divine and the holy by which ultimate concern is given its content, but there is also a primary mystical *a priori*, a direct and self-evident awareness that is the presupposition of every religion, every state of ultimate concern.

The moral type of religion knows the ground of being as judgment and demand. The Unconditioned confronts us with moral claim and shows us what we ought to be. Standing over against us, he commands and claims us. He comes to us as demand and as promise in the teleological sense. Always the Unconditioned stands above us and ahead of us. There is a legalistic element, but the laws are moral, not ritual and ascetic as in the first type of religion. In their own distinctive ways, Islam, Talmudic Judaism, the religion of the Old Testament prophets, and even Confucianism fall under this heading. Often here the mystical emphasis on "being" is replaced by "ought to be," although elements of the first type of religion are often found in the second type and vice versa.

Tillich regards humanism as a religion falling in most contemporary forms under the second type. He is thinking of our Western progressive-utopian type of humanism. He holds that there is a basic faith here in the perfectibility of human nature by man himself, a state of ultimate concern and of total devotion to that concern.

In addition, Tillich labels as quasi religions those which have what we have referred to earlier as false ultimate concerns—nationalism, fascism, and communism, for example. These bear all the marks of a state of ultimate concern including surrender and promise of fulfillment, and the living religions are in vital encounter with them.[61] Tillich points out that in practice, no world religion is purely one type. Furthermore, there are religions, such as Hinayana Buddhism, in which the idea of God is absent but that are still religions because they describe a state of ultimate concern and still fall within the range of these two types of faith.

In actual world faiths, Tillich sees a tension in all religions. He finds that all religions have a sacramental basis which they transcend. They then move in one of two directions—either toward mysticism and the experience of the holy as "being" or toward ethical religion and the experience of the holy as what "ought to be." "There is no holiness and therefore no living religion without both elements, but the predominance of the mystical element in all India-born religions is obvious, as well as the predominance of the social ethical element in those born of Israel." [62] Thus the dialogue between the religions is grounded in a more basic dialogue within the religions themselves. Christianity in discussing the relation of the mystical and the ethical with Buddhism is driven back to an interior discussion of the relation of the same two elements in itself.[63]

In the Christian revelation the two types of religion should attain real unity. Tillich indeed sees all types of faith as united in the Pauline experience of the Spirit, although such unity has been largely lost in both Catholicism and Protestantism. Paul understood the Spirit "as the unity of the ecstatic and the personal, of the sacramental and the moral, of the mystical and the rational." [64] Christianity needs to regain the real experience of this unity if it is to "express its claim to answer the questions and to fulfil the dynamics of the history of faith in past and future."

Thus Tillich has another approach to religion in his understanding of the spiritual presence. He sees religion as "the self-transcendence of life under the dimension of Spirit." [65] The Spiritual Presence brings to men the New Being, fully manifest in Christ, but mankind is never left alone, for there is a common experience of the Spiritual Presence in all religions.[66] Only in Jesus Christ, however, is the divine Spirit present without distortion. "His human spirit was entirely grasped by the Spiritual Presence." [67] Hence Tillich can declare that "Jesus, the Christ, is the keystone in the arch of Spiritual manifestations in history." [68] Tillich thereby emphasizes in yet another way that religion has a revelatory and objective dimension; it expresses a Spiritual Presence and cannot be reduced to a man-made projection. Further, he emphasizes again the finality of the revelation in the Christ in whom "the New Being appeared as the criterion of all Spiritual experiences in past and future." [69]

## The Contribution of Tillich

Like Schleiermacher, Tillich is ontological and not cosmological in his philosophical approach. He belongs to the Augustinian-Franciscan tradition and has a warm place in his thought for mystical piety. He tends toward an "ontological identity" and is panentheistic in his presupposition. In consequence, he preserves the significance of personal being, refusing to allow it to be merged in any absolute. He is very concerned to protect man's freedom and integrity against any heteronomous authority. His approach to sin as a basic estrangement bound up with the dialectic between essence and existence, freedom and destiny, has many profound insights. Yet his panentheistic approach leads him to tie in far too closely the Fall and the Creation. Indeed, the creation of man as a *finite* being gives to non-being in man a leverage against being that makes estrangement a reality. We have almost an identification of the Fall with the act of Creation and of sin with finitude, and that despite Tillich's attempt to emphasize the place of human freedom in the act of sin.[70] If man participates in the ground of being to the point where the infinitude of the latter is poured in its dual aspect of being and non-being into his finitude, we must not be surprised if that finitude inevitably begets sin. A panentheism that rejects absolute creation will always have difficulty, especially if it employs mystical ideas of the *Ungrund* to project the demonic back into the divine being.

Hamilton [71] declares that Tillich is the victim of his system, and at points just mentioned, this is true. Yet let it also be said that he was a devout and committed Christian thinker who was honestly striving to speak to the intellectual despisers of his day. At times limited by the straitjacket of his system, he offers more creative insights than perhaps any other thinker of this century. Hamilton [72] attacks, among other items, Tillich's basic method of correlation, holding that the questions arising out of Tillich's philosophical system dictate the theological answers that Tillich finds in the revelation. His metaphysical scheme is the authoritative center of his thought and his religious thought is subordinated to his ontological analysis. As a result, his correlation is simply the bringing together of elements already forced into agreement by his system. The theology is so controlled ontologically that the correlation is predetermined. This criticism is unfair to Tillich, for there is little doubt that an unprejudiced observer will recognize how much the insights of Christian theology have shaped the system, even while the system has shaped some of the emphases of the gospel. Standing on the boundary between philosophy and theology, Tillich has, throughout his thinking career, developed the two approaches side by side so that they have mutually influenced each other. The truth is that, like every other Christian philosopher, he has been passionately concerned with the ultimate, and his ontological quest has mingled with his theological answer, so that speculative influences cannot be ruled out from his theological formulations. But then that is exactly what happened in the case of Augustine, in whose tradition Tillich stands. We would rather recognize that Tillich himself does not rigorously follow his methodology and really confine his ontology to questions and his theology to answers.

Let us note, however, that fundamental as these issues may be to Tillich's consideration of the nature of religion, his insights on this latter theme are significant. He recognizes that religion is both subjective and objective in the fullest sense and that revelation is operative at every level of the religious consciousness. Further, he holds that such revelation of the Unconditioned in and through the media of things, persons, or events, requires a prior awareness, a mystical *a priori,* in which man is aware of the presence of the Other. Thus, true to his ontological presupposition, Tillich sees a fundamental *a priori* kinship between the finite and the infinite without which religious response would be impossible. Religion is no mere outreach of the human imagination, no man-made creation, but a response to and a grasping by the "ground of being" in a revelatory situation.

Again, Tillich sees religious faith as an act of the whole self, transcending all the divisions of psychological analysis. He thus refuses to identify its uniqueness with some particular dimension of the human consciousness such as "feeling." He steadfastly refuses to isolate religion from knowing or willing. Yet more, he recognizes that the language of religion is mythicosymbolic and that in religious knowledge, the imagination is central, under the influence of the symbols provided by the media of a particular revelatory situation. Finally, he wants to affirm both the finality of Christianity and yet its continuity with other faiths.

In all of this, he is helped by his definition of religion as the state of ultimate concern. This enables him to find religious response in the quasi religions produced by secular thought and to include more easily in his religious category religions like Hinayana Buddhism which themselves are basically atheistic. In all such, as well as in the faiths that are more obviously "religious," he finds that ultimate concern which is objectively in the Unconditioned and is subjectively experienced as a state of ecstasy whereby a man's estrangement is overcome and he is reunited with the ground of being. Thus Tillich sees salvation as a healing of the estrangement and a promise of final fulfillment. Man is on the way to becoming a real person, a genuine self, theonomous man. Faith is both surrender and fulfillment as the Unconditioned approaches man in revelation.

Tillich is quick to assert that Christianity shows all the characteristics of a religion, but like every state of ultimate concern it is also a response to revelation and it is this revelation for which he claims finality. Of the two poles of Christian ultimate concern, the subjective and the objective, the latter is final revelation, but the former shows many varieties of response within the range of Protestantism and Catholicism. There is needed, as he rightly sees, an internal dialogue within Christianity itself whereby the transcendence of the sacramental emphasis by either ethical or mystical emphases may be brought into true balance in relation to the Christ.

In suggesting that all religions, including the varieties of Christianity, need to come under the judgment of the final revelation in the Christ, Tillich is meeting the position of Barth and Bonhoeffer head on. He readily agrees that Christianity is both a religion and not a religion. He points out that religion in the narrower sense is characterized by two essential expressions—myth and cult. Now if Christianity denies its nature as a religion, it will have to fight these elements in its own expression. It has done this across its history. Periodically it has attempted processes of demythologization only to seek new mythical expression. It has criticized its ritual only to devise new ritual. It has sought the mystical way of transcending both cult and myth, only to return to them. For in a real sense cult and myth are the necessary means of self-expression, if the religious experience is to continue. They are present even in the most secularized forms of the quasi religions. Tillich notes that

you cannot escape them, however you demythologize and deritualize. They always return and you must always judge them again. In the fight of God against religion the fighter for God is in the paradoxical situation that he has to use religion in order to fight religion.[73]

We must return later to Tillich's application of this to the secular challenge. It is sufficient here to emphasize a valuable insight, on the basis of which he contends that "religion cannot come to an end, and a particular religion will be lasting to the degree in which it negates itself as a religion." [74] We have noted already that even Bonhoeffer still observes the ritual aspects of the Christian faith and finds spiritual support through them, while even to talk in a secular way about God will involve us in new myths that may be no final advance on the Biblical images!

# IV

## *From Moral Value Judgments to a Religious* A Priori

KANT's *Religion Within the Limits of Reason Alone* set the line of thought for one approach to religion in the next century. His critical philosophy, awakened by Hume's skepticism, set boundaries for the movement of the theoretical reason. Man's pure reason could not advance from the phenomenal world to the noumenal, from the realm of things as known through the senses to the realm of the thing-in-itself. The *a priori* equipment of the pure understanding with its intuitions and categories invalidated any attempt to pass beyond the phenomenal to the noumenal. Hence Kant rejected all metaphysical attempts to establish the existence and reality of God. Although, in his *Critique of Judgment,* he sought to give some validity to the aesthetic judgment and to find some objective place for teleological movement in the universe, Kant fell back ultimately upon the moral judgment and the practical reason. In the categorical imperative with its moral oughtness man was in touch with reality, moving beyond his phenomenal to his noumenal self. This experience of unconditional obligation became for Kant the basis on which the practical reason could postulate the reality of freedom, God, and immortality, the trio beloved by rationalistic theology and affirmed by rationalist thinkers to be the essence of religion.

Be it noted that Kant's scheme offers no place for revelation *per se* and is exceedingly skeptical about "judgments for fact." At the theoretical level, man can make no affirmations beyond the phenomenal. The "world" is always the world which has passed through the alembic of the mind of the knower. Theoretical judgments can affirm nothing about the reality of their statements. Only in his moral judgments can man begin to grasp clearly the nature of reality at any level, and then the approach is anthropocentric. In his religious affirmations a man starts from himself, and such religious affirmations are grounded in his moral experience. Religion is reduced to morality.

We have seen Schleiermacher's reaction to the moral emphasis but noted also his reaction to Hegel's attempt in his idealistic monism to transcend Kant's critical idealism by a new rationalism. We must now turn to the stream of thought that shows marked Kantian influence and to later developments which employ Kant in a way that basically inverts his own methodology. We have for this reason included Ritschl and Otto in the same chapter, for in their own distinctive ways they show Kant's influence.

## Ritschl—Religion and Value Judgments

Ritschl's background embodies the influence of two figures who dominated Protestant thought until the time of Barth and whose impact is still felt—Hegel and Schleiermacher. They represent the speculative or rationalist and the mystical or pietist strains in Christian thought, and against both Ritschl reacted.

Hegel's influence reached Ritschl through his teacher Frederick Christian Baur. The speculative rationalism of Hegel, unlike the rationalism of the eighteenth century, had not rejected Christianity. Rather, it had sought to universalize it by fitting the characteristic insights of the Christian faith into a metaphysical framework and by merging the particularity of the Christian revelation into the general concepts of a philosophical scheme. As a result, theology had become the bondslave of metaphysics, and the emphasis on the historical particularity at the heart of faith was lost. Ritschl affirmed that the final court of appeal for Christian thinking must be, not philosophy, but the historical Jesus and his revelation. He did not reject philosophy completely; he was prepared to use it to give philosophical consideration to the meaning of the concepts that he employed. But he would not allow it to exert any influence on the basic meaning of what faith affirmed.

Ritschl's preoccupation with the Christian faith means that he has less to say about religion in general than the thinkers so far discussed. His emphasis on the historical particularity of Jesus of Nazareth did mean that he rejected all forms of natural theology, as one aspect of his rebellion against speculative theism. Such thinking is concerned with general ideas having no connection with revelation. Speculation starts from outside the aegis of the Christian faith, and it has no possibility of bringing men within that reconciliation which God has effected in Christ. Arguments for divine existence at the best establish a probability; they cannot open up God's inner nature and bring forgiveness. God is known only in his revelation. That revelation is in Christ, and to begin elsewhere is futile.

Yet one positive result of the influence of Hegel and Baur is important. They brought to Ritschl, especially through Baur, a concern with the historical. If Hegel had rehabilitated the historical consciousness, Baur applied the Hegelian dialectic to the history of Christianity.[1] Baur saw a movement in the history of the church, a continuity through the antithetic poles of successive stages. He gave to Ritschl a very real appreciation for the significance of tradition and a recognition of the importance of the historical basis and development of Christian thought. With all his rebellion against the Hegelian straitjacket, Ritschl retained the emphasis on history. Hence we have his concern with the historical particularity and givenness of the Christian revelation. Like Baur, Ritschl looks for continuity in the history of the church. He finds it, not in some abstract principle—being and becoming, spirit and matter, perfectly united in Christ, but in the total human condition of a *Lebensführung* "in which God's prevenient reconciling action and man's subsequent ethical response are held together in equilibrium." [2]

The ethical and historical emphases bring us to Ritschl's rejection of Schleiermacher. The latter, although Christocentric, had placed his emphasis on the subjective. He began with the religious consciousness and its feeling and found little place for the objective givenness of revelation. Emphasizing experience, he had seen theological formulations as expressions of the believer's pious feelings. Ritschl rejected this purely subjective base with its lack of concern for the historical. He emphasized the historical givenness of the revelation of God in Christ and historical formulation of that givenness in the developing tradition of the Christian church.

Along with pietism, he rejected mysticism, for it too transcended the historical, merely, at the best in Christian mysticism, employing Christ as a ladder by which to climb to the final absorption in the "beloved." Furthermore mysticism isolates; it negates fellowship. Real relationship with God is possible only within genuine fellowship with others. Yet again, mysticism pays little or no attention to the emphasis on the forgiveness of sins that Ritschl regards as central in the Christian faith. Let us note, at this point, that Ritschl fails to differentiate between pantheistic and panentheistic mysticism with its emphasis on absorption and theistic mysticism with its emphasis on communion. The former interprets mysticism in terms of identity with the deity, whereas the latter retains personal being within the experience of oneness with God. The latter is the approach that we find in Paul and the Fourth Gospel, and only a narrow definition of mysticism would bar such experiences from that category.

In rejecting rationalistic speculation, Ritschl also rejected any attempt to define a universal essence of which all religions were particular embodiments. He was a nominalist, concentrating on the particulars of historical experience and refusing to regard universals as other than useful classifications of the human mind. Universals were not in things but were the creations of the knowing mind, the products of memory and association. Particulars alone corresponded to reality. Hence any definite general definition of religion could be at best regulative and not constitutive in the interpretation of any particular religion.[3] Thus Ritschl writes:

In the investigation of Christianity the general conception of religion should be used *regulatively*. I desire to distinguish myself very precisely in this respect from those who, in interpreting Christianity, make a *constitutive* use of the general conception.[4]

A general idea of religion will serve "as a clue by which to determine the chief characteristics of the various species of religion." [5] Each religion is a particular historical phenomenon and must be understood as such. "The qualities by which *Christianity reveals its religious character* should be brought out with that distinctness which they claim to possess at the level of Christianity." [6] Here Ritschl partially agrees with Schleiermacher.[7] He refuses to look for some abstract essence of religion present in all religious phenomena. The difficulty of finding a universal generic concept is seen when we recognize that various elements of such a concept undergo considerable modifications in different religions.

As . . . the historical religions offer, under each (such element) . . . a rich supply of specific and sub-specific characteristics, which have no place in the general conception of religion, language can furnish no terms sufficiently neutral and indeterminate to express the general conception of religion desired.[8]

Here Ritschl is thinking of the nature of the Godhead, the relation of the Godhead to the world, the believer's concept of blessedness.

In rejecting speculative idealism at this point, Ritschl was also rejecting the position of Kant with his view of the three postulates of the practical reason. For he believed that every religion had a revelatory aspect. Again, he agrees with Schleiermacher that such revelation is tied to a specific historical situation.

Yet on the positive side, Kant's influence is also evident. His phenomenalism is a presupposition to Ritschl's approach. The latter's emphasis falls upon relations to the knowing subject. Entities are known only in their relation to us, and Ritschl shows a measure of skepticism about knowledge of things in themselves. This is true of God, who is known only as he relates himself to us. Thus like Schleiermacher and Kant, each in his distinctive way, Ritschl is anthropocentric. He begins with experience, which alone brings knowledge. He can write: "We know the nature of God and Christ only in their worth for us." [9] Even theology must not be speculative, for we can speak only of what faith can apprehend. Kant's phenomenalism issues in Ritschl's theological positivism.

Kant's influence on Ritschl is seen again in the latter's emphasis on will in his understanding of religion. For Schleiermacher knowledge in religion is subordinated to feeling. For Ritschl it is subordinated to willing. Religion exists in its own right, and its objective pole cannot be established by rational and discussive argument. Man has to be aware of the divine other, and this awareness comes through the practical side of man's nature, his experience of value and the unconditioned demand that it makes upon him. Like Kant, Ritschl therefore turns to value judgments and especially to moral value judgment, but not exclusively, as shall be seen immediately.

In thus turning to value judgments, Ritschl was following Kant and actually denying the direct experience that mysticism and pietism emphasized. Hegel's rationalism had a mystical dimension. It was an identity ontology in which the human spirit through religion became conscious of itself as Absolute Spirit. Schleiermacher's emphasis on "feeling" had made pious experience central, and, as Tillich points out, "experience means having the divine within ourselves, not necessarily by nature, but yet given and felt within our own being." [10] By emphasizing history,

Ritschl's anthropocentric approach avoided subjectivity and turned to judgments of value on the historically given. Man is a moral person. The emphasis falls not on mystical identity, but on man's capacity for value judgments.

It is here that Ritschl was stimulated by the thought of Lotze, who differentiated between theoretical and practical judgments. Theoretical judgments are judgments of fact; they are concerned with what exists, with what is in relation to us. Practical judgments are judgments of value; they are concerned with significance and meaning, with what ought to be. Lotze had differentiated radically between the two, relating judgments of fact to the sphere of nature and judgments of value to the personal sphere, and making the two entirely independent. Thus the real and the ideal, that which "is" and that which "ought-to-be" were only united in God for Lotze.

Ritschl accepted this differentiation of judgments, but he held that judgments of actual existents, factual judgments, were never without some associated value judgment. The fact that a subject made any propositional statement or judgment about existents inherently carried some judgment of their significance for that subject. A man is only concerned with some fact because it holds his interest and is of value to him. This is, of course, especially evident when we are confronted by a collection of historical material. We choose some happenings as more significant than others and do not judge all our facts on the same level. Ritschl, particularly concerned about history, termed such judgments of value that are involved in judgments of fact, *concomitant* judgments of value. As John Baillie has put it:

There can be no description apart from some rudimentary kind of appreciation. Our attention to "that which is" is directed by some elementary sense of "that which ought to be"; and hence not even physical science can be carried on altogether apart from value-judgments.[11]

In other words, however impartial or objective we try to be in judgments of fact, there is always some degree of partiality. To quote Ritschl's own description:

Value judgments . . . are determinative in the case of all connected knowledge of the world, even when carried out in the most objective fashion. Attention during scientific investigation, and the impartial examination of the matter observed, always denote that such knowledge has a value for him who employs it.[12]

Today, indeed, we might say that the form of the knowledge itself reflects the attitude of the observer. We are much more suspicious of what Ritschl and his contemporaries felt to be the impartiality and objectivity of science. Selectivity in the highly diversified area of theoretical cognition makes concomitant value judgment a necessity, according to Ritschl. This is still more evident today. Nowadays this is increasingly recognized. All knowledge is personal knowledge.[13]

Ritschl then proceeds to distinguish between such concomitant value judgments and *independent* value judgments that he associates with moral and religious experience. By such a description he means judgments that are concerned with what ought-to-be rather than with what is, with the spiritual order of things and not with the perceptual, factual order. Yet he does not mean by the description "independent" that the moral and spiritual order is not real or that such judgments are not bound up with factual judgments. As Baillie puts it:

Sometimes our interest is not in actual perceived fact at all but in an ideal order of things; and these direct affirmations of the ideal are independent value-judgments.[14]

But this ideal order is not just a subjective creation. As Ritschl sees it, it has objective reality and our independent value judgments are thus directed upon reality in its ultimate sense. He writes:

. . . Theoretical cognition must simply accept the fact that while spiritual life is subject to the laws of mechanism so far as it is interwoven with nature, yet its special character as distinct from nature is signalised by practical laws which declare spirit to be an end in itself, which realizes itself in this form.[15]

These two heterogeneous orders of reality, nature and spirit, coexist, and independent value judgments are concerned with the latter. The Kantian dichotomy between the phenomenal world that science studies and the inner and noumenal realm of the moral imperative and personal obligation is thus expressed in a new and more realistic fashion.

This applies especially to Ritschl's identification of religion with such judgments. He tells us that "religious knowledge moves in independent value judgments." [16] Baillie notes that Ritschl's disciples, such as Kaftan, clarified his view about the reality of the world of values, and in particular, of the object of religious judgments, by holding that religious judgments were not themselves judgments of value but rather based upon such judgments. He believes that this is what Ritschl himself intended. "Faith . . . does assert the reality of its own objects, but its conviction of their reality is always grounded in a prior recognition of their value." [17] The word "conviction" in this statement emphasizes one aspect of Ritschl's approach. By *independent* value judgment, he sought to bring out the convictional element in religious judgments and to underline that such personal conviction referred to objective reality. All judgments of value imply an existential judgment. "The judgment that a thing is good presupposes or includes the judgment that the thing is real," writes H. R. Mackintosh. He continues: "In our living experience, fact and value never exist apart; both are presented together as a complex whole which is indissociable, or dissociable only for thought." [18]

We must then ask what are the independent value judgments with which religious faith is associated. Once more the Kantian dichotomy is evident. Ritschl rejected the Hegelian approach, among other reasons because it had too closely identified nature and spirit. His definition of religion in the light of his emphasis on value judgments turns rather to the opposition of nature and spirit. Putting his stress on the voluntary and practical dimensions, he sees a distinction between man's religious and moral aspirations and the realm of phenomena. Ritschl is concerned with a very practical tension. Man finds himself both as a part

of and involved in nature. But he knows himself also to be a
spiritual personality with hopes and aspirations. He claims to
dominate nature, and yet he is hemmed in and limited by nature
on every hand, both the natural aspect of his own psychosomatic
wholeness and his natural environment. Because he is a spiritual
being, man regards himself as of more value than the world in
which he finds himself. Religion is man's attempt to solve this
practical contradiction. He seeks the aid of superhuman powers
to overcome the tension. Ritschl writes:

In every religion what is sought, with the help of the superhuman
spiritual power reverenced by man, is a solution of the contradiction
in which man finds himself, as both a part of the world of nature and
a spiritual personality claiming to dominate nature. For in the former
*role* he is a part of nature, dependent upon her, subject to and confined by other things; but as spirit he is moved by the impulse to
maintain his independence against them. In this juncture, religion
springs up as faith in superhuman spiritual powers, by whose help the
power which man possesses of himself is in some way supplemented,
and elevated into a unity of its own kind which is a match for the
pressure of the natural world.[19]

Ritschl is seeking to emphasize the worth of the individual and
his spiritual values over against a naturalism that merges him in
nature and an idealism which merges him in the Absolute Spirit.
In nature, Ritschl includes also society in its natural effects, and
thus he regards religious belief as the affirmation of individual
worth against the mass as well as against a heartless and overpowering nature.

Now in the value judgments that are basic in religion, the central emphasis falls on the ethical. The values that man pursues
over against the environment, social and natural, that tends to en-
gulf him are basically ethical goods. Ritschl's emphasis on religious values as values of personality makes this almost inevitable.
Yet he does give Kant's practical reason a broader base, and he
does, at times, include other goods besides the moral within the
gamut of religion. This is especially evident, as we shall see
shortly, in a passage in which he considers the development of religion in the human race and indicates that, in the early stages,

morality was not necessarily constituent of religion. In one striking passage he suggests that moral and religious values are not
identical and he paves the way for what Rudolf Otto expressed
in another way later:

Religious knowledge forms another class of independent value judgments. That is, it cannot be traced back to the conditions which mark
the knowledge belonging to the moral will, for there exists religion
which goes on without any relation whatever to the moral conduct of
life. . . . For only at the higher stages do we find religion combined
with the ethical conduct of life. Religious knowledge moves in independent value judgments, which relate to man's attitude to the world.[20]

This passage has been variously explained by Ritschl's disciples
and opponents. It would seem, however, to be an intrusion, for
the general trend of his thought is an emphasis on ethical judgment. If pressed, however, he would probably have agreed that
reality should vindicate all values.

It would appear then that for Ritschl religious faith is not an
intuition but a postulate grounded in our moral judgment about
the worth of the personal. Religion emerges out of the struggle
for existence, and the deity is bound up with the preservation of
personal values. Commenting of Luther, Ritschl declares that
"knowledge of God can be demonstrated as religious knowledge
only when He is conceived as securing to the believer such a position in the world as more than counterbalances its restric-
tions." [21] Again, he writes that "in religious cognition the idea of
God is dependent on the presupposition that man opposes himself to the world of nature, and secures his position, in or over it,
by faith in God." [22] Mackintosh interprets Ritschl as meaning
that "God is the needed prop of ethical aspiration, the trustee of
our moral interests." [23] Faith affirms the reality of that which personal values require. Religion enables us to be moral persons.

## The Religions and Christianity

Such a view of religion might support Bonhoeffer's dismissal of
religion as man-made. It would certainly agree with the sociolog-

ical description of religion. But there is another side to Ritschl's thought. He is also concerned with revelation, although he does not say very much about it at the non-Christian level. In discussing the significance of worship, he writes: "No idea of a religion complete after its own order can be formed if the characteristic of revelation which belongs to it is either denied or even merely set aside as indifferent." [24] Revelation is bound up with the characteristic elements of time and place associated with any particular religion. It does indeed form "the organic center of every connected religious view of the world." [25] Every religion takes shape within a community of believers who recognize the divine operations on them, in accord with the revelation borne by the founder of their faith.[26] Furthermore, Ritschl carefully defines religion in a very general way. At the commencement of Volume III of his *magnum opus*, he describes the circle by which religion is fully represented as determined by three points which are interrelated—God, man, and the world. He then continues in accord with the ideas developed above but significantly stresses the divine operation. "The central point is always this, that the religious community, as situated in the world, endeavors to obtain certain goods in the world, or above the world, *through the Divine Being, because of His authority over it.*" [27]

This emphasis on revelation and his concern with history are evident in Ritschl's attempt to deal with the historical development of religion in which he sees three stages—paganism, Judaism, Christianity. Hök, in an outstanding study,[28] has shown how Ritschl associated each of these stages with a development in the divine revelation. In paganism, God reveals himself as absolute power. In Judaism, God is disclosed as absolute will requiring obedience of man within the covenant. Thus here the divine will is directed on a particularistic goal. In Christianity, God reveals himself as concerned with a universal purpose, the Kingdom of God. Thus the development of religion is grounded on the transcendent, and each stage of religion has a concrete goal. In his earlier lectures on dogmatics of 1854 and 1856, Ritschl interpreted this goal as the inner transformation of man. As Hök puts

it: "Ritschl has here combined the thought of an objective revelation with the effect of the revelation which consists in the inner transformation of men." [29] In his later lectures, he omits this
consideration of the religious stages. Yet, as Hök contends, in
*Justification and Reconciliation* there is the same connection of
the transcendent ground with the thought of revelation, even
though the content of the revelation is expressed in a different
way.[30]

Here the effect of the revelation is thought of in terms of
"blessedness" rather than "inner transformation." Ritschl moves
to the thought of redemption from the contradictions in which
man finds himself involved as his personal values are in tension
with his natural environment. The goal of religion is essentially
the same, but now transformation gives place to the state of being freed from the contradictions. In paganism, we have a sensual
salvation, emphasizing man's dependence on the forces of nature.[31] In Judaism, man's blessedness is given a political flavor for
it is concerned with man's place in the particularity of the Jewish covenant. In Christianity, we reach a fully spiritual understanding of blessedness, in which man's salvation moves out of a
national into a universal setting and is concerned with his place
in the Kingdom of God.[32] In *Justification and Reconciliation* we
have a summary of this development:

As regards blessedness, we have to consider the different cases in
which what is sought through adoration or adjuration of the superhuman powers is merely some chance benefit, or the idea of a supreme good is formed, and this again is sought in the world, or apart
from the world, or in a combination of both forms.[33]

Later in the same work, Ritschl sees a movement from orgiastic
religions with little or no moral content in their understanding of
blessedness to Christianity where an explicitly moral character is
central. He finds that in Christianity "there emerges the value
judgment that our blessedness consists in that elevation above the
world in the Kingdom of God which accords with our true destiny." [34] Thus we have revelation linked up with the subjective

effect of blessedness and with the religious value judgments that are concerned with it. A kind of Schleiermacherian preoccupation with dependence on God has been replaced in Ritschl's thought with a more dynamic and voluntaristic emphasis on value judgments.[35]

It would be unjust therefore to say that Ritschl has little place for revelation and that faith is a postulate. He was anxious to preserve human freedom over against the idealistic and pantheistic tendencies toward determinism in Hegel and Schleiermacher. In consequence, he tended himself to put undue emphasis on religious value judgments without always indicating their revelatory source. We need to remember also that Ritschl's anthropocentric and positivistic approach led him to hold that God is known only by his effects on us. Hence the divine revelation would be emphasized by its effect within man himself. It is man's response that really indicates the presence of the divine operation, and such a response will be seen in his value judgments and concomitant ethical activity.[36] Hök's judgment is worth recording:

Ritschl has represented the development of the history of religions . . . as a history of salvation grounded in a transcendent revelation of God which has as its goal the blessedness of mankind and which is accompanied by the development of humanity towards that goal.[37]

Ritschl admits that in his approach to the stages of development of religion he presupposes that the Christian religion is the supreme and final manifestation of the religious consciousness.

Christianity claims to be the perfect religion, as distinguished from all other kinds and grades of religion, and to furnish man with that which in all other religions is striven after but only dimly and imperfectly realized. That is the perfect religion in which a perfect knowledge of God is possible.[38]

It is impossible, he contends, when arranging the religions in a series of stages, to evade the claim of Christianity to occupy the highest place. The qualities that are characteristic of religion in other faiths are judged by their perfection attained in the Chris-

tian religion. When we arrange the religions in stages we are
making "a scientific attempt to promote mutual understanding
among Christians," so that "assent to the statement that Christianity is the highest and most perfect religion is . . . no ob-
stacle to the scientific character of the theory." [39] He thus endeavors to deal somewhat weakly with the issue of how Christianity can be both final and within a continuous development.

In all this study of the development of religion, Ritschl does
not lose his appreciation of the historical, derived from Hegel
through Baur. He sees history as a movement toward the conser-
vation of personal values, the attainment of blessedness. Man's
spirituality must be conserved over against nature. The primary
principle in all religion and that by which it must be tested in
history is its concern with the conserving of spirituality. The
claims of the human spirit and their fulfillment are the grounds
on which any historical religion must be judged. Its founder must
be considered as a historical phenomenon and examined as to his
meeting such claims. Hence Christianity too must be verified on a
historical base. Ritchl's historical positivism demanded this, and
thus his theological thinking is basically Christocentric. He places
the historical revelation in Jesus Christ in the center. He makes
Christ's benefits to the continuing believing community a dem-
onstration of the validity of Christianity's claims to possess the
full truth of religion.

Ritschl defines Christianity as:

the monotheistic, completely spiritual, and ethical religion, which,
based on the life of its Author as Redeemer and as Founder of the
Kingdom of God, consists in the freedom of the children of God,
involves the impulse to conduct from the motive of love, aims at the
moral organization of mankind, and grounds blessedness on the relation of sonship to God, as well as on the Kingdom of God.[40]

This is in keeping with his declaration that Christianity is not to
be represented by a circle centered in Christ with his redemption. It is an ellipse that is determined by two foci—Christ and
his redemptive power at one focus; the Kingdom of God as a

kingdom of moral ends at the other focus.[41] Hefner has argued
persuasively that Ritschl's long preoccupation with the history of
the Christian tradition was a formative factor in this view of the
Christian religion. Christian history witnessed continually to this
bifocal nature—God's reconciling action and man's ethical response.[42]

The presentation certainly brings out the factors that we have
already delineated in Ritschl's understanding of religion. True
to his argument that each religion must be understood from within
and not from some universal essence of religion, holding also to
his Christian presupposition that Christianity was the true religion, he derives from the latter the characteristics that he looks
for elsewhere. He finds in Christianity a blessedness or spirituality that is essentially moral. Man overcomes the contradictions
and tensions due to his natural setting, within and without, by
finding release in a fellowship of love and moral concern, the
Kingdom of God. Such redemption is made possible through Jesus
Christ who does for him what only God can do.

Ritschl holds that Christ has the worth of God for our souls,
and he has this because he does the work that God alone can perform. The knowledge of Jesus as uniquely divine and the supreme
and final revelation of God to man is attained only through the
experience of His benefits, of what he can do in us and for us.
"But if Christ," Ritschl writes, "by what He has done and suffered for my salvation is my Lord, and if, by trusting for my salvation to the power of what He has done for me, I honor Him as
my God, then that is a value judgment of a direct kind." [43]

Ritschl refuses to begin with any dogmatic statement about
Christ as God-man or with any metaphysical straitjacket into
which the gospel has to be fitted. He begins with the historical
givenness of Jesus Christ and the value judgment which this historical revelation evokes. All dogmatic statements begin here
with what we apprehend of Christ, and this apprehension has
been constituted by the personal convictions, judgments of worth
for us, which the revelation kindles in our minds. The emphasis
falls not on some dogmatic speculation about the person of Christ,

such as the Chalcedonian Definition, but upon the work of Christ
in our lives and the judgment he evokes. But this judgment upon
Jesus must be based on the historical revelation. The judgment
must be exhibited in his earthly life. What he does now for us,
for his church, is the posthumous work of what he did in his
historical existence. Jesus was himself conscious of a relation to
God that had never been known before, and his vocation was to
lead his disciples into the same attitude to the world and the same
self-judgment.[44] His influence with us is a prolongation of the
effects of this earthly existence; he does for us now what he did
in his historical life. That life was one of perfect obedience to
God and of lordship over the world. As the bearer of God's revelation, he creates faith in us and reproduces his life in us. On the
basis of such work in us, we affirm his deity. Ritschl writes:

Thus what in the historically complete figure of Christ we recognize
to be the real worth of His existence, gains for ourselves, through the
uniqueness of the phenomenon and its normative bearing upon our
own religious and ethical destiny, the worth of an abiding rule, since
we at the same time discover that only through the impulse and direction we receive from Him, is it possible for us to enter into His
relation to God and to the world.[45]

Thus in accord with his basic approach, Ritschl ties up Christian faith with a value judgment. He tells us, as above, that

if Christ by what He has done and suffered for my salvation is my
Lord, and if, by trusting for my salvation to the power of what He has
done for me, I honor him as my God, then that is a value judgment
of a direct kind.[46]

Our value judgment here takes two forms. He heads one of his
sections: "The ethical estimate of Christ according to His vocation carries with it the religious recognition of Him as Revealer of
God." [47] He states this explicitly in these words:

Since the aim of the Christian is to be attained under the form of personal freedom, therefore the two-fold significance we are compelled to

ascribe to Christ as being at once the perfect revealer of God and the manifest (revealed) type of spiritual lordship over the world, find expression in the single predicate of His Godhead.[48]

The ethical dimension of the value judgment is concerned with Christ's fidelity to his task, whereby he becomes the archetype of moral personality. His historically complete existence, with its perfect obedience to death, becomes normative for us, because we find that he gives to us the impulse and direction to enter into his relation to God and the world. But the ethical dimension is accompanied by a religious one. We affirm that in him we have a disclosure of God as loving will. We are reconciled to God as we see Christ's faithfulness to his vocation even to death. "As Bearer of the perfect revelation, Christ is given to us that we may believe on Him. When we do believe on Him, we find Him to be the Revealer of God." [49]

The foci of the religious ellipse become evident in the religious value judgment of the Christian faith—the redemptive and the ethical. Christ as revealer stands at one focus, and the other is the ethical way of life within the Kingdom of God. Reconciliation lifts the believer into that lordship over the world which he sees exemplified in Christ. Thereby he moves out in obedience to take his part in the Kingdom, a community in which human activity is inspired by love and which acknowledges Christ as Lord. Life in the Kingdom is characterized by love and elevation above worldly motive.[50] Such love is a universal love to man. The Kingdom is the "idea of the moral unification of the human race, through action prompted by universal love to our neighbor," [51] and love is "that will which accepts, as belonging to one's own end, the task of advancing permanently the end of other personal beings of like nature with oneself." [52] In true Kantian tradition, Ritschl endeavors to preserve human freedom within such a setting. The absolute idealism of Hegel and the panentheistic approach of Schleiermacher denude this. Ritschl can, therefore, speak of freedom as consisting "in self-determination by that end which, by possessing the most universal content, makes it possible to subordinate to it all individual impulses and all moral aims which may be particular in their range." [53] The standard for this end is the law of universal love for man. Man has to be permanently self-determined by the Kingdom of God as final end.

## An Assessment

Ritschl's rejection of metaphysics is really a rejection of Hegelian idealism and, to some degree, of Schleiermacher's romanticist panentheism. But he forgot that there are other forms of metaphysics, and his adoption of so much of Kant's ethical ontology has put him in a metaphysical straitjacket quite as firmly as the condition of those whom he criticizes. On every hand the Kantian influence is very evident, modified though it be by the insights of Lotze.

Ritschl's understanding of religion is essentially utilitarian. It is an instrument for the preservation of the worth and the values of human personality against the opposition of "nature," both within man's embodied nature and in his social and natural environment. Spirit and nature are set in opposition in a typical Kantian dichotomy, and belief in God is the guarantee that Spirit will rise triumphant over the world. Hence religion is involved with value judgments, and all religions, at various stages, seek to establish man's blessedness in accord with what their founder and religious community have received in revelation. The emphasis on man's "blessedness" or "spirituality" and its definition as the conquest of the tensions and contradictions due to existence in the world make religion anthropocentric. Man occupies the center of the stage, and man's value judgments are the determinative factors.

Such a view pays little heed to the adoration of and communion with God that are accentuated in all forms of mysticism to the point of absorption in the deity, but which are also present in, at least, all higher forms of religion. But then, his opposition to pietism leads Ritschl to reject arbitrarily any experience that he can label "subjective." Communion with God and prayer are not ends in themselves. They are practiced with the ulterior motive of conserving man's ethical ends and personal values. Man does not pray out of a desire for fellowship with God but because of the value of prayer in furthering his own self-improvement. Religion is a way of making use of God. This is a denial of what all religion stands for in its finest moments, although it is quite in keeping with the kind of religion that Bonhoeffer dismisses. What matters for Ritschl is man's attitude toward the world, not his attitude toward God.

The value judgments with which religion is concerned are fundamentally ethical—again we see the influence of Kant. The noetic element is present in religion, but it is practical, and it issues in ethical conduct. Ritschl reduces religion to the level of morality. Even the religious dimension of his Christian value judgment is basically ethical, as we have seen. In his effects on us, Christ makes a completely moral life possible, a life of self-giving love, and thus he is morally indistinguishable from God. We have already noted that Christ's perfect life awakens us to his deeper import as revealer of God. The religious dimension of the value judgment rests upon the ethical. This holds at all stages of religion.

Once more we have to ask whether this meets the distinction of religion from morality. Is our faith grounded in our moral capacities? Schleiermacher attempted to keep religion in the realm of "feeling," evidently intending an intuitive aspect in this and not relegating religion to a mere emotive state. Tillich more carefully suggests a "mystical *a priori*," without which no historical revelation could gain secure lodgment in the human consciousness and which underlies all man's conscious response to his world. Both these thinkers, in true Augustinian tradition, had sought for some point of contact between God and man, some divine-human kinship, which, however broken and distorted, gave entrance to the divine self-disclosure through the world. Furthermore, they looked for something in the religious response that would not allow it to be reduced to rationalism or morality, for a distinctive dimension. Ritschl saw the revelation coming at the Christian level through One whom we could morally recognize

as identical with the Deity. Then our standard of judgment is a
moral one. But is it, rather, a divine illumination whereby we
recognize as coming to us in history One who is already present
to us, however obscured, in the deep places of our own soul?

Yet there are positive aspects in Ritschl's treatment of religion.
Our difficulty is that generally his reading of the Christian religion provides the norm, and his treatment of religion at other
stages is colored by his Christian presuppositions, a fact which,
as we have seen, he is ready to acknowledge. For one thing, he
does not deny a givenness in religion. However subjective "value
judgment" may appear to make religion, he reminds us that the
object of religious value judgment is also a reality. Value judgments are also judgments of existence. Ritschl's concern with history made him emphasize the givenness of revelation in history.
But he kept the revelation *in* history and did not recognize that
it is also *through* history. The transcendent reference is thereby
weakened.

Let us look at his Christian norm. Jesus of Nazareth is a historical figure. He is in history. Yet the historical explanation of
Jesus is concerned with his historical background, with the con-
tinuum of historical events in which he was involved. Ritschl's
religious value judgment in its ethical dimension stays just there.
But faith declares that the transcendent and eternal has become
especially immanent in Christ's historicity and temporality. There
is a hiddenness about him that the historian *qua* historian cannot
unveil and which our human judgments at the rational and ethical
level cannot probe. The deep in Jesus reaches out to the deep in
ourselves. There is, as John Baillie suggested, a mediated immediacy here in which the depth beneath history, the ultimate Reality, is disclosed and lays his claim upon us. The insight of faith is
more than historical perception and moral judgment.

Revelation becomes for Ritschl little more than the static givenness of history and our religioethical value judgment upon that
givenness. There is little real sense of the dynamic self-disclosure
of God in and through history and of the human response of
faith at a deeper level than ethical judgment. Again, this applies

at all stages of religious development.

This concern with the historical givenness, together with his bias against Hegelian metaphysics and with the Kantian emphasis on man's finitude, led to an approach to revelation that shows many similarities to current theological thought. For it led Ritschl, in his value judgments, to ignore the mysterious element in religion, to emphasize the ethical, and to regard theological propositions as simply expressions of man's relation to God. Ritschl will say nothing about God's essential nature, and the Trinity is for him an economic Trinity.

Again, Ritschl is concerned with a "this-worldly" emphasis. In these days when we are concerned with secularity and are thinking in terms of a "theology of hope," it is refreshing to turn back to his thought on the Kingdom of God and that of his disciple Adolf von Harnack. However regrettable was Ritschl's failure to note the eschatological dimension in the Christian religion, he did at least suggest that religion is fundamentally concerned with life in this world and with life at the social level. Here we can be grateful for his ethical emphasis. His interpretation of the Kingdom of God in purely ethical terms needs to pass through the alembic of much subsequent New Testament scholarship, but he did see that religion is at its best, at all levels, when it is concerned with man's human existence in this world. To this also we must return later. At this level, he speaks to our time. "Blessedness" is life here and now in the community of love which is the Kingdom. He failed to see the Kingdom fully as an eschatological miracle that the continued coming of the Christ makes possible. But, then, here too his theological positivism made it difficult for him to find any place for such continuing activity other than as the posthumous effect of the historical existence of Jesus of Nazareth, a kind of prolongation down time.

One last comment needs to be made. Convinced that Christianity was the final and supreme expression of that spirituality or blessedness that man sought through religion, Ritschl assessed all other stages of religious development and identified their distinctive characteristics in terms of it. His was no phenomenolog-

ical study of the religious consciousness such as Otto was to undertake. Nor did he resolve in any way the dilemma caused by regarding Christianity as within the continuity of religious development and making absolutist claims for it. The issue facing
Schleiermacher remained. How can Christianity be a religion and
yet be above all religions?

## Rudolf Otto and the Religious A Priori

The thought of Rudolf Otto in the first decades of the present
century represents quite a different phase of Kantian influence,
while showing marked relationship to the thought of Schleiermacher. Otto undertook a phenomenological investigation of the
religious consciousness, seeking to find the distinctive element in
the human self-consciousness in which the religious response was
grounded. Kant, followed by Ritschl, had grounded religion in
man's moral *a priori*. Schleiermacher, dismissing knowledge and
morality from the primary response of religious man, had
grounded religion in man's "feeling" of absolute dependence.
Otto sought to establish a distinctive religious *a priori* on the
lines of Kant's *a priori* of the pure understanding and moral *a
priori*. Yet he saw this as constituting an actual encounter with
reality, and not as a point from which reason might operate toward the establishment of ultimate reality, as had Kant at the
level of the practical reason. Thus Otto did not suffer from the
Kantian dichotomy, and it would be unjust to regard him solely
in Kantian terms. Actually, he *mis*uses Kant much more than uses
him, as we shall see later.

Rather, because of his real admiration for Schleiermacher, much
that Otto says follows the line marked out by this great thinker.
He describes Schleiermacher as the one responsible for the "rediscovery of religion." He can write that "it will be a task for
contemporary Christian teaching to follow in his traces and again
to deepen the rational meaning of the Christian conception of
God by permeating it with its non-rational elements." [54]

Schleiermacher had sought to locate the primary religious re-

sponse in the feeling of absolute dependence. Hegel's suggestion
that this made Schleiermacher's dog more pious than its master
is beside the point, for Schleiermacher's emphasis was on the
word "absolute" or unconditioned. Thus he did attempt to specify
a peculiar type of feeling. Otto criticizes Schleiermacher as failing to differentiate the religious or pious feeling sufficiently from
other feelings of dependence, holding that the difference is not
merely one of degree, namely between "absolute" and "relative"
dependence.[55] There is a measure of analogy between the religious state and the state of dependence, but the former involves
something more, and Otto calls it "creature feeling." He suggests
that this expresses "the note of self-abasement into nothingness
before an overpowering, absolute might of some kind." [56] It is a
feeling that cannot be expressed verbally and must be directly
experienced to be understood. Furthermore, it is not, as with
Otto's understanding of Schleiermacher, a self-conscious valuation, but it is directly related to an objective situation. We have
sought to show that Schleiermacher implied the latter in the way
he early used the word "intuition." [57] The creaturely feeling is,
in any case for Otto, a response to objective reality.

Otto finds this object described in the distinctive category of
interpretation and valuation which is peculiar to the religious
realm, "the Holy." This cannot be identified with the valuations
the Good, the True, and the Beautiful, although the Holy is a
composite valuation involving such elements. It has, indeed,
strong ethical connotations in most developed religious experience and comes to mean the perfectly good. Yet such rational
elements are secondary and do not provide the core of "the
Holy." There is also present a nonrational element, one which
cannot be rationally expressed and conceptualized. Otto calls this
element "the numinous." It is "the holy" stripped of the secondary rational and moral concepts which are closely associated with
it, and it lies at the center of the religious response to reality.
Thus, in essence, religion is nonrational and nonethical, and its
characteristic evaluation of reality is "the numinous."

The state of mind which is purely numinous or religious is *sui*

*generis,* and it is characterized by the numinous feeling or creature feeling. Otto describes the object of such an evaluation by
the phrase *mysterium tremendum et fascinans.* It is *mysterium,*
"wholly other," transcending all conceptual expression. As such it
fills the mind with blank wonder and amazement before its overpowering majesty. Thus there is a constituent feeling of stupor in
the human response. The subject is struck dumb with astonish-
ment. Otto qualifies the "mystery" with the term *tremendum.* It
possesses an awesome and overpowering majesty. It produces a
condition of abasement and awe, a consciousness of creaturehood,
a feeling of utter self-abasement and nothingness. Otto also finds
in this aspect an awareness of life, energy, urgency, evident from
the level of the demonic to the idea of the "living" God. Finally,
the "mystery" is qualified by the description *fascinans.* It not only
daunts; it also attracts, fascinates, allures. Thus the religious object is an awesome mystery, daunting and overpowering in its
majesty and yet strangely fascinating and attractive. The feeling
evoked by this *mysterium* is described by Otto as the "numinous
feeling." The deity as basically experienced at the religious level
is unapproachable mystery, the "wholly other," and the numinous
feeling is essentially nonrational. That which is felt belongs to a
preconceptual level of cognition. It is an affective state of mind
that transcends conceptual expression.

Otto finds this numinous feeling in the religious consciousness
at all levels. His far-reaching phenomenological analysis estab-
lishes it as the unique dimension in mankind's religious response,
that which differentiates it from all other responses to reality, including the ethical and the rational. It is, indeed, *sui generis.* It
cannot be reduced to any other natural feelings, and here Otto
would disagree with anthropologists like Marett,[58] who regard
the religious response as a special composite of natural urges like
fear, love, and reverence. Thus Marett identifies the religious feeling with awe and writes that

awe is not the same thing as "pure funk." *Primus in orbe deos fecit
timor* is only true if we admit wonder, admiration, interest, respect,

even love perhaps, to be, no less than fear, essential constituents of this elemental mood.[59]

Otto rejects any such reduction. The "elemental mood" is irreducible and uniquely characterizes man's religious response. His judgment on his analysis should be cited:

The two qualities, the daunting and the fascinating, now combine in a strange harmony of contrasts, and the resultant dual character of the numinous consciousness, to which the entire religious development bears witness, at any rate from the level of the "daemonic dread" onwards, is at once the strangest and most noteworthy phenomenon in the whole history of religion.[60]

The holy in its original form of the numinous is an *a priori* category of the human mind. Otto describes it as "a hidden predisposition of the human spirit, which awakens when aroused by divers excitations." [61] It manifests itself in propensities that may ultimately become a search and a driving religious impulsion that finds peace only in attaining its goal. Otto connects this *a priori* with what he terms, using Schleiermacher's terminology, a faculty of divination. It is "the faculty, of whatever sort it may be, of *genuinely* cognizing and recognizing the holy in its appearances." [62] Genuine divination "is not concerned at all with the way in which a phenomenon—be it event, person, or thing—came into existence, but with what it *means*, that is, with its significance as a 'sign' of the holy." [63] In divination we have an intuitive outcome of feeling, something that may legitimately be described as cognition, "the apprehension of a ground and meaning of things in and beyond the empirical and transcending it." [64] Otto holds that this is what Schleiermacher was feeling after in his emphasis on the pious "feeling." He suggests that the intuitions describable under the term "divination" are "*surmises* or *inklings* of a Reality fraught with mystery and momentousness." [65] The religious *a priori* is often dim and obscure rather than explicit and overt, but it is the guiding principle in the religious response and belongs to this intuitive level of divination. It is a capacity *sui generis* for judgment and valuation, so that religion has "its own independent roots in the hidden depths of the spirit itself." [66] In an expression that echoes the thought of Schleiermacher and Augustine and is echoed also in Tillich, Otto declares that the *a priori* category of the numinous springs "from the deepest foundation of cognitive apprehension that the soul possesses," [67] even though it comes into being amid the sensory data and empirical material supplied by man's sensory perception of his world. Religious valuations take us beyond the empirical to the transcendent mystery.

This *a priori* religious valuation has an objective reference in contrast to Kant's categories of the pure understanding. The numinous feeling matches the reality of the *mysterium*. There is no phenomenalism in the structure of Otto's thought. Nor is the *mysterium* an inference, as with Kant's postulates of the practical reason. We have here a primary and rudimentary cognition of reality, preconceptual and nonrational, yet a real apprehension of deity. By holding that the numinous feeling is *sui generis* and not compounded of feeling aroused by natural objects, Otto avoids also the suggestion that the object of such a feeling is an imaginative projection, such as Feuerbach and many others have suggested. It is no effort of the human consciousness to create an imaginary object by a special aggregation of natural feelings.

How, then, does the nonrational numinous valuation become the category of "the Holy" with its moral and rational elements? Otto again falls back on Kant, even though he still further misrepresents him. The misrepresentation begins of course by the contradictory idea of a nonrational category. Paton [68] has exposed this at some length. He points out that Otto has mixed up Kant's "Ideas of Reason" with the "categories of the understanding." The former are concerned with ideas like absolute reality and absolute power and are concepts of the unconditioned that we can never experience. Hence such ideas have no object in experience. The categories are the ordering concepts for every object experienced in space and time. Otto speaks interchangeably of the "Idea" and the "category" of the Holy, and further holds that this Idea or category can give us knowledge of what transcends sensual experience. At this point, as we have just indicated, Otto is really going his own way while using Kantian terminology.

This misuse becomes more evident when he seeks to explain the way in which moral and rational elements are associated with the numinous. He makes use of Kant's idea of schemata. The rational and moral elements are the schemata of the nonrational numinous. They add a rational dimension to the nonrational numinous. Kant had conceived this process in the reverse direction. He believed that the pure understanding was so patterned that spatiotemporal schemata such as succession, enable us to apply a category like causation to the real object of experience. For Kant the schema is the nonrational element, nearer to perception and providing the material to which the category can be applied. The schemata make it possible for a rational concept to gather into itself a nonrational element. But Otto places the schemata after the category or Idea and regards them as adding rational dimensions to what is originally nonrational. Paton comments: "Otto no doubt talks as he does because he wishes to regard the non-rational element in religion as somehow 'higher'—in an unspecified sense—than the rational. But Kant must have shuddered in his grave." [69]

This very valid criticism notwithstanding, Otto has added considerably to our understanding of the religious consciousness. Paton acknowledges this.[70] He points out that Otto's work, though it suffers from a faulty use of Kant, could yet have been presented in a similar way if he had regarded the numinous feeling as the schema which was incorporated in the Ideas of absolute goodness and unconditioned reality to give the complex concept of the Holy. Thereby the feeling and groping after a dimly perceived *mysterium* behind the world of sense and the Ideas by which we can conceive such an object of our yearning are brought together in an intelligible whole. What in the Ideas is purely rational and not religious, becomes in this way an object of adoration and worship. The nonrational numinous becomes the schema which, when combined with the rational concepts, yields the complex *religious* category of the Holy.

The non-rational element of feeling remains essential to religion; but it has become purified into a feeling, not of the merely dreadful or fascinating or daemonic, but of the august and the holy; and through this purified feeling or direct awareness our empty Ideas of reason can find their object in a living and holy God.[71]

H. D. Lewis [72] likewise finds real significance in Otto's approach, despite the cumbersome mechanism by which he seeks to give the numinous a rational and moral coloring. On lines parallel to those of H. J. Paton, he suggests that Otto misled his readers by suggesting too close an affinity with Kant and that actually he was endeavoring to characterize the elusive idea of the holy by "felt analogies." Even in describing the *mysterium* as *tremendum et fascinans,* he was applying to the transcendent numinous reality two "felt analogies" taken from the familiar emotions of fear and admiration. As analogies the latter pointed to the peculiar and unique character of the numinous feeling and yet are not identical with the elements which characterize that feeling. The difference is not one of degree, but such finite feelings give some clue to "the distinctive experience of the transcendent" that prompts such descriptions. There are, however, other "felt analogies" that we are prompted by religious experience to ascribe to the deity. Here "particular importance attaches to the sense of transcendent worth in our experience of the holy, for this provides a link at the very center with moral ideas as we find them in normal experience." [73]

C. A. Campbell [74] takes a similar line in support of Otto's approach. He finds an inner necessity of the mind to think about the numinous, since the numinous experience is not merely emotional but is directed toward an object, however dim. There is a *numen praesens* that evokes the numinous feeling. If this be the case, there is also an inner necessity to apply "felt analogies" from ordinary emotional experience, otherwise we could say nothing specific about nor give significant determination to the numinous object. We are aware of the analogies at the ordinary level and thus "we naturally . . . think the numinous object as the bearer of qualities analogous to the nameable qualities that evoke the or-

dinary emotions of wonder, dread, and entrancement." [75] Analogy
carries the connotation of difference as well as of identity. Thus
symbolic language is the only way to speak about the numinous,
for the numinous experience is enveloped throughout with an
"aura of the *supra*-natural, the *supra*-human, the *supra*-ra-
tional." [76] This means that there is an inner necessity of the mind
"*to refrain from* interpreting the numinous object in these rational
terms," and yet there is also an almost irresistible temptation to
rationalize. The resolution of the dilemma lies in the recognition
that we are not dealing with something greater *merely in degree*.
To interpret the deity in terms of the highest we know involves
the recognition that such descriptions have no more than symbolic validity and must not be given their literal validity. Thus
Otto recognized that the rational and moral are as indispensable
as strands in the idea of the holy as is the suprarational element.
Yet this must not lead us to a rational theism, and the implication
of Otto's work is that only *symbolic* theology is a viable option.
As H. D. Lewis comments:

Otto is quite correct in holding that when we use particular terms of
God, or ascribe attributes to Him, we do so in a symbolic way. . . .
In his emphasis on this, as in other ways, Otto has done a great ser-
vice to religion.[77]

Here the contribution of Otto links on with that of Tillich. The
"felt analogues" do aid in pointing to and evoking the numinous
experience.

John Oman [78] has criticized Otto and at the same time formulated his own viewpoint. He likewise holds that there is an immediate conviction of the presence of a special kind of objective
reality, the supernatural, that creates a unique kind of feeling.
This religious consciousness involves the sense of the holy, which
at the primitive level has more to do with awe than with moral
reverence. Oman interprets Otto as regarding the awesome holy
as the one essential religious feeling, and holds that the sense of
the holy involves far more than the awesome *mysterium*. Accord-

ing to Oman, Otto's idea of the numinous describes "the mere impression of an awe-inspiring something, the mightier for stirring intense feeling the vaguer it is." [79] He argues that though this element is present, we can only interpret the sense of the holy aright when we pass beyond mere feeling and relate the feeling "to sacred value and the existence of the supernatural." The numinous feeling has to be distinguished by relating it to the absolute value of the sacred. By the sacred, Oman means "absoluteness of value, that which is of incomparable worth, and incomparable is not merely super-excellent, but what may not be brought down and compared with other goods." [80]

C. A. Campbell points out that Oman's criticism arises from a misinterpretation of Otto. Far from concentrating on the awesome and separating it from valuation, Otto carefully includes *fascinans* as well as *tremendum* in the description of the *mysterium*. Oman ignores the former and concentrates on the latter in his criticism. But his criticism falls, when it is recognized that Otto thinks of the numinous consciousness as having two poles, and speaks of the *tremendum* as *one* element or factor in the total response. Otto speaks of "the dual character of the numinous consciousness," [81] and clearly regards the *fascinans* aspect as "that in virtue of which the numinous consciousness is enraptured and entranced by the transcendent *worth* or *value* of the numen." [82]

If we follow Oman's misreading it is easy to present Otto as entirely dividing the religious from the ethical. This he valiantly tries not to do, despite his involvement with the cumbersome Kantian machinery. The roots of the ethical valuation of the holy lie back in the element of *fascinans* in the basic feeling of the numinous. As Campbell points out: "It is precisely the *fascinans* aspect that provides the link between the two, ensuring that we cannot but think the object of religious experience as endued with supreme excellence." [83] Oman contends that the sense of the holy can be "the most overwhelming of human emotions, even to the abject sense of nothingness as a creature. But it may also be the calmest of all responses to a reality in which we find our true independence." [84] But the latter is what Otto devotes so much attention to in his treatment of *fascinans,* and to this treatment Oman seems strangely blind.

Oman's approach does recognize, like Otto's, that the religious object creates a feeling of a unique character and has a unique value for us. Although he is not so ready to separate the numinous from the ethical and the rational as Otto might appear to do—although the above discussion suggests that this is more appearance than reality—he does give to religion a distinctive place. The religious response is no aggregation of responses made to the natural environment. It is *sui generis* and has a characteristic content. It is the virtue of Oman's discussion that he sees man's environment as both natural and supernatural. The two are not in opposition—we note the contrast here with Ritschl's approach to religion. They are "so constantly interwoven that nothing may be wholly natural or wholly supernatural." [85] Oman sees awareness and apprehension as basic in man's approach to such an environment and more important than conceptualization and explanation, even though the latter make it possible for him to deal with and control that environment. This explains his preparedness to accept an intuitive base for religion and to accept a feeling for the sacred as the fundamental judgment of the religious consciousness. He tells us:

Both the Natural and the Supernatural are distinguished by the way in which they make themselves known, which is by the meaning or, in other words, the value they have for us. As the natural world is known by sensation and its varied comparative values, so the supernatural world is known by the sense of the holy and its sacred or absolute values; and for practical purposes, the distinction between the Natural and the Supernatural is between comparative value and absolute.[86]

We may sum up this section by suggesting that the positions just outlined point to two things. First of all, they hold to the underived nature of the religious capacity in man and its independence from his other conscious capacities. Secondly, they hold that, from the beginning, religion is organic with and basic to all man's other activities, so that the moralization and rationalization of the sense of the numinous is no artificial and imposed process but a normal development of the human consciousness. We believe that is what Otto sought to make it and this his friendly interpreters have made plain, while critics like Oman have moved in the same direction.

# V

## *Projection, Relativism, Rejection*

WHILE Schleiermacher and Ritschl, each in his own way, were seeking to validate the religious consciousness and uphold the finality of Christianity as the supreme expression of religion, other forces were at work whose effect was evident in the last century and is still more so in this. Feuerbach and the left wing Hegelians were at work turning Hegel's system upside down and preaching a materialism that transformed religion into a human creation and God into a utilitarian projection of the human mind. By the end of the century we find a new form of historical emphasis emerging in which religion is increasingly bound up with culture, so that a specific form of religion reflects its cultural milieu. Thereby the search for absoluteness is replaced by a relativism, a movement very evident in the intellectual pilgrimage of Troeltsch.

The left wing Hegelianism of Feuerbach and his disciple Marx have produced a materialistic and atheistic philosophy that has captured many intellectuals of this century. It was reaction to the

Marxist attack on religion and also to the relativism of thinkers like Troeltsch that was influential in Barth's rejection of religion and his declaration that Christianity was not a religion. So we come back to Bonhoeffer, who in many respects is a disciple of Barth despite his criticism of that master theologian.

## Religion as Man-made and God as a Projection

Feuerbach inverted the approach of Hegel and reduced Hegel's system to a materialistic base. Hegel had made the Absolute Spirit immanent in the process of nature and history and argued the latter were moments in the self-determination and self-realization of Spirit. But he ought, Feuerbach held, to have eliminated the speculative concept of the Absolute and come to anchor in man himself. The superhuman should have been reduced to the human and the process of spirit to the process of nature. Hence Feuerbach sought an approach that employed the empirical method of science and sought to explain the religious consciousness on the basis of man. He claims that he posits no general propositions that have not been derived from the analysis of religion and that they are

generalizations from the known manifestations of human nature, and in particular of the religious consciousness — facts converted into thoughts, i.e., expressed in general terms, and thus made the property of the understanding.[1]

On this basis he made a study of religion in its manifold historical manifestations.

In this study he inverted the whole Hegelian position and dialectic. He was prepared to admit that the Hegelian philosophical system marked the highest level that philosophical thought could attain, and hence he held that his criticism of it was at the same time a criticism of all metaphysical systems that sought a transcendent or spiritual base. He claimed to put an end to such speculation by explaining it.

Speculation makes religion say only what it has *itself* thought, and expressed far better than religion; it assigns a meaning to religion without any reference to the *actual* meaning of religion; it does not look beyond itself.[2]

This is a very evident reference to Hegel's attempt to fit the Christian religion into his system by universalizing and sadly misinterpreting its affirmations. But it is at the same time a statement of Feuerbach's own "blik," for he too wants religion to be what his own naturalistic position makes of it, as we shall see shortly.

Not only did Feuerbach confuse the issues by making Hegel's system the representative climax of all philosophical speculation, but he also made the mistake of identifying Hegel's Absolute Spirit with the God of religion and of regarding the latter as the controlling element in Hegel's thought. Collins describes Feuerbach's judgment on Hegel as follows:

Historically and genetically considered, the Hegelian system is nothing more than the ultimate refuge and rationalizing support of theism and Christian theology, the last great attempt to restore Christian dogma under a philosophical guise.[3]

Hence Feuerbach can say that "the secret of speculative philosophy [is] theology." [4] The doctrine of the Absolute in Hegel is essentially dependent on the doctrine of God, rather than itself being the controlling factor in the development of the monistic system. In consequence, Feuerbach attacks religion and the whole idea of God on the basis of an attack directed upon absolute idealism.

Claiming to be a realist, he begins with man and with nature. He replaces Hegel's absolute spirit by man and reduces theology to anthropology. In *The Essence of Christianity* he writes: "This philosophy has for its principle, not the Substance of Spinoza, . . . not the Absolute Mind of Hegel, in short, no abstract, merely conceptional being, but a *real* being, the true *Ens realissimum—* man." [5] Again he tells us that "the *absolute* to man is his own nature." [6] Hence we must "exalt anthropology into theology." [7] This means that Feuerbach's approach is a naturalistic humanism that denies the reality of the transcendent order of spirit and of the supernatural. It is a purely immanentist approach and, as Feuerbach's thought progressed, it devolved ultimately into materialism.

He begins in his thought process with human self-consciousness, like Schleiermacher and Hegel and yet so unlike them. The reason for this unlikeness is Feuerbach's psychological premise—this is that in his self-consciousness and in his knowing, willing, and loving, man never actually gets beyond himself. Man is himself the measure of reason, and, even when his thinking is concerned with some object, in knowing that object man is really knowing himself. "In the object which he contemplates," Feuerbach writes, "man becomes acquainted with himself; consciousness of the objective is the self-consciousness of man." [8] His human nature is evident in the object, and the object is his true objective ego. Even in feeling man is dealing with himself, for "feeling is only acted on by that which conveys feeling, i.e., by itself, its own nature," [9] and still more does this hold of willing and thinking. But man is essentially constituted by willing, feeling, and thinking, and so in these activities man is, as it were, looking in a mirror and finding himself in the object.

It will be noticed how Feuerbach has inverted Hegel's approach, for Hegel had taught that in man's knowledge of his objective world, the Absolute Spirit, subjectivized in man, is knowing itself, objectivized in nature and society. What Hegel affirmed of his absolute, Feuerbach affirmed of man himself. "Consciousness consists in a being becoming objective to itself." [10] So Feuerbach can declare: "Whatever kind of object . . . we are at any time conscious of, we are always at the same time conscious of our own nature; we can affirm nothing without affirming ourselves." [11]

Yet Feuerbach does not completely invert Hegel, for he does accept the reality of the things of nature, and ultimately he was to move to a complete materialism. In knowing things through the senses, man knows himself, and yet the things are not just appearances. In Hegel's system they are appearances of the Spirit, but Feuerbach could not do this—he is not a solipsist. He carefully distinguishes man's mind from the lower orders of the natural process. Man, as the principle of Feuerbach's philosophy, "generates thought from the *opposite* of thought, from Matter, from existence, from the senses; it has relation to its object first through the senses, i.e., passively, before defining it in thought." [12] Here his naturalistic realism is evident, but so also is a remnant of the Hegelian dialectic of opposites. Hence Feuerbach, commenting on the Christian sacraments from his humanistic standpoint and trying to keep religion even within his atheistic standpoint, can argue that the bread and wine are symbols of our difference from nature. We are distinguished from nature, and in the sacraments we celebrate this distinction. They remind us that "Nature needs man, as man needs Nature" and that "man can do nothing without Nature." [13] So nature gives the material, and mind gives the form.

This break with the Hegelian understanding of the complete identity of the objective and the subjective is removed when Feuerbach turns to religion. Having attacked the Hegelian system as the last refuge of Christian theism, he now declares that in religion man is not dealing with some ultimate reality beyond himself, God, but in actual fact only with himself. Our religion is purely subjective. It reflects our own inner dispositions. Man is actually relating himself to himself in religion. Feuerbach, keeping up the distinction just noted, can write:

The object of the senses is out of man, the religious object is within him, and therefore as little forsakes him as his self-consciousness or his conscience; it is the intimate, the closest object.[14]

He quotes Augustine in support, but out of context. For he is not thinking of that inner awareness of God which both Schleiermacher and Tillich, as disciples of Augustine, regard as a necessary constituent of self-consciousness. Feuerbach is thinking of man's inner knowledge of himself, howbeit "a human nature purified, freed from the limits of the individual man, made objective." [15] The divine being is a human being. Man projects himself upon the backdrop of the universe. In religion he is actually revering and contemplating himself. God is man's ideal nature abstracted from himself as he actually is and worshiped as an objective reality. The ideal self is split from the empirical self and is seen as outside the latter. Even in his finitude, man is aware of his infinitude in his essential nature, and so in religion he expresses his desire to be this ideal, freed from the limitations of nature and society. Feuerbach writes:

Nature, this world, is an existence which contradicts my wishes, my feelings. Here it is not as it ought to be; this world passes away; but God is existence as it ought to be. God fulfills my wishes;—this is only a popular personification of the position: God is the fulfiller, i.e., the reality, the fulfilment of my wishes.[16]

So "God is my hidden, my assured existence; he is the subjectivity of subjects, the personality of persons." [17] He expresses my yearning for a more perfect condition and is a projection of my own aspirations whereby I hope to attain salvation.

We note that this psychogenetic explanation of religion and of God is purely a presupposition. Feuerbach, as with all such absolute presuppositions, can give no proof of its validity, any more than can his disciple Freud many years later. Feuerbach does, however, seek to show that his position is a viable one by offering an interpretation of man's developing religious experience. He does this, as his thesis demands, by inverting the traditional Christian position.

One element in his interpretation is marked by his general understanding of the anthropomorphisms that religious faith employed in the description of God. He argues that the recognition that the descriptions of the deity are anthropomorphisms should logically imply that the subject of such descriptions is himself an anthropomorphism. God is actually man himself. He argues that "all the attributes of the divine nature are . . . attributes of the human nature." [18] But if we negate the divine attributes, then God becomes a being without qualities and such a being cannot be an object to the mind; it is virtually nonexistent. Yet the negation of the attributes is not regarded as irreligion, whereas the negation of their subject is. Hence religion can be retained while it is affirmed that God is unknowable. Now such religion, Feuerbach contends, is unreal and without practical consequences in human behavior. Such a God ceases to count in man's actual living. Nor is it any way out to say that the anthropomorphic attributes are due to our human limitations, and that God in himself is distinct from what he appears to be in relation to me. Religion must have a complete deity, a God without reservation. "Religion gives up its own existence when it gives up the nature of God; it is no longer a truth when it renounces the possession of the true God." [19] The only way to interpret the religious use of anthropomorphisms and to retain the reality of religion is to identify God with man himself and set religion in the framework of atheism. "If thy predicates are anthropomorphisms, the subject of them is an anthropomorphism." [20]

What Feuerbach failed to see is that religious language is neither univocal nor equivocal but analogical. It uses analogues or models in seeking to point to and communicate man's experience of the ineffable. What, in discussing Otto, we have described as "felt analogues" had no place in Feuerbach's thought about religion.

This becomes quite evident in Feuerbach's discussion of the history of man's religious consciousness. Here he, in some sense, prepares the way for *Kulturprotestantismus* as we find it in Troeltsch. He sees the development of religion as taking place *pari passu* with that of human culture, such that the two are intimately bound together. Men's ideas of their God or gods at any stage of their development reflect their ideas of themselves.

The qualities of God are nothing else than the essential qualities of man himself, and a particular man is what he is, has his existence, his reality, only in his particular conditions. [21]

So for the Greek, the gods were Greek beings. For the ancient Germans with their understanding of themselves as warriors, Odin was the god of war. Whatever men regard as the most significant attribute of themselves they apply to their deity. Hence, for Feuerbach, the development of religion leads to the conclusion that "religion is that conception of the nature of the world and of man which is essential to, i.e., identical with, a man's nature." [22]

There is a viable alternative to such an interpretation, but Feuerbach was inhibited from this because of his basic presupposition. Men always use the highest human qualities that they recognize in themselves as models to interpret the ultimate reality, their deity. As man grows culturally, the models change and become more refined. They are moralized and spiritualized. But this in no way suggests the unreality of God or denies the reality of divine disclosure.

In defending his view of religion as a projection of man's own being and thus as best understood in atheistic terms, Feuerbach argues that religion as normally practiced enriches its deity at the expense of man himself. The glorification of the divine nature is only possible when human nature is devalued. This view is of course in keeping with the Hegelian dialectic which exalted the Absolute Spirit and reduced human personality to the level of an adjectival existence. Hence Feuerbach is actually attacking Hegel and his system rather than Christian theism. For the latter, by its emphasis on the divine image in man and on God as love, gives to man a dignity and a freedom that actually enrich rather than deprive human nature. Man in the incarnation is restored to divine kinship and made a partner in God's Kingdom—extreme predestinarianism excluded!

Feuerbach argues, however, that the more the divine is pictured in human terms, the greater the distinction between God and man while the identity between God and man is denied.

The reason of this is, that as what is positive in the conception of the divine being can only be human, the conception of man, as an object of consciousness, can only be negative. To enrich God, man must become poor; that God may be all in all, man must be nothing.[23]

Man denudes himself and yet enjoys what he renounces in a higher form in God. Man in religion denies sensuality, knowledge, even goodness to himself that he may attribute them in a higher form to God and thereby enjoy them in God without the limitations that attend them in man himself. Thus the nun is married to a heavenly bridegroom; the human reason listens humbly to the higher wisdom of the divine revelation; human nature corrupted by sin finds goodness as its destination and law in the eternal goodness. So Feuerbach comments: "So long as man adores a good being as his God, so long does he contemplate in God the goodness of his own nature." [24] The whole argument is based upon the psychological presupposition and the inverted Hegelian dialectic that provide the basic structure of Feuerbach's thought. Furthermore, as we have suggested, it may apply to Hegel, but it is a falsification of the actual insights of Christian theism at its best.

Always Feuerbach is seeking to establish the positive values of religion within an atheistic setting. He wants to be religious—and we need to remember this—but without God! He is a striking parallel to Auguste Comte who, having dismissed religious mythology and metaphysical speculation and enthroned scientific positivism, finishes with an ambitious attempt to found a religion of humanity. Feuerbach too remains *homo religiosus*, so he inverts religion by his naturalistic humanistic bias and provides a striking parallel to contemporary "God is dead" theology.

He even suggests, like some moderns, that "love is God himself, and apart from it there is no God. Love makes man God and God man." [25] Or again, he writes of the incarnation:

Who then is our Saviour and Redeemer? God or Love? Love; for God as God has not saved us, but Love, which transcends the difference between the divine and human personality. As God has renounced himself out of love, so we, out of love, should renounce God; for if we do not sacrifice God to love, we sacrifice love to God, and, in spite of the predicate of love, we have the God—the evil being—of religious fanaticism. [26]

God is just human love, and "Christ is the love of mankind to itself embodied in an image—in accordance with the nature of religion as we have developed it—or contemplated as a person, but a person who (we mean, of course, as a religious object) has only the significance of an image, who is only ideal." [27] God is simply the nature of man regarded objectively; therefore "if human nature is the highest nature to man, then practically also the highest and first law must be the love of man to man." [28]

Religion, indeed, becomes coterminous with life in all its complex of relationships. All are of a divine nature. This is an interesting parallel, again, to contemporary religious radicalism—a this-worldly religion, without God, but very much concerned with the social conditions and relationships of humanity. No "God of the gaps" is needed. Morality can do well without any transcendent support, and man can lift himself to his own social heaven by his own bootstraps. In all religions, God is simply a projection of man's own ideal self. But religion must not be abolished. Abolish God and substitute a religion of humanity whose sacraments are constituted by the nobler relationships of men.

Feuerbach sought to remain religious. Those who followed him proclaimed a triumphant atheism and denied religion too. The one the closest to his line of thought was Karl Marx, who denied any validity to religion whatsoever and regarded it as the opiate of the people, a drug administered by the ruling caste with the intent of keeping the proletariat contented with their impoverished lot. Religion offered "pie in the sky when you die" and thereby sought to direct attention away from the absence of pie in the here and now. It is, of course, true that religion has often provided an escape from the intolerable situation of the present, that other religions than Christianity as well as Christianity have tended to emphasize the hereafter and a realm beyond death, that religion does find its god in the limit-situations rather than in the midst of life. Yet this perversion of religion does not mean an impugnment of all religion. Of Christianity at its best, it can be said that it has shown a very real concern with man's earthly lot and has endeavored to establish some degree of economic and social justice. That Christianity is also a perversion of true religion at times should not blind our eyes to another fact. Christianity's real concern with God has led, in its finest moments, to a real concern with the conditions of human life in this world.

Nearly all the social reforms of our Western world can be traced back to the crusading efforts of Christian groups. Yet Marx has left his mark on the current secular scene.

More recently we had Sigmund Freud classifying religion as an illusion and explaining it away in the light of his psychological presuppositions. We need to remember that the latter, as in the case of Feuerbach, were never demonstrated but were dogmatically affirmed. In a more subtle and scientifically informed way than Feuerbach, Freud regards religion in terms of the mechanism of projection.[29] Man, disappointed in and frustrated by the failure of his earthly father, projects the father image upon the backdrop of the universe and finds consolation in the worship and contemplation of this ideal figure. Religion becomes a matter of wish fulfillment.

Baillie's comment on Feuerbach and Freud bears repeating:

If all that Feuerbach and Freud say were true, we should expect to find in historical religion a glorification of self-seeking instead of what we do find—the most rigorous self-denial and self-sacrifice and the belief in a God who demands of men things almost impossible to perform. Had these writers said that religion stands not for what man wants to be true but for what he feels *ought* to be true, our criticism of them would read very differently; but the distinction that is here indicated is an entirely vital one.[30]

The influence of such a view of religion is still, however, strongly evident. Undoubtedly it underlies Bonhoeffer's very narrow definition of religion and dismissal of it. It has activated the viewpoint of many self-styled "secular" theologians who have often out-Feuerbached Feuerbach and out-Comted Comte in their efforts to father off a new religion on humanity or a much distorted and atheistic version of Christianity. Even Ritschl in the last century shows marks of Feuerbachian influence.

## Religious Relativism

By the end of the nineteenth century, Ritschlian influence had produced a *Kulturprotestantismus* in which scholars such as Harnack had sought to present the founder of Christianity as the teacher of an ethicoreligious ideal like that held by respectable bourgeois society. Harnack himself had sought to show, in his famous *Dogmengeschichte,* that the original teaching of Jesus had been overlaid and distorted by the inroads of Greek philosophical speculation and, indeed, by the apostles themselves. As a result, the religion of Jesus, with its concern for the fatherhood of God and the brotherhood of man, had been superseded by a religion about Jesus reaching its flower in Catholic Christianity.[31]

In reaction to this, there appeared the school of *Religionsgeschichte* which sought to show that the bourgeois picture of Jesus offered by *Kulturprotestantismus* was not authentic, but that he was a typical man of his time, subject to the cultural and religious influences of his milieu. So Johannes Weiss,[32] Ritschl's son-in-law, and Albert Schweitzer [33] saw Jesus in the light of Jewish apocalyptic and brought to light the eschatological aspect of his thought which Harnack had lightly dismissed. In this school, New Testament scholars sought to set Christianity in the religious environment of its day, and other thinkers sought to relate Christianity to the historical religions. From A. Deissmann to Nathan Söderblom we find a tremendous variety in the advocates of this approach, some more orthodox and others less so. Günkel [34] in his book on the Holy Spirit frankly regarded Christianity as a syncretistic religion, finding parallels between Christian and pagan worship. Ritschl and his followers had almost isolated Christianity from the environmental influences of other religions. Now the Christian religion was so immersed in the latter that the faith of the New Testament was often presented as almost the product of the mythology and religious speculation of its Greco-Roman environment. The ideas and concepts in the New Testament were traced back to similar patterns of thought in the Jewish, Hellenistic, and Oriental setting of the early church.

The towering figure in the school, one among many giants, and the theologian of the movement, was Ernst Troeltsch. Ritschl had concentrated on Christianity and shown little deep concern for religion in general. So also had his disciples. Now attention was turned again to the more general issue of the religious consciousness. We have already looked at one thinker who was on the fringe of the *Religionsgeschichtliche* school and who left an intellectual heritage for this century on the issue of the religious consciousness—Rudolf Otto. He, like Nathan Söderblom,[35] was more central in his attitude to the significance of Christianity in the history of religions. With Troeltsch, we find a man whose intellectual pilgrimage led him ultimately to complete relativism.

Troeltsch began as a disciple of Ritschl but soon moved away from this position. While Ritschl vitalized his thought about the dynamic and ethical nature of Christianity, he soon came to reject the attempt to modernize the Reformation and Luther's theology and also the narrowed use of the Biblical disclosure without reference to outside religious influences. He became increasingly concerned with the problem of history and the place of Christianity within the historical process. The new "history of religions" school, in which most of his intimate friends were numbered, convinced him that a full understanding of Christianity was possible only when it was viewed within the history of religion itself and within the general movement of historical life. Christianity was one religion among many in the history of man and it must be studied as a historical phenomenon. This meant that Troeltsch was led to reject thinking based on the supernatural and to direct his attention upon the immanental factors in history.

He quickly began to reject the idea emphasized by Ritschl that the Protestant Reformation marked the beginning of the modern age.[36] Rather, he found the modern secular world beginning with the Enlightenment and placed Protestantism along with Roman Catholicism as both being more closely related to the medieval period than to the age of science and technology. While acknowledging "the great significance of Protestantism for the arising of the modern world," [37] he held that "Protestantism cannot be supposed to have directly paved the way for the modern world." [38] In spite of its many new ideas, it appears as "a revival and reinforcement of the ideal of authoritatively imposed Church-civilization, as a complete reaction to medieval thinking, which sweeps away such beginnings of a free and secular civilization as had already been toilsomely established." [39] He felt that both Protestantism and Catholicism had hindered the advance of culture, especially in the areas of social ethics, science, and the history of religion. The Enlightenment with its struggle for freedom at every level brought the Middle Ages to an end. The forces that shape our modern secular culture are not to be traced to the forms of life fostered by the Reformation and its progeny of Protestant churches.

Troeltsch thus recognized what is now very evident, that the role of the Christian religion in our secular culture is very different from that of Catholicism in the Middle Ages and Protestantism in the Reformation period when they controlled life and society authoritatively. In this sense he speaks to our contemporary situation. If Christianity was to be understood, Troeltsch held, it must not be by a return to Luther and the Reformation. It must be by a psychological and epistemological analysis of the religious consciousness and by an examination of Christianity's place within the historical movement of that consciousness.

Thus Troeltsch became concerned with the historical in a far more comprehensive way than Ritschl. The latter's historical concern had concentrated on Jesus of Nazareth. Troeltsch turned his attention to the whole movement of history and regarded the Christian religion as a historical phenomenon within the total movement. In *Die Absolutheit des Christentums und die Religionsgeschichte* [40] he emphasized the relativity of all historical phenomena. History is always open to the future, a developing movement ever throwing up the new and disclosing fresh adaptations as the situation changes. Hence all the values of history are relative, and there can be no absolute in history.

Despite the relativism of history, Troeltsch did not view it as chaotic. He was helped here by the influence of Hegel to whom he turned from Ritschl. From him, Troeltsch gathered the conviction that history is pervaded by reason. He believed that history is process directed by infinite Spirit and moving progressively as an unfolding of the thought of that Spirit within space and time. There is no hint in his thought of the Hegelian dialectic or of idealistic speculation. However, the Hegelian flavor is evident. God is the ground of the world, the immanent reason. The supernatural is banished and theistic transcendence in the sense of Otto is denied. Troeltsch admits that the Absolute is a supersensible reality standing beyond all historical appearances, even though it is the source of them. Yet, although the Divine Spirit transcends history, it is also present in history so that all history is a revelation of its life. At no point is the Absolute present in history in an absolute sense, but in a relative sense it is present throughout history as a source of the relative values manifested in history, including those of the historical religious consciousness.[41]

Because all history was included within this display of the divine reason, culture and religion were intimately bound together in Troeltsch. Furthermore, because all historical values are relative and the Divine Spirit is never absolutely present in history, even at the religious level, Troeltsch could ultimately find no absolute manifestation of the religious consciousness. Yet again, he had no place for a special and final revelation. He could take refuge only in a general revelation. He wrote:

The whole of the world or God can only manifest itself through itself, through the inner feeling and certainty of the whole and its being, which we call religious feeling or religious sense, and which we clearly feel as the presence of the whole within ourselves.[42]

Thus revelation is identified with the inner movement of the human spirit; it is the work of the immanent divine reason in man's consciousness and is practically synonymous with human discovery. The idea of the supernatural must be banished from the understanding of the historical religious consciousness for Troeltsch. There is no special divine disclosure, but rather all religions play their part in the elevation of humanity to God within the process of human history. If there are to be any norms or standards for the judgment of the religious consciousness, they must arise from a study of process of history itself. Here all history is on the same level.

Alongside his concern with the historical, Troeltsch thus placed a psychological and epistemological analysis of the religious consciousness. While strongly commending the psychological investigations undertaken by thinkers like William James,[43] whom he greatly admired, he sought to move to a deeper level and examine the epistemological dimension. Here the empiricism of the psychological studies must give place to rational investigation. Troeltsch looked for the rational within the phenomenal, for the truth content in the data that the psychology of religion had amassed and analyzed. In all this concern we can trace the influence of Schleiermacher, and Troeltsch regarded his own task as in part the completion of Schleiermacher's program. Yet it was to Kant that he turned when he sought for some clue to the epistemological significance of the religious consciousness.[44]

Kant had postulated an *a priori* structure in the mind by which all human experience was conditioned. He had differentiated between the theoretical and practical dimensions of reason, assigning scientific and empirical knowledge to the former and morality, aesthetics, and religion to the latter. Each dimension was furnished with its own *a priori* categories, but Kant had, as Troeltsch noted, handled the *a priori* of the practical reason differently from that of the pure or theoretical reason. In the case of the latter, he had made the matter of experience a necessary element as well as the form of the experience that was provided by the *a priori* structure. In the case of morality, however, he had made the form—the categorical imperative—all sufficient and had not united it in any way with the human desires and the concrete situation that evoked them. Furthermore, he had linked religion closely with morality and made knowledge of God a postulate of the practical reason operating upon the sense of moral oughtness.

Troeltsch held that there is a distinctive religious *a priori* structure in the human mind. Here we see the influence of Schleiermacher, also taken up by Rudolf Otto. The religious consciousness was not grounded in an ethical *a priori,* the compulsion of duty. It was grounded in its own distinctive *a priori* categories. "Religion," Troeltsch declared, "as the special category or form of those psychic states which result from the more or less apprehended presence of the Divine in the soul—the sense of the presence and reality of the Superhuman and Infinite—that is, beyond all doubt, a far truer starting-point for the analysis of the rational a priori of religion." [45] Without carefully supporting his case for such an *a priori,* Troeltsch postulated an element in the structure of the human consciousness out of which religion takes its rise. Like all *a priori* structures, it develops under the impact of experience and brings its own kind of certainty.

This *a priori* involves, as we noted with Seeberg earlier,[46] the intrinsic capacity for becoming aware of the being and activity of God. In this sense it is the point of contact in man that makes possible the reception of the divine revelation. There is that in man which makes him inherently religious. But Troeltsch means more than this by his use of the term. He believes that religion is the focal point of the awareness of the absolute in human experience, and he regards the religious *a priori* as "the basis upon which he asserts the validity, the truth, and the meaning of religious life and experience." As Ogletree points out: "It is the awareness of that Ground of our religious life which gives it normative significance." [47] He cites James Luther Adams' definition of the religious *a priori* in the thought of Troeltsch—it is "the law . . . of the self-apprehension of the unity of consciousness in a transcendent ground, a mystical immediacy with the transcendent ground." [48] There is a primary awareness of the divine and absolute, prior to all other knowledge—a point of view that echoes the thought of Schleiermacher. The deepest thing in all religious experience and the root of all expressions of religious life is a mystical and intuitive contact with the ground of being. Tillich, commenting on Troeltsch, writes:

It is impossible for me to understand how we could ever come to a philosophical understanding of religion without finding a point in the structure of man as man in which the finite and the infinite meet or are within each other.[49]

Barth would disagree as we shall see shortly, and Bonhoeffer is, at this point, a disciple of Barth. Troeltsch's weakness lay in his weakened view of revelation which was primarily the all pervading presence of the supersensible grasped intuitively by the religious *a priori* at its primary level.

In his later writings, especially *Der Historismus und seine Probleme*, Troeltsch dropped the term "religious *a priori*." He had by then so closely integrated religious expression with its cultural milieu, however, that he retained the idea, but spoke of it in more general terms. Religion had by now become the key to the understanding of man's cultural life. He sees every historical cultural synthesis as built around religion. The norms or values that govern such a synthesis are rooted in an *a priori* element in the human consciousness, "which in a general way is the basis for the autonomous validity of cultural norms." [50] For Troeltsch, any synthesis of culture is an *a priori* in its rootage. In *Der Historismus* he describes this *a priori* as "spontaneous creation, in so far as it actually brings forth the new of its inner depths and validates itself only by means of its inner self-certainty and its power that determines will." [51] He adds that the synthesis is no creation out of nothing nor does it result from the constructive activity of reason. It is both a transformation and a continuation accompanied by "the inspiration of a new soul and a new spirit." He thus sees cultural movements as accompanied by a spontaneity grounded in a-priority. In every synthesis of culture, something new emerges that cannot be explained in terms of antecedents. This a-priority is valid only as it is a decision of the will.[52] Furthermore, it has an objective base, and here he differs from Kant's view of the *a priori* structure of the consciousness. Since the historical development in its relativity is yet the expression of the all-pervading and directive absolute spirit, the a-priority is related to and must be seen in this objective setting.[53]

The religious *a priori* has been generalized, and Troeltsch can

now think of an *a priori* awareness of the absolute in the midst
of the relativities of history. It is this which makes possible the
genuine values pursued by historical cultures despite the relativity of all historical processes. As Ogletree comments:

Because Troeltsch sees such an interplay between the relative and the
absolute, between the historical and the transcendental, he can acknowledge the relative validity of the naïve claims to absoluteness
found in the religious and moral and cultural values of history.[54]

Values are significant and valid in the relativity of the historical
process because they are grounded in an *a priori* awareness of the
absolute in the human consciousness.

Troeltsch brought his analysis of religious knowledge to his understanding of history in his assessment of Christianity and the
other religions. Here his understanding of revelation becomes
plain. He viewed God as immanent spirit, the ground of all
values, the universal consciousness of the historical process. As
such, his presence is continuous, and every culture is grounded in
him as absolute. Hence Troeltsch denied any special revelation
and the presence of any supernatural element in history. In addition, he could attribute no finality or absoluteness to any event
or cultural phenomenon within history itself. History, as the expression of the absolute, was open ended, and its characteristic
throughout was relativity. Another mark of history was its integral continuity. All events are explicable solely in terms of the
forces immanent in history itself.

Troeltsch found three principles operative therefore, in the historical process, including, in particular, the historical manifestations of the religious consciousness. The first is the law of criticism which means that, at the most, the examination of history
offers probability, although we can have moral certitude. The
second principle is that of relativity, with its denial of uniqueness and the operation of the supernatural. We have basic continuity in history. The third law is that of analogy. At the religious level this means that all manifestations of the religious consciousness have basic similarities. Even the new dimension that

he found in each culture with its spontaneity and peculiar values was not a novelty, for the emergence of such newness was a familiar pattern of history. Troeltsch sees incarnation, resurrection, miracles, etc., as symbols in which the intuitions of the soul are clothed. They do not possess historical truth and are common to all religions. Similarity makes it possible for us to learn from history.

When such principles are applied to Christianity, certain deductions are inevitable. Its historical basis contains no certainty. Its claims to special revelation and a supernatural dimension have no validity. It has no absolute character. It is one religious phenomenon among the rest, a part of the relativity of the historical process. Troeltsch does not, however, view the diverse manifestations of the religious consciousness as contingent occurrences. Because history is directed by the divine spirit, there is development and movement. This is not to be interpreted in terms of evolution, for he does not see a single line of development. But the development is there, and it is directed toward the goal set by the divine ground of the whole process. Hence, in typical Hegelian manner, Troeltsch can tell us that

as all religion has . . . a common goal in the Unknown, the Future, perchance in the Beyond, so too it has a common ground in the Divine Spirit ever pressing the finite mind onward towards further light and fuller consciousness, a Spirit Which indwells the finite spirit, and Whose ultimate union with it is the purpose of the whole many-sided process.[55]

In his earlier thinking [56] Troeltsch had been prepared to give some measure of finality to Christianity. He saw it as the religion in which the two great types of the historical religions met—the religions of law exemplified in Judaism and Islam and the religions of redemption exemplified in Hinduism and Buddhism. Mackintosh quotes him as writing of Christianity, "It is thus not only the climax, but the converging point of the two great kinds of historical religion." [57] All religious development found both its point of convergence and its point of culmination in Christianity.

He had regarded it as having "the highest claim to universality of all the religions, for this its claim is based upon the deepest foundations, the nature of God and of man." [58] But the individuality and relativity of the historical process led him to move from this position.

As he increasingly bound up religion with culture, Troeltsch saw each religion as the integrating center of a cultural phenomenon. Christianity, therefore, was viewed as a new synthesis arising out of syncretistic Judaism and embodying aspects of other religious faiths. It is the religious center of Western culture, and distinctive as such. So Troeltsch tells us that the divine life constantly manifests itself within history in ever-new and peculiar individualizations and that we must not look for unity or universality among them. Rather the tendency of the divine life is "towards the fulfilment of the highest potentialities of each separate department of life." [59] Hence, when we turn to religion, this "makes it quite impossible to characterize Christianity as the reconciliation and goal of all the forces of history, or indeed to regard it as anything else than an historical individuality." [60] Troeltsch now sees Christianity as the only religion that the Western world can endure because it has grown up with us. Its validity *for us* lies in the empirical fact that it could not so influence a highly developed racial group, were it not, to some degree, a manifestation of the divine life. It is the way in which we receive and react to God's revelation, allowing for the kind of beings Westerners are. "It is final and unconditional for us, because we have nothing else, and because in what we have we can recognize the accents of the divine voice." [61] But other groups in different cultural situations "may experience their contact with the Divine Life in quite a different way." [62] So the great spiritual religions persist in their distinctions because of their historical destiny. Their relative value is bound up with the cultural context in which they are found. They will, however, always remain distinct in history, and the issue of their relative values "will never be capable of objective determination, since every proof thereof will presuppose the special characteristics of the civilization in which it arises." [63] We are left with the truth for us, and we can only look at other manifestations from within our own religious consciousness and its truth claims for us. Troeltsch leaves us with polymorphous truth, each racial group striving to attain its own highest potentialities and, at the same time, striving to get nearer to the others.

Troeltsch thus held that the fortunes of Christianity are bound up with Western civilization and that its final claim for validity must be found here, for the power and authority of every religion lie within its own cultural context of which it is a constituent element, indeed the point of concrescence. Once the West denies Christianity, it destroys itself. Because history is open to the future, we have no right to say that this may not happen. The Christian gospel is only one facet of the absolute truth, one manifestation of the divine life. Yet the purpose of the whole historical process is the ultimate union of the finite spirit with the Divine Spirit that indwells it.

It was the virtue of Troeltsch that he recognized the era of secularity into which the Western world was entering. The empiricism of the scientific method which had led to the secularization of society came to dominate his own thought. While he recognized the difference between the causative structure of natural science and the element of freedom and voluntary causation in history, he adopted an immanentist stance toward the latter. Furthermore, he saw history as a process in which individuality occurred within continuity. Though it was characteristic of history that the new should emerge, yet this was a repetitive pattern, and the forces that made history were the forces within history itself.

Once such a stance had been adopted, a man of faith, such as Troeltsch was and remained, must adopt a corresponding viewpoint with regard to God. So God was the Absolute Spirit, the supersensible reality that pervaded the whole process and directed it toward the attainment of goals still future. Such a "divine life" (and Troeltsch often preferred this term to God) provided the absolute dimension behind the relativity of history. It was the ground out of which all cultural values arose. The con-

tact point at which the divine Spirit met and indwelt the finite
spirit was the religious *a priori*. Yet the divine presence was everywhere the same. The supernatural and special revelation
could have no place. Revelation was uniform and took place
within the human spirit, in which the immanence of the divine
was felt. Divine transcendence in the full theistic sense could
have no place. Granted such a position, it was inevitable that
Christianity should be a particular and individual phenomenon,
valid only for the Western culture of which it was the soul.

It is understandable that Troeltsch gave up the search for the
essential norm of religion. Since history is open to the future, this
is impossible. Fresh autonomous expressions of religion may yet
arise. Allow Troeltsch's presuppositions, and the rest of his
thought falls into pattern.

Because of his preoccupation with the scientific dimension of
modern culture, Troeltsch barred true transcendence and the supernatural from his understanding of history. He turned to Hegel
for inspiration, instead of recognizing that, even within the relativity of history, there could arise disclosure situations in which
men were confronted by a power and presence that were beyond
history as well as dynamically active in history. In the Augustinian tradition so far as his acceptance of an *a priori* awareness
of the divine, he carried Schleiermacher's program out to its logical implications provided that only immanentism be accepted.
The knowledge of the divine life springs out of man's inner life
and its intuitions. It is not enriched to fuller comprehension by
revelatory disclosures in and through the historical. Here we meet
his evident reaction to Ritschl, yet he did recognize the universality of the religious consciousness.

Troeltsch's failure to recognize historical revelation as distinct
from a kind of inner discovery accounts for his treating religions
as pure autonomous cultural flowerings, individual manifestations
of the divine ground of all historical life. Had he appreciated the
significance of the resurrection and had he that sense of the eschatological that Ritschl too lacked, he might have combined the
finality of the Christian disclosure along with his understanding

of the openness of history. The Christ is the eschatological disclosure within the relativity of history who gives some comprehension of the God who stands unveiled at the goal of the historical process. Furthermore, had Troeltsch been able to emphasize the givenness of the historical disclosure in Christ, he would have had ground for bringing all religions, including the varied flowerings of the Christian religion, under the judgment of that eschatological event that points to the ultimate destiny of every one of them. For, at least, he recognized this—that every religion has some measure of revelation. It is not just man-made.

## The Abolition of Religion

With Karl Barth we have an all-out attack on religion as such and a separation of the Christian faith as unique and quite apart from man-made religious structures. He leans on Feuerbach's view of religion as a human creation in which man projects his ideal humanity as an objective entity that he can worship and which helps him overcome his frustrations. Hence Barth says of religion: "It is the attempted replacement of the divine work (in revelation) by a human manufacture. The divine reality offered and manifested to us in revelation is replaced by a concept of God arbitrarily and wilfully evolved by man." [64] Again, Barth can define religion as "the realm of man's attempts to justify and to sanctify himself before a capricious and arbitrary picture of God." [65] Thus he would deny any measure of revelation to the world's religions and regard revelation and religion as essentially contradictory. "In religion man bolts and bars himself against revelation by providing a substitute, by taking away in advance the very thing which has to be given by God." [66] While he agrees with Feuerbach's description of religion as the projection of man's wishes and desires, he yet escapes from this thinker's illusionism by rejecting his thesis that the true theology is anthropology. Rather, Barth turns to a theology grounded in the Word of God.

By the Word he means the communication of God to man that centers in Christ. Its movement is the direct opposite to that of scientific thought and philosophical reasoning as well as of human religion. It comes from God to man, not from man to God. For, as Barth sees it, there is no way from man to God. The only way that man can know the living God is through the revelation in which he freely and graciously discloses himself. "The truth that God is God and our Lord, and the further truth that we could know Him as God and Lord, can only come to us through the truth itself. This 'coming to us' of the truth is revelation." [67] In such revelation the initiative is with God, and all that man does is to respond to this divine address in faith and commitment. Such faith has no ground in man's religious quest. Indeed, as Barth sees it, if man had been able to find God through religion, there would have been no need for the revelation in Christ. Religion has been shown to be inadequate by this divine "coming to man."

All this is of one piece with Barth's condemnation of natural theology. He can say in his Gifford Lectures: "I am an avowed opponent of all natural theology." [68] So far as philosophy is concerned, there can be no true knowledge of God. In his majesty and freedom God is completely free of all earthly structures. Barth insists that God is the "wholly other," qualitatively different from man, his fallen creature. By his fall, man has completely lost the divine image, so there is no point of contact where man can lay hold on God, either in his reason or in his religion. Barth sees the only evident possibility and reality of man's existence as "the attempt to preserve and affirm himself." [69] He finds in man no evidence of "an openness for the grace of God and therefore a readiness for the knowability of God in His revelation."

Natural theology, as he sees it, is simply the unavoidable expression of just the human condition. "It is the man closed to the readiness for God who cannot and will not let himself be deprived of the fact that a readiness of God is at his disposal even apart from the grace of God." [70] It becomes, indeed, the expression of man's opposition to grace. In it man does not know the real God. What is "God" to the natural man and what he calls his "God" is a false god, an idol. Such an idol will, moreover, not bring him to any knowledge of the divine reality, nor will it in any way prepare him for such knowledge. Rather, it will keep him from it, and thus natural theology will make him an enemy of the real God.[71]

As with natural theology, especially in its association with Christianity, so with religion. Barth argued that the status of religion in relation to faith must be determined. Faith is man's response to God's gracious self-revelation in Christ. As such it is God's gift. Men have been led by God himself, through the work of his Holy Spirit within them, to a conviction about the revelation. "The work of the Holy Spirit is that our blind eyes are opened and that thankfully and in thankful self-surrender we recognize and acknowledge that it is so: Amen." [72] The Holy Spirit, indeed, sets man free for God.[73] Furthermore, the work of the Holy Spirit "cuts away from us the thought of any other possibility of our freedom for God." [74] So man in his freedom is yet able to hear the Word of God because the Spirit makes this possible. In the hearing of the Word, man knows that he does not of himself possess the possibility of communion with God. With all his freedom and possibilities, this possibility is not open to him by his own right. Here he is not free, but the Holy Spirit makes this possible for him.

When the Word of God is acknowledged, it is also acknowledged that man is not free for God. . . . It is not grounded upon any freedom or possibility for this acknowledgment which he possessed in his own right. It is grounded solely upon the freedom of the Word of God which has come to him.[75]

With such an understanding of revelation and faith, Barth proceeded to demolish religion, yet he did so with some degree of charity.

Barth is careful to set limits to his attack on religion. For one thing he agrees that religion is a universal phenomenon. It is difficult to find any historical time or locality where men have not felt obligated to offer worship to God or gods and to shape cultic forms. Indeed, "human culture in general and human existence in detail seem always and everywhere to be related by men to something ultimate and decisive, which is at least a powerful rival to their own will and power." [76] It seems to be universal also that men have believed that they heard the voice of the deity, while piety is by no means limited to Christianity. Hence Barth agrees that, at the level of human experience from the subjective aspect, revelation "seems necessarily to be only a particular instance of the universal which is called religion." [77] Christianity would appear to be one species of the genus "religion." So faith in its outward appearance is of the same order as the religious responses elsewhere and belongs to the same area of human competence, experience, and activity. In other words, it can to some degree be classified as a religious act. God utters his Word in an area filled with more or less adequate parallels and analogies. His divine particular is hidden in a human universal. His givenness in revelation is accompanied by a hiddenness "which is obviously given to it along with its true humanity as a religious phenomenon." [78]

Here we are touching upon one of the most difficult issues of theological thought. Christianity seems to fit, as a religious phenomenon, within the series of world religions, but the Christian claims that in the revelation that is the center of Christianity there has been a unique divine disclosure. Hence Barth sees the theological either/or as follows. Either we make our knowledge of the nature of religion in general the norm by which to judge the Christian revelation, or we make the latter the standard by which all religions, including the Christian religion, are brought under judgment. Here he echoes, in a more exclusive sense, the view of Tillich. [79] Barth claims that the revelation is not open to discussion. We must begin with the Word in its sovereign power. Jesus Christ is Lord. Barth sees the frequent mistake of theologians as talking about "the revelation of religion" rather than "the religion of revelation." [80] But revelation must not be explained in terms of religion. Rather the reverse is the case. The revelation stands in judgment.

Yet in our theological assessment of the religions, we must proceed with great caution and charity. We must treat man and his religious capacity with all seriousness, for he is the man for whom Jesus Christ was born, died, and rose again.[81] But this does not mean that we must make the Christian religion the norm for all others, as if man has achieved something unique. The Christian religion is not the true essence of all religions. It is not the true religion superior to all religions that man has created. We cannot therefore speak, like the early Troeltsch, of the absoluteness of the Christian religion. Rather the Christian is also a religious man. His distinctive mark is that he has responded to the divine grace in Jesus Christ, who has reconciled to God "godless man and his religion." [82] The Christian should, therefore, place himself alongside his fellowmen in their religiousness in the forbearance of Christ. For he knows that his own religion, which has been overcome by divine grace in Christ, is as much in need of such tolerance and forbearance as are the religions of his fellows.

On the human side, Barth can thus describe religion as unbelief.[83] It is the one great concern of godless men. In it man is asserting himself, trying to grasp at the truth by his own powers, and thereby directly contradicting revelation. The attitude of the religious man is the opposite to that of faith.

He does not believe. If he did, he would listen; but in religion he talks. If he did, he would accept a gift; but in religion he takes something for himself. If he did, he would let God Himself intercede for God; but in religion he ventures to grasp at God.[84]

What he attains by his grasping is not truth, but a complete fiction. He knows an antigod, which must be discarded when the truth comes to him and evokes the response of faith. Apart from revelation and faith, religion, like natural theology, is concerned with idols. So revelation does not connect on to religion as it is already practiced. The Word in Jesus Christ rather shatters religion and overcomes it.

Jesus Christ does not fill out and improve all the different attempts of man to think of God and to represent Him according to his own standard. But as the self-offering and self-manifestation of God He replaces . . . all the different attempts of man to reconcile God to the world, all our human efforts at justification and sanctification, at conversion and salvation.[85]

Here is the nub of Barth's attack on religion. It is man's attempt to replace what God alone can do by something of his own contriving, to substitute a human product for the divine Word, to create his own images of the God who is to be known only in His free chosen disclosure. Religion is man seeking to justify and sanctify himself, to put himself on friendly terms with the higher world, and to interest it on his own behalf by his own works, "to come to terms with the world, to make the world serviceable to him." [86] Thereby instead of reaching God, he locks the door against God. The pious element in such pious efforts to reconcile God to man is, indeed, an abomination to God. Under the impact of the divine revelation, religion becomes self-righteousness and idolatry. It is an inescapable and universal aspect of man's existence, and yet, despite its spirituality at its best, it remains a human achievement and as such it stands condemned before the Word in Jesus Christ.

Even religion can at times become aware of its own failure, quite apart from the impact of revelation. Barth sees mysticism and atheism as two ways in which religious man reacts in self-criticism. As he reflects upon himself as religious, man may revolt against his false gods by turning within and finishing often in a comprehensive negation. Mysticism retreats from the outward religion and yet still retains it as material for spiritualizing. It is the starting point of the mystic's great withdrawal, in which the mystic queries God, the cosmos, and the individual. Yet like a parasite, mysticism is kept going by the religious forms against which it rebels.

The revolt of atheism is less astute. The mystic still has his retreat to inwardness and still derives strength from the religion he criticizes. The atheist denies the God of religion, but does not see that, "apart from religion, there are other dogmas of truth and ways of certainty, which may at any moment take on a reli-

gious character." [87] Hence in denying its God, atheism's revolt
may help unintentionally to foster other religions, oftentimes in
disguised forms. It would appear that Barth implies that atheism
creates a religious vacuum which other and new religions will rise
to fill because man is inherently religious. Now what both these
products of religion's self-criticism do is to perpetuate the error
of all religion—man's assertion of his ability to determine his own
existence and justify himself. They do not achieve the negation
of religion, for their own existence demands the existence of religion.

Barth's attitude toward religion is not, however, completely
negative, for he recognizes that even faith is nurtured within the
soil of religion and that those who receive the divine revelation
clothe their response in religious dress. The real crisis for religion arises not in its own self-reflection but under the impact of
the divine revelation. Yet, even then, religion is both abolished
and retained. For Christian religion is under judgment with all
religion and yet it is also the "true" religion. It is true religion
because it has been overcome by the divine Word. It remains
true religion only insofar as it stands under God and, like the
sinner, is justified by grace. It is religion shaped and sustained
by, subservient to the revelation. It is not acquitted because of
any inherent worthiness. As *our* Christianity it stands condemned
with all religion as unbelief. Such a description makes Christianity
our work, serving our aims. Hence continually the religion of revelation has stood under the judgment of the revelation and has
been preserved, like the sinner, only by grace. Barth comments
upon the prophetic ministry in Israel that we see "at every point
the inevitable struggle of revelation against the religion of revelation, a struggle in which the prophets did not even spare prophecy
itself." [88] Directly it vaunts itself and boasts of its superiority, it
ceases to be the true religion. Always such religion is true only
as it exists for faith and under revelation. Its truth rests in no
human quality or capacity but solely in Jesus Christ. Barth points
to the Amida Buddhism of Japan and, to a lesser degree, to the
Bhakti religion of India as apparent parallels to Christianity, and

argues that the one decisive element which they lack is Jesus Christ.

It is not merely a matter of prudentially weighing the various possibilities of heathen development, which might eventually catch up with the differences we teach, but of a clear insight that the truth of the Christian religion is in fact enclosed in the one name of Jesus Christ, and nothing else.[89]

Once Christian people forget this and turn their faith into a religion, subserving the divinely given truth to man-made aims and manufactured forms, they become an abomination to God. Only in Christ is the religion of the church created and elected as the one and only true religion. Such religion is justified religion and the sin of religion is pardoned, even though the hands that carry the treasure are continually stained with sin.

By his opening definition of religion, Barth very evidently has adopted the stance of Feuerbach. He sees nothing divine in religion but only the products of man's contriving. That, at the same time, he affirms revelation over against Feuerbach is possible because of his exceedingly narrow view of revelation and because of his ultra-Protestant view of the fallen nature of man. Any criticism of him must commence at this point.

As we have seen, Barth denies any point of contact in man that makes possible any "hearing" of God. Even the great protagonist of Reformation theology, Calvin, had spoken of a *sensus divinitatis* which God had implanted in the human soul. For him belief in a divine being was no product of human devising, even though "designing men have introduced a vast number of fictions into religion." [90] He furthermore declares that this sense of divinity is *indelibly* engraven on the human heart. It is by nature inherent, as it were, in our very bones. Now Calvin sees that this implanting of the seed of religion in men's minds is also accompanied by a divine manifestation in the whole structure of the universe. God daily places himself in our view and "we cannot open our eyes without being compelled to behold him." [91] It is true that Calvin believes such possibilities to have been hopelessly corrupted, but he does not deny that all religions have some degree of revelation, however much man may have distorted it and dressed it up in his own fictions. Still more basically he can speak of man's sense of divinity, his religious *a priori,* as a permanent constituent of man's consciousness. A true knowledge of God is possible for Calvin only in Christ.

We have emphasized this approach of Calvin in order to remind ourselves that Barth's radical position has little justification in the Reformation thought to which he would continually have us turn. Furthermore, in the light of our own examination so far, his position is far from justified. If it be argued that Barth later modified his position, as he himself confesses in *The Humanity of God,*[92] let us remember that the point of contact is only in the conjoining of man and God in Jesus Christ, in whose humanity all men are rejected and all men are elected. His exceedingly peculiar view of redemption at this point would suggest that all men have been redeemed in Christ, but are not aware of it. As Brunner points out, faith then becomes an awakening to our actual condition, almost a Platonic viewpoint.[93] This might presumably make some difference to Barth's radical *Nein* in his debate with Brunner as to some point of contact between God and man. If so, Barth never spells it out. Actually his highly commendable and fundamentally sound polemic for the divine grace has led him to postulate an extreme position that he can only defend by continually affirming it.

The result is a one-sided view of the nature of religion, which, in true dialectical style, Barth almost negates when he can describe Christianity as the "true" religion. At this point, we must look at Barth's understanding of revelation. He is emphatic in affirming that the sole revelation is Jesus Christ. Kraemer, who was much nearer to Barth in *The Christian Message in a Non-Christian World* than in his later writing, can in that volume criticize the Swiss theologian as not breathing the atmosphere of Biblical realism. He writes:

Whosoever by God's grace has some moderate understanding of the all-inclusive compassion of God and of Christ rejoices over every evidence of divine working and revelation that may yet be found in the

non-Christian world. No man, and certainly no Christian, can claim
the power or the right to limit God's revelatory working.[94]

Barth was rightly Christocentric in his theological thought, and
we can rejoice in the way in which he makes the incarnation the
focal point of his understanding of faith. Furthermore, his emphasis on the grace of God in Jesus Christ makes it clear that
Christianity is distinctive because it is the response of "godless
man and his religion" to God's saving act. It is divine grace that
makes it possible for Christianity to be the "true" religion—strange
dialectical twist! Yet has he any right to eliminate the working
of the divine grace elsewhere if the Christ be truly the incarnate
presence of a redeeming God?

The Greek apologists and the fathers of the early church recognized the activity of the divine Logos elsewhere. Although we
try to stick to the empirical and shun the speculative these days,
dare we say that he who by becoming incarnate and wrought our
redemption thereby, did not work elsewhere? Kraemer sees this
and emphasizes it in his later thinking. He delineates various areas
where revelation may be found in other religions and would not
dismiss other religions as purely human products. He writes:

It would be fascinating to go deeper into the Greek tragedians, the
inner dialectic of the great philosophers, the pointers to God-en-
counter, to the activity of the life and the light of the Logos everywhere in Man's entire cultural enterprise.[95]

Thus Kraemer would have us employ the Logos concept as it
comes in the Prologue of the Fourth Gospel. The Word is the
light which lightens every man coming into the world. Yet he is
careful to refuse any Stoic flavoring of this concept, and he specifically rejects any attempt to talk about all religions as being the
product of revelation, the results of the *logos spermatikos* in every man or the embodiments of a *praeparatio evangelica*.[96] He
rightly comments that this leads to a form of relativism and blunts
our concern for the truth. Yet he is concerned, as he finds Barth
is not, with whether God has anything to do with this whole business of religion,[97] and he reminds us that the Biblical testimony

does recognize other modes of revelation than Christ.[98] We cannot easily use the term "general revelation" or suggest uncritically that all religions are true. He writes that "all religions are huge systems of manifold, partly more or less positive, partly more or less negative, responses to God." [99] Hence we must not indulge in facile explanations. Equally we cannot turn our back on the problem and take refuge as Barth does in the Christ event as the sole revelation. Kraemer writes of Barth that

> if he says that all modes of revelation find their source, their meaning and criterion in Jesus Christ, and that the revelation of God's righteousness in Christ is the final revelation in the light of which Jesus Christ is the Truth, the only Truth, without whom no man comes to the Father—then he is quite right and we ought to be *Christonomists* [Christ-alone-ists].[100]

This would seem to be what Barth does not say, although Kraemer does not make any judgment on this. Of course, it may well be that Barth may have modified his position on religion in the light of his anthropology developed in *Christian Dogmatics*, Volume III, Part 2, and of his understanding of the "humanity of God."

We have looked at Kraemer's work because it offers a criticism of Barth from one who has much sympathy with his theological thought. We must now, however, follow up with further strictures. To suggest, as we just have, that there is some measure of revelation in other religions is not to do away with the finality of the revelation in Christ. And, at this point, Barth rightly indicates that Christianity can only be the "true" religion insofar as it possesses, is shaped by, and responds to the grace of God that comes in the incarnate Word. In itself, it possesses nothing by which it can claim exclusiveness. Apart from this grace, it stands with all other religions. It must always be religion justified by grace, for at its best there always remains the human aspect of religion in its cultic forms, its theological expressions, its churchly patterns. What we would claim is that other religions are not just the work of godless men.

Unless such historical faiths have some measure of revelation, dialogue with them would be of little avail. Now it is true that Barth advocates they be treated with a tolerance that is activated by the forbearance of Christ, but tolerance is not what the situation requires. If the grace of the Lord Jesus is the way of the Servant, then we are required to listen to others, not with any patronizing air, but with the humility of our Lord himself. If we would share with them our riches in Christ, we must listen also to what they have to offer, for even to them the "light that lightens all men" may have spoken. Only if we so share with them our common human conditions as godless men in need of grace, can we hope to make any judgment upon the relation of their religious insights to our own revelation. We need in sympathy to stand alongside them, understand the conditions under which they find themselves, and see from within, in Christian charity, the religious response which they make. Furthermore, in judging them we must also bring ourselves under the judgment of the Christ, before whom all godless men and their works must stand.

Barth's description of religion as the concern of godless men really does not face the issues, for we cannot say that God's grace is not operative and that there is no divine disclosure. Yet his analysis of religion is a warning that religion may become an escape mechanism by which men may seek to evade the responsibilities of a vital faith in God. Christianity may become the true religion when it is justified by grace, but it may itself also be a way of evading the way of costly discipleship. In this sense, religion needs to be abolished. Yet when such false religion is abolished and living faith takes its place, faith must take on the garb of religion as it did with Bonhoeffer during his years in prison. Piety that seeks to defend a man against the movement of grace and institutionalism with which men may shut out the living God needs to be abolished. But true religion, religion overcome by grace and transfigured to be the expression of living faith, remains as the response of the man who is justified in Jesus Christ. In his faith he may transcend religion, and yet still he has to assume a religious garb.

As this chapter has progressed, we have faced three pitfalls that confront the Christian theologian. The first is complete secularism and the adoption of a secular theology without the God of religion. The second is total relativism and the acceptance of a position that sees no finality in the process of history. The third is an exclusive absolutism that concentrates on the Christian disclosure and regards all other faiths as purely human devisings. We must now examine these, for they were faced by Bonhoeffer in his prison letters.

# VI

## *Christian Faith and Religion—*
## *The Contemporary Crisis*

IT WOULD SEEM that any attempt to arrive at a thoroughly defini-
tive description of religion is not likely to be successful. Yet the
strenuous thinking of theologians in the last century and a half
has at least brought to a focus certain important aspects of the
religious consciousness. Efforts to separate a distinctively religious dimension in the human consciousness have been mod-
erately successful. Schleiermacher's emphasis on God-consciousness as a feeling of absolute dependence, Tillich's attempt to define religion as the state of ultimate concern, Otto's isolation of the
sense of the numinous and its accompanying feeling tone—all indicate that religion has to do with something more than can be
arrived at by rational speculation or reduced to the level of ethical valuation. In the religious consciousness we are dealing with
an intuitive and feelingful awareness of the mysterious and transcendent depths of the universe. It would seem that here Otto's
analysis, supported in large measure by the thought of Tillich,
Oman, Lewis, and Campbell, indicates one basic dimension of the

religious approach to the reality. Religion involves an apprehension of a transcendent and powerful presence in and behind the universe. Furthermore, there is an axiological aspect in this apprehension. For this mysterious presence is apprehended, not merely as the numinous but also as supremely good and true. Much could be made of the suggestion that in religious experience, the primary awareness of awesome mystery gathers around it "felt analogies" in which man is led to give content to the apprehension by models borrowed from the intramundane and intrapersonal levels of experience.

Evidently religion is a highly complex phenomenon, and we cannot fix on a few defining characteristics. As far as the object of the religious consciousness is concerned, we might define it as that which, in its power and transcendent mystery, is apprehended as of such infinite value that it evokes the response of worship. Yet the response of worship is accompanied by one of commitment and belief, for that which is worshiped makes unconditioned demands upon the worshiper. Tillich brings this out in his emphasis upon the association of the holy with ultimate concern, and in his differentiation of the true ultimate by its unconditioned nature. The religious man manifests faith in that which is ultimate in the form of total commitment. The religious consciousness is aware of the mysterious and awesome power of the holy and yet also drawn to it in a rapture and wonder that issue in love and commitment.

Such commitment finds expression in the ritual of worship but also in the relationships of society. Religion is a cultural phenomenon, as Troeltsch clearly saw. The values of a culture have their roots in the fundamental religious response of its members. Alongside worship, ritual, and ethical conduct, the element of belief, of distinctive cognitive content for the object of faith-commitment, is central.

Because of his idealistic emphasis on reality as thought, Collingwood in his earlier philosophical work identified religion with philosophy and regarded its distinctive element as the notion or concept of God that any particular religion embodied. He dis-

missed all anti-intellectual views of religion, including the emphases on conduct and on feeling, and noted that one common use of
"feeling" includes intellectual content, as we have already seen
in the case of Schleiermacher. Our critique of Otto has, we hope,
sufficiently indicated that any true understanding of religion must
include the "felt analogies" of truth and goodness, rational and
moral content, but also an awareness of transcendent mystery.
Collingwood,[1] however, dismisses all such except the rational and
reduces religion to a view of the whole universe. Religion cannot
exist apart from a specific belief as to the nature of God. He defines religion as "the theory of God and of God's relations to the
world and man." [2] This is in keeping with the whole development
of his philosophy in which he seeks always for the thought behind
feeling. We would agree that belief is an important aspect. There
is intuitive awareness filled in by specific divine disclosures. Every religion has intellectual content, but the belief is intimately
bound up with an emotive aspect of the religious consciousness
and involves the voluntary aspect of commitment. Faith is more
than belief and is akin to the best manifestations of love at the
human level. Religion is not reducible to philosophy.

Yet, as we shall see later, the differentiation of one religion
from another may well best be undertaken by a dialogue in which
each faith gives internal reasons for its own characteristic approach to reality. Ninian Smart agrees with Collingwood to the
extent that "there does not appear . . . to be any clear line between theology and speculation; for both are concerned with the
kind of cosmos we live in." [3] He proceeds in his essay just cited,
and more fully in his book *Reasons and Faiths*, [4] to examine the
historic religions empirically and to discuss their doctrines in a
dialogic manner—giving the religious reasons for the view of the
universe embodied in each specific religion, and thus moving to
an apologetic for one's own specific viewpoint. He holds that "any
appeal to religious experience (whether intuitive or otherwise)
must inevitably lead to a consideration of the experience not
merely of Christians but of Buddhists and others, and thereby to
an examination of the way experience is linked to different sorts

of doctrines."[5] Any consideration of the relation of the various religions involves us in a serious dialogic examination of their belief content. An emphasis on emotive aspects and faith as commitment does not suffice. Any understanding of the phenomenon of religion requires more than a concern with the vague awareness or God-consciousness of which Schleiermacher speaks. It necessitates a concern with the deeper cognitive content expressed in the specific world view that is carried in the beliefs of any particular religion.

Thus the religious consciousness manifests emotive, cognitive, and conative aspects. It is a feelingful awareness of that which is of such transcendent power and worth that, despite its awesome mystery, it evokes commitment and worship and issues in specific forms of belief and conduct.[6] Basic to this there would appear to be, despite the protestations of Bonhoeffer, an *a priori* structure in the human consciousness that makes possible a vague awareness. This does not necessarily mean that every man has this awareness, but every man *may* have it. Ninian Smart's comment is apposite:

I am inclined to feel that there may be some intimation of divinity which every man may have; but such intimations *may* not occur at all, and in any case may well be of less evidential value than certain profounder revelations to the comparatively few.[7]

It is this primary apprehension which is filled with content in the world's religions, as symbols and myths, static and dynamic models, are shaped to account for man's religious experience. Furthermore, such specific content would seem to arise in particular disclosure situations in which the transcendent presence evokes an imaginative response in the mind of man. Here Feuerbach's suggestion that religion is purely man-made is countered by the recognition that religion, like all knowledge, arises out of a relationship between man and the givenness of his world. In religion there is the human response, but there is also a givenness from beyond man, a disclosure that evokes in him the awareness of unconditioned demand, the urge to commit himself to that which comes to him, the desire to worship and the response of love for that which in its mystery and overpowering presence yet strangely draws him to itself. In the Jacob's ladder of the relationship of man to the divine, we cannot easily ascribe all to man's designing. The common stock of static symbols and dynamic models, which is everywhere drawn on, might suggest that no religious response is without some measure of divine disclosure. The issue that arises is how we are to define religious truth and avoid the pitfalls outlined at the end of the last chapter.

## The Radical Theologians

We have seen the first pitfall arise in the last decades. Feuerbach's reduction of theology to anthropology and Nietzsche's celebration of the death of God have found an echo in the company of those thinkers who likewise would reject any idea of God and any significance for the religious consciousness. Obsessed with the secularized environment of our time, such "theologians" (*sic*) would eliminate the word "God" from their vocabulary and regard the Christian church and its structured worship as irrelevant to the needs of secular man. They believe that in so doing they are following up the insights of Bonhoeffer, but certainly not Bonhoeffer as we have sought to interpret him in the first chapter. Bonhoeffer, at the point where he speaks about God and religion, is much more evidently heir to some of the insights of Karl Barth. As we have seen, Bonhoeffer is attacking the metaphysical speculations, pious notions, and divorce between religious practice and worldly activity that so often characterize Christianity. What he labels as religion is hyperindividualism and overconcern with one's own redemption, a preoccupation with the otherworldly, a lack of concern for this world, and a commitment to temporally-influenced presuppositions of metaphysics. Identifying religion in this way, he declares that men "simply cannot be religious any more," [8] and looks for the stage of human development when men shall be radically without religion.[9] Yet his concern with real prayer and worship, his commitment to

Jesus Christ in whom the transcendence of God is manifested in the midst of the world, his emphasis on costly grace, are expressions of the religious consciousness as we have just sought to define it.

The radical "God is dead" theologians [10] have found inspiration in their own interpretation of some of Bonhoeffer's enigmatic, but also prophetic, utterances. Still more, however, they have been influenced by Nietzsche, for whom contemporary culture had obliterated the thought of God. He could boldly assert that God is dead and that the future lay with the superman who rose above the slave morality of Christianity and determined his own destiny. He analyzed the doctrine of God along the lines of Feuerbach, and associated the meaning of the "death of God" with the decline of effective belief in God. For him there was a cultural decay at this point, and this meant the end of the kind of being that "God" enjoyed, since "God" was a function of man's own self-consciousness. Hence Nietzsche is concerned with the cultural death of the idea of God, and with its consequent uprooting of the intellectual and moral values associated with it. Actually men themselves are the deicides, and they must now attend God's funeral. They have created the idea of God, and now they have to let it die. "We have killed him—you and I. All of us are his murderers." [11] The only hope now is the ruthless way of the superman, the self-chosen path of the will-for-power. Religion is out.

Thus Nietzsche celebrated the cultural death of God because God is a product of culture. Modern culture is passing into a period when the idea of God is no longer widely accepted. God is no longer believable, and man no longer feels a need for him.

That we find no God—either in history or in nature or behind nature— is not what differentiates *us*, but that we experience what has been revered as God, not as "godlike" but as miserable, as absurd, as harmful, not merely as an error but as a *crime against life*.[12]

Paul van Buren [13] is strongly influenced by the school of linguistic analysis that has developed, under the influence of the later Wittgenstein, out of the earlier logical positivism. The contention of such thinkers is that it is legitimate to play language games but that we must be clear about the rules for the game concerned and about its meaning. The linguistic analyst requires us to show exactly what part a word like "God" plays in sentences making theological statements. Unfortunately, van Buren is more a logical positivist than a linguistic analyst. His attitude is fundamentally empiricist, and he seeks to retain the verification principle of the logical positivist in a modified form. The later Wittgenstein had sought to evade this principle according to which any statement, to have meaning, must be empirically verifiable.

Van Buren, however, believes that theological statements must be either cognitive or noncognitive. If they are cognitive, they must be verifiable publicly by examination of empirical data. Obviously statements about "God" do not fall in this category. All that we can verify are the historical statements about Jesus Christ, and language about transcendence can convey no meaning at this level.

The other type of sentence, the noncognitive, expresses an attitude toward reality rather than being a statement about reality as such. Here we have a subjective aspect—the point of view of the one making the statement. The only possible public verification would be that the person's behavior is consonant with his stated point of view. Men's attitudes are verified by their "fruits." But here, again, statements about "God" would seem to have no referent. All they really do is to express a human attitude. It would be best then, van Buren contends, to avoid the use of the word "God" and to speak about man.

In consequence, van Buren covers the Biblical and historical development of theological language, only to finish with statements from which all transcendent reference must be removed. In quite a different way from Feuerbach, he turns theology into anthropology. Beginning as a Barthian, with the belief that God's Word is beyond all cultural phenomena, he has now come to the position that contemporary culture is so empiricist that the word

"God" and the idea of transcendence must be permanently banished from the Christian message.

He wants to remain "Christian," however. Just as Nietzsche's desire to return to pre-Christian paganism was only realized in his post-Christian paganism, so all the radical theologians who in some form advocate atheism yet have to do so in a Christian dress. Thus van Buren focalizes his attention in Jesus Christ. He tries to retain the Christological formulations of the church to the degree that Christians affirm Jesus as Lord and find a source of vitality and purpose in the life and death of Jesus of Nazareth. Jesus was so uniquely free that he gives that freedom to the believer. His freedom has a "contagious" character, and his "resurrection" is simply the affirmation that "the disciples were changed men. They apparently found themselves caught up in something like the freedom of Jesus himself, having become men who were free to face even death without fear." [14] To be committed to Jesus as Lord is to live his life of freedom.

Van Buren, because of his linguistic approach, is still concerned with the idea of God. It is this idea which has died, and the word "God" should be discarded as useless. Yet though he dismisses transcendence, this theologian is still sufficiently Barthian to want to retain some measure of Christology. In consequence, his attempt to give meaning to the Lordship of Jesus carries implications of the very transcendence that he seeks to banish. He ought, in the light of his argument, to be content with Jesus as Teacher and Example.

This is where William Hamilton is content to rest. For him frankly and avowedly God is dead, not just the idea of God. It is difficult to understand what he means in such language, since a true atheism, understanding the significance of the name "God," simply affirms that there is no God. But Hamilton is, like his fellow radicals, bound up with our post-Christian and secular culture. He himself seems to have passed through a pilgrimage into which the chronological succession of his fragmentary writings give some insight. It is difficult to build up from such writings any coherent position, probably because he is doing his thinking as he writes and is ready to take up a new position in every new literary effort. He seems to have moved from an attitude in which he felt the impossibility of faith in God even for the Christian.[15] Vexed by the problem of suffering, he sought, in *The New Essence of Christianity*, to expose his own feeling of the presence and absence of God. God seems to be present in our godless existence, troubling us, and then to be absent and not reveal himself when we commit our lives to him. Hamilton writes:

In one sense God seems to have withdrawn from the world and its sufferings, and this leads us to accuse him of either irrelevance or cruelty. But in another sense he is experienced as a pressure and a wounding from which we would love to be free. For many of us who call ourselves Christians, therefore, believing in the "death of God" means that he is there when we do not want him, and he is not there when we do want him.[16]

Hence he reduces Christianity to a Christological minimum and still confesses that man "cannot live as a Christian for long with the suspicion that God himself has withdrawn." [17]

In "Thursday's Child," [18] Hamilton moves beyond this initial position, stating that no contemporary theologian (*sic*) actually believes in God or that God exists.[19] Such a theologian does not go to church, nor is he interested in ecclesiastical questions. "At the centre of his thoughts and meditations is a void, a disappearance, an absence." [20] Yet this is not traditional atheism, for there is a wistful hope that one day God will come back again.[21] Hamilton is still preoccupied with the absence and presence of God, yet he is prepared to make the extra step and affirm that the absence of God means the death of God. Thus we are left with the enigmatic idea that God has died and that he may come to life again. Kenneth Hamilton interprets this to mean that "Hamilton's God dies when he is not to be found, and He will rise again when he is to be found once more." [22] The only logical deduction would seem to be that the atheism of Hamilton follows a Feuerbachian pattern. God is somehow bound up with the believer's consciousness, a kind of function of it. We are not dealing with the Holy

Other of the Biblical revelation but with a God who is a phenomenon of the religious consciousness, who dies and rises again as that consciousness waxes and wanes. R. Gregor Smith cogently suggests that Hamilton is "thinking essentially of the death of an *idea* of God, rather than speaking of the direct experience of the death of God." [23]

This is not Nietzsche's nihilism, for Hamilton still wistfully turns to Jesus and seeks to retain thereby some modicum of theological comfort. While he denies that Jesus can now be associated with divine revelation, he yet, like van Buren, regards him as the one to whom he repairs and before whom he stands. Jesus as the "man for others" is the ethical pattern for Hamilton's behavior.

There is something then, in his words, his life, his way for others, that I do not find elsewhere. I am drawn and have given my allegiance.[24]

But the last phrase betrays the wistful yearning for Christ's Lordship which gives an eschatological twist to Hamilton's "Christian atheism." He can write: "Our ethical existence is partly a time of waiting for God and partly an actual Christology." [25] For he tells us that Jesus is being disclosed in the world and may be concealed in the relationships and concerns of the social structure. Thus, like van Buren, he implies some transcendence. Indeed, since he so focalizes all his attention on Jesus, he apparently thinks of him as the embodiment of all meaning, meaning of personal existence, meaning for the whole social structure, meaning for the totality of history. And once he begins to do this, he is already, as Ogletree points out, "moving in the direction of formulating a doctrine of God in order to attest the reality disclosed in and through the person of Jesus." [26]

We may say of Hamilton that his thought is confused. He seeks for an approach to a secular society that has no place for transcendence and thus for God. Yet his atheistic stance cannot help being Christian, both because he is himself bound to Jesus of Nazareth and because the culture he is addressing is itself post-Christian, shot through with secularized Christian values. Furthermore, once he acknowledges his commitment to the historical Jesus, he cannot avoid some degree of transcendence and thus a tacit acknowledgment of the God whose death he deplores and for whose return to life he wistfully hopes. But that God never dies! It is only the idea of God in the consciousness of Hamilton that dies.

When we turn to T. J. J. Altizer we find yet another form of this radical theology. In many ways, he makes more sweeping statements than Hamilton. One such statement is quoted on the cover of the book *Radical Theology and the Death of God:* "God has died in our time, in our history, in our existence." Here it would appear that Altizer is talking about the cultural death of God, that is to say, the disappearance of the idea of God from the consciousness of secular man. He is falling into the same error, then, as Hamilton, and identifying such absence from consciousness as a basis for atheism. But, as we have continually emphasized, there is a difference between cultural atheism and real atheism. This becomes increasingly evident as Altizer seeks to develop a theology. For he is very much concerned with God and with God's involvement in this world process and in our common life. What he is really attacking is the idea of God as an alien deity, the Other who in his transcendence is not involved with personal beings, their joys and their sorrows, not concerned with their deepest affirmations and profoundest commitments. But then such a deistic image of God never has been central in the Christian understanding. Bonhoeffer was attacking the same idea of transcendence as associated with abstract ideas like omnipotence and was calling for a transcendence that was involved, so that Jesus Christ, the man existing for others, became for him the true disclosure of transcendence.[27]

Nietzsche calls on us to kill "God," this transcendent Other who saps our own personal vitality and creates a slave morality. But, as Altizer's thought has developed, the emphasis seems to be on the idea that this God has killed himself. Hence Altizer has moved from the "death of God" as a cultural fact to the declaration that God, the transcendent God, died in the life, death, and resurrection of Jesus, and that in this secular age we are just coming to realize it. He writes:

The radical Christian proclaims that God has actually died in Christ, that this death is both a historical and a cosmic event, and as such, it is a final and irrevocable event, which cannot be reversed by a subsequent religious or cosmic movement.[28]

He proceeds to indict *religious* Christians as those who still know a resurrected Lord of the ascension and who may be bound to an almighty and distant Creator and Judge. This original or primal death of God in the incarnation must be distinguished from "the actualization or historical realization of his death throughout the whole gamut of human experience." [29] Thus the incarnation and the crucifixion are not merely isolated events but "primary expressions of a forward-moving and eschatological process of redemption, a process embodying a progressive movement of Spirit into flesh." [30] Altizer is thus turning into a process theologian. His thinking is still confused, but its trend is now evident.

The roots of his thought must now be traced back behind Feuerbach and Nietzsche to Hegel himself, who more negatively than positively influenced both of them. Hegel's Absolute Spirit, which moves to self-realization through the rational dialectic wrought out in nature and history, provides a positive framework, however, for Altizer's thought. Hegel thought of the world process as involving a negation of Being in which the given actualities of the world had to be annihilated to make way for new possibilities. This negation might be symbolized as "death." The Absolute Spirit in its primordial essence is pure Being isolated and beyond all relations, but there is within it a drive to concreteness. Thus it actualizes itself in the world-process. In so doing it negates itself as pure Being. Hegel could describe history as "the Golgotha of Absolute Spirit, the reality, the truth, the certainty of its throne, without which it was lifeless, solitary, and alone." [31] For Altizer this negation of Being is manifested in the incarnation. Here the Spirit becomes flesh, the divine is negated in the human. God dies, and after the crucifixion, he never lives again. Through Jesus, divinity becomes the heritage of humanity. Now the Christ is embodied in every human fact. The primordial God has annihilated himself in Jesus.

Altizer supports his case by a radical kenotic Christology, in which he takes the ideas of Phil., ch. 2, and celebrates them as describing the divine self-annihilation, whereby the transcendent divine spirit poured himself totally into the flesh of Jesus and took an incarnate mode of existence. The sacred has thus come to dwell in the profane, and Jesus Christ is the initial point of a new movement of the divine within the secular. Now contemporary man must be this-worldly, saying Yes to this world, as Nietzsche bade him. The sacred has emptied itself into immanence. The historic Christian gospel fails here because its faith can be real only in the negation of the world. Thus Altizer tells us that "the disappearance of transcendence actualizes a new immanence, as a total Yes-saying to an immediate and actual present transforms transcendence into immanence, and absolute immanence dawns as the final kenotic metamorphosis of Spirit into flesh." [32] Altizer finds inspiration for his viewpoint in Blake, the mystic poet,[33] as well as in Hegel, while his studies in Oriental mysticism reinforce his view of a primordial totality or Nothingness which, in his view, has annihilated himself and poured himself into historical existence.

Altizer appears to be moving in the direction of process thought in a radical way. For him, so-called Christian atheism means the purging of Christian religious belief in the existence of a unique and absolutely autonomous God. Men must understand "the Christian God as dialectical process." [34] His position is a complete denial of the whole Christian tradition, but Altizer glories in it. The Biblical testimony, the creedal confessions of the church, centuries of theological thought are cast on the junk heap. Oriental philosophy, the mysticism of the Orient, the mythological poetry of Blake, the philosophical monism of Hegel, and the nihilism of Nietzsche provide ingredients for a new "witches brew" that is to provide the good news for modern man!

It has been pointed out that the kind of radical theology that is emerging in the above cases may well be a new religious phenomenon. Despite the denial of God, we have here certain elements that have a religious coloring. Such thinkers may deny Christianity as a faith and as a religion, yet theirs is a Christian or post-Christian atheism. For one thing, every one of the writers just discussed still professes an allegiance to Jesus of Nazareth which makes the latter more than a teacher and a paradigm. There are lingering remnants of the historic Christology in the way they speak about him. This is especially evident in the use made by Altizer of the kenotic idea. Also, they speak of allegiance to the Christ in terms that suggest his contemporaneity in the sense of a personal presence. In some way, whatever they mean by the symbol, the "death of God" is bound up with the historical actuality of Jesus of Nazareth and involves a commitment to his person that has religious overtones. W. C. Smith notes that we have the possibility of a new kind of Unitarianism, in which, of the three Persons of the Trinity, the Son alone is retained. He cryptically remarks:

They can call themselves Christians because they take the man Jesus, whom they even call Christ (though I think that is cheating a little), as a kind of model for moral behavior, for all men. There are echoes here of the classical saying of Athanasius; God "became man, in order that we might become divine"—or perhaps they are revising this to read, "God became man, in order that men might become modern." [35]

This brings us to the second feature of their thought. Quite evidently, the idea the "death of God" is a symbol that has religious content. It is pregnant for them with a kind of numinous significance. We have seen how significant in the religious consciousness are the symbols or models expressed both theoretically in belief and practically in the ritual of worship. W. C. Smith suggests that this holds of the symbol so central in the radical theology. He notes the strange juxtaposition of the words "death" and "God" that seems to outsiders absurd. But "for those for whom it has become religiously significant, the very act of bringing to-

gether these two polarities has resulted in the emitting of a whole
shower of sparks, emotional and in some cases intellectual." Smith
continues: "And from these sparks some fires have been lit, to
burn through the walls of the purely mundane, making openings
through which they have again caught sight of a transcendent
realm from which they had previously felt themselves shut in." [36]
He suggests that we may be seeing the emergence of a new cultural religious symbol. It may actually be a flash-in-the-pan "akin
to Comte's religion of humanity." What is significant, however, is
that the enthusiasm, commitment, and evangelistic fervor that
have accompanied the phenomenon point to the very presence of
that which its exponents would deny—the religious consciousness.

We note, in the third place, that the very symbol itself has
Christian overtones. Such a way of thought could arise only
within a Christian context with its historical emphasis upon the
death and resurrection of Jesus of Nazareth. The peculiar symbolism thus possesses connotations that would appeal to the religious consciousness of Western man.

Finally, while the note of despair is struck, we find an element
of hope, wistful and ultimately lost in the case of Hamilton, much
more positive in the thought of Altizer. As Smith notes: "One de-
tects a certain sense of men waiting for something to happen; or at
least of their leaving the door open just in case it might." [37] Here
we have something akin to notes struck much more positively by
Jürgen Moltmann, Wolfhart Pannenberg, Teilhard de Chardin,
and the process theologians, with their emphasis on hope, on the
open-ended nature of the universe, and on the God who also
waits in the future. We shall consider such thought later, for it
points toward a this-worldly repatterning of the Christian faith.

The thought we have been considering is a theology of revolt.
It is strongly opposed to the patterns of ecclesiastical organization
and rejects the positive theology of the Christian revelation. Yet
its rebellion strangely takes a religious form and its symbols and
commitment seem to point to a transcendence which, in its positive language, it is so anxious to reject. At the same time, it points
positively to some dimensions of the religious consciousness that

traditional Christianity has either neglected or sadly underemphasized. The theme of kenosis, the emphasis on this world, the concern with immanence all point to traditional elements present in the Christian understanding of the incarnation and the work of the Holy Spirit. Whatever religious and theological form Christianity takes in this secular society, such dimensions of religious concern will have to become central.

## Secular Christianity

The revolutionary situation of our contemporary human condition is responsible for the kind of religious aberration that we have been considering. Its mark is the increasing secularization of our Western culture, a process that by now is affecting also the peoples of Africa and the Orient with their own distinctive expressions of the religious consciousness. We have seen religion excluded from area after area of cultural activity and social organization, until it seems now confined to the realm of individual and ecclesiastical life. The dominant force in our time is the impact of science and technology upon our common life. This more than any other factor has made us aware of the secularity of contemporary culture. By its very terms of reference, science is concerned with the realm of sense experience and not with the supernatural or transcendent. In itself neutral, it has tended to fix men's eyes upon the natural order. Its success has made men wonder whether there is any need for a transcendent reference or a concern with the issues of which religion speaks. What once fell within the province of the church, from politics to healing, has been taken over by activities that have seemed to need no support from a religious concern. Science has taken over areas like disease, famine, and mental disorder that once were the objectives of religious activity and prayer. Charitable activities, concern for the poor and indigent, have become the responsibility of the state. Bonhoeffer's haunting phrase, "man's-coming-of-age," indicates what is involved. Man feels himself to be standing alone and able to cope with his world without a religious referent.

The words "religious" and "secular" would appear to be mutually exclusive, yet our contemporary secularity is the child of the Christian faith. The Christian emphasis on creation and incarnation show the involvement of the divine referent of Christianity with this world and its order. The Christian God is one who is involved with his world and its history. It is within the historical that he fulfills his purpose, and the Old Testament prophets as well as Jesus of Nazareth were concerned with man's condition in this world. The otherworldly reference stands *pari passu* with this-worldly concerns. In his inaugural sermon at Nazareth, our Lord reads from the prophet of the old covenant and declares that his task has to do with the healing of the sick, the restoring of sight to the blind, and the preaching of the "good news" of the Kingdom to the poor. Here Ritschl's insight and that of his followers was a genuine recovery at the theological level of the this-worldly dimension of the Kingdom, even though the estchatological emphasis was almost ignored. Furthermore, as van Leeuwen [38] has shown in his comprehensive analysis of world history, the Biblical revelation involved an attack upon the ontocratic form of society in the name of the living God.

The major theme running right through the Old Testament is that which proclaims the kingship of the Lord and the unremitting struggle against the challenge of the ontocratic state. Fundamentally, the decision which faced the people of Israel was a choice between ontocracy and theocracy.[39]

In such a condition of ontocracy man is subject to deified forces of nature or of society. He is dominated by mundane and intramundane authorities and is an element in a cosmic divine totality. The Biblical witness is concerned with the freeing of man from such a totality that he may stand free in his human dignity before and under God. The only authority left for Biblical men is that of the living God. Ontocracy has to give place to theocracy. As van Leeuwen sees it, history is Christian history in the sense that it portrays the stages in which man is being set free from intramundane authorities that he may stand on his feet, a being who is "coming-of-age," under God.

Significantly the agent of secularization in the last three centuries has been the development of science with its technological applications, and science too is a child of the Christian faith. The roots of science in Greek rationalism, with its mathematical base, are matched by the roots in the Christian revelation. The transcendent presence of the divine mystery implies in the Hebrew-Christian tradition that the divine ordering of nature may be understood only by observation and (implied) experimentation. The freedom of God means that his nature and purpose can be known only as he chooses to disclose something of his mystery as transcendent power and wisdom. Neither man nor his world are divine. The universe is no divine totality. Its being is derived being, and man cannot discover its rational patterning by contemplating the patterns of his own mind. The mind of the creator can be grasped only by investigating his works. Furthermore, for the Biblical disclosure, man is given under God the power and wisdom to understand and subdue his world. His creaturely being yet gives him a dignity within the cosmic order. He shares in the divine creativity and may be a cooperator with the creator in the completion of the creative process. His "coming-of-age" as scientist and technologist thus sets him free to exercise his "divine image" within his world.

Troeltsch rightly sees the Enlightenment, not the Reformation and Renaissance, as the turning point at which the new and secular era emerged. The Reformation-Renaissance was a stage in the process of the emancipation of man. It freed man from churchly authority but put him under the authority of a sacred book. It began the freeing of man from monarchical authority with the claim of divine right. But in the Enlightenment, the appeal was to man himself with his scientific and rational powers, and now this movement is moving apace. Man is set free from mundane and intramundane social, political, and religious authorities, be the latter papal, churchly, or Biblicist. He is no longer surrounded by the sacral structures of society, and he is in rebellion against the churchly establishment, for this also has its sacral structures. His religion, because it has its human aspect, has its ontocratic patterns. The Christian gospel has set him free directly by its proclamation and indirectly by the forces that it has released in world history. But he is set free under God! Gogarten cites Paul's thought in Romans and Galatians at this point. Christ has inherited the world and we have inherited it along with him. He writes:

If the world is on loan to man as his inheritance, then, as Paul would say, man is a mature son, independent of the world. He is no longer subjugated to "the elemental spirits of the universe," as the heir in the order of the earthly world is who, not yet of age, is placed under guardians and tutors retained by his father. . . . With the knowledge that the world is granted to the man who has come of age as an inheritance, the relation of man to the world is fundamentally changed. The world no longer rules him. He has become its master.[40]

Now, at this stage, it is easy to affirm that secular man is set free from religion and to claim that Christianity is not a religion, but a faith, a way of life. It is true that in the process of history, the man-made dimension of religion, including its Christian form, has been subject to demonic distortion. Christianity has served the ends of human aggrandizement and the ontocratic claims of social and political institutions. Yet Christianity has always centered in its revelatory dimension and always been subject to the judgment and purificatory reformation of the incarnate Word, the divine disclosure in the Christ. Granted that the man-made elements in the belief, ritual practice, and institutional organization of Christianity have been subject to distortion, does this mean that we must dismiss the whole religious posture and call essential Christianity by some name other than religion? As we have seen, it is difficult to think of the Christian faith without worship and individual piety, without the acknowledgment of transcendent power and grace, however much piety may become hyperindividualistic, belief may be put in a metaphysical straitjacket, and worship may become dead and formalized in structure. We agree with Lesslie Newbigin that "religion is much too great and permanent an element in human experience to be swept out of sight." [41] Man's worshipful response and his creedal and rational understanding are alike necessary concomitants to the gracious and awesome transcendent presence, however large the dimension of human contrivance may loom in them.

Furthermore, to set Christianity apart in this way savors of an arrogance quite remote from the attitude of the focal point of its revelation, the Christ who came in the form of a Servant. Those who advocate a nonreligious Christianity emphasize the latter, but so often they forget that all religions have some claim to an element of transcendent disclosure. Their human dimension may be very evident, but dare we deny a divine dimension, a sense of the presence of the other and the coming in them too of the Christ, the light which lightens every man coming into the world?

There is an alternative to setting Christianity and religion apart and adopting the stance of Barth. It is to see secularization as making possible a desacralized form of the Christian religion, in which commitment to the Christ and concern for the this-worldly can be expressed in worship and fellowship. Newbigin speaks of "the religion of a Christian who accepts the process of secularization and lives fully in the kind of world into which God has led us." [42] But, if such a reformation of the Christian religious consciousness can take place under the pressure of the secularizing movement of world history, we dare not say that a like change may not be possible in other expressions of the religious consciousness in which divinely given insights may be found. Van Leeuwen suggests that Islam may prove itself able and willing "to adapt itself, however drastically, to the requirements of modern society." [43] Again, he reminds us that "Hinduism" is not a timeless entity; it is much more like a river the current of which has now reached a state of tremendous acceleration, bringing the Hindu pattern of life into the dynamic onrush of Christian history. It is possible, of course, that Hinduism will be swept away by a technocratic ideology. It is also possible that India will remain Hindu for the rest of time. [44] There may be a degree of Christianization, conscious or unconscious, in such reconstitutions of the religious consciousness, as in the case of some forms of Mahayana Buddhism, but we cannot, *ipso facto*, assert that religious expressions will disappear. Religion may take a new and truer form under the process of secularization. We may see a dynamic process of enrichment and the opening of new dimensions in the expression of worship, piety, belief, and religious fellowship.

With this general discussion, let us turn to some typical expressions of religionless or secular Christianity. Harvey Cox, in his challenging book, *The Secular City*, has launched on one such attempt. He sees three stages in the social aspect of man's historical existence—the tribe, the town, and technopolis. At the tribal level, Cox finds a *pre* I-Thou type of relationship, in which the ties of kinship predominate and in which individualization is deficient. The relationship to God was envisaged in symbols taken from family titles. The authority was predominantly horizontal, and "some kind of mystical, often exotic, union with the deity was this era's characteristic relationship." [45] At the urban level, the tribal kinship ties are broken up or rather broadened into an I-Thou type of relationship. The deity is envisaged in political terms, as king or ruler. Individualism predominates and relationship to God is envisaged in vertical rather than horizontal terms. Man does not participate in God; he encounters God. God is one who has authority over him. Within this urban level, Cox sees a new form of I-Thou relationship emerging, a relationship of alongsideness. This characterizes the technocratic and contemporary level. No longer must we speak of God in terms of participation or confrontation, but in terms of mutual membership of a team. God is met as "you," as part of the work team that characterizes a technological culture. God is to be thought of as our partner in a joint venture, and the model must be the Servant image exemplified in the life of Jesus. [46]

Hence, Cox sees little place for "experiencing" God, or for becoming "fascinated with God himself." He tells us oracularly that "God wants man to be interested not in Him but in his fellow men." [47] He sees the religious quest ending in Jesus of Nazareth and finds little place for that mystical commitment to God and worship of God that is the heart of religion. For him, the gospel is working in a team with God to build the social structure, and he seems to forget that the capacity to work in a team without friction and with loyalty is not characteristic of sinful man. Indeed he ignores this latter element of alienation and estrangement, of which contemporary existentialism is so aware and with which the religious consciousness is very concerned. The technological culture is always tittering on the edge of the totalitarian anthill. Without the renewing presence of God, made available in prayer and worship, any team bent on social reformation and political renewal can easily fall apart. Without a loyalty that transcends our intramundane relationships we soon fall back into the morass of the collective. It is no solution to reduce the transcendent presence to the level of our intramundane team relations. Even Harvey Cox has, of late, realized the need for personal piety. Without religious springs, social reform can fall apart.

Van Leeuwen, like Harvey Cox, is captured by the technocratic nature of contemporary culture. We have already commended his association of secularity with Christian roots. Now we need to note the thesis that he builds around this. His examination of world history is directed by the conviction that religion is a cultural phenomenon from which man must be set free and by the idea that Christianity and contemporary secularity so belong together that they may almost be identified in essence. He has drunk deeply at the Barthian springs and falls into the same snare of condemning all religion. He sees that the secularity of the West is becoming worldwide, and celebrates the possibility that Christians and non-Christians can cooperate in building a new tower of Babel, each bringing his particular treasure, reinterpreting the past creatively, and making use of the wisdom and experience of the many cultures.

This will be possible "once the religious myth has been blown away." [48] Religious forms, Christian and non-Christian, now impede the advance of Christian history which is identified with the development of technocratic culture. Van Leeuwen is typically Barthian in his rejection of the non-Christian religions. They are cultural forms now to be superseded by the secular technological forms. Van Leeuwen sees the latter as the bearer of the Christian message that he seems to identify with an attack upon social evils. Prayer and worship in the presence of a transcendent mystery and power from which come the streams of true personal and social renewal find little place in his thought. The Christian and non-Christian have in common, not worship, divine disclosure, commitment, but a stock of cultural building stones retrieved from their past and outmoded cultural forms and capable of being built into the new "tower of Babel" of a technocratic culture.

Like Harvey Cox, van Leeuwen becomes exceedingly nebulous about the form that a religionless and secular Christianity should take, except for social concerns. We would seem to be hearing too much of the secular and too little about "honest religion," to quote John Oman's phrase. John Macquarrie pungently comments:

It is the man who prays and is aware of a transcendent reality who, in the long run, is likely to be most concerned with other men as persons; while the man whose mind is fixed on some impersonal ideal, even if it happens to be an admirable one in itself, is the man who can be most inhuman towards his fellows and can use them as means for the realization of his ideal.[49]

No one can read the two closing chapters of R. Gregor Smith's *Secular Christianity*, entitled respectively "Secular Christianity" and "Prayer," without feeling that this advocate of religionless Christianity is seeking to express what we have called "honest religion." Having dismissed religion, in the typical style of Bonhoeffer, as "the attempt to use God as a completion to man's life," he bids us turn to a real prayer in the Spirit.

Without this basic awaiting of the Spirit the forms of prayer are vacuous. Only by way of the utter desolation of Christ's historical being on the Cross is prayer possible at all. It is thus the impossible possibility which is only found in the utmost mystery of the Spirit being with us and speaking for us.[50]

He defines religion as a cultural phenomenon and rejects it, yet, what he is talking about above is real religion as we have sought to express it. The reason is that Gregor Smith's more balanced view of secularity retains a very real sense of transcendence without which man has no equipment to deal with the secular.

## Christianity and the World Religions— Relativism and Syncretism or Finality

Another pitfall that faces any view of the religious consciousness and of the significance of its Christian expression lies in relativism and syncretism. In our contemporary scene this has been exemplified in the thought of the metahistorian, A. J. Toynbee.[51] He commences his massive study of world history as a Christian thinker, but he finishes in a relativism that hopes for some emergent religious syncretism. His thought falls into two periods. After the first six volumes of his monumental study of history, a change occurs, and in the remaining volumes of his work we have an increasingly relativistic viewpoint. Religion quite evidently is central in his thought. He is sure that religious history should be given primacy in the study of history as a whole, "for religion . . . is the serious business of the human race." [52] He interprets world history in terms of challenge and response, finding in it a dynamic movement in which there are alterations of strife and peace. And it is significant that he finds the clue to this interpretative principle in the myth-making aspect of the religious consciousness. He holds that the accumulated wisdom of the human race is enshrined in the structures of the religious mythical consciousness and that the latter manifest the depths of man's thinking, the thinking of the heart. Hence human history is to be understood in terms of spiritual, not material factors.[53] The primordial images referring in various ways to the struggle of two superhuman personalities reflect the movement of the human spirit as this is expressed in world history.

Toynbee's work has debatable theological deductions, but he does emphasize the significance of the religious consciousness and its mythical contents in the formation and destruction of cultures. What is important in history, as he sees it, is the encounter of man with God in the rise and fall of cultures. Indeed, the successive cycles of civilization, like the turning wheels of a chariot, move history forward to ever more adequate expression of that religious consciousness that is the core of history.[54] A higher and more developed religion lies ahead. "The breakdowns and disintegrations of civilizations might be stepping stones to higher things on the religious plane." [55]

In the first six volumes of his *Study of History*, Toynbee differentiates between what he classifies as mythical religions and those he describes as historical.[56] Of the former, only Mahayana Buddhism now survives, whereas the historical group includes Islam, Judaism, and Christianity. The former have a nonhistorical, prescientific, mythical basis for their religious consciousness. The latter have replaced this viewpoint by a personal and historically mediated encounter between God and man. Actually, even Mahayana Buddhism has survived only by borrowing personal and historical categories and thereby transforming the original Hinayana Buddhism in a Christian direction. The three historical religions believe that "God as well as mankind is at work in history in this world, though this world is only one part of the field of God's activity." [57] The divine-human encounter is mediated by the acts and events of history. These three religions come to a focus in Christianity, in which the Judaic understanding of God is given a distinctive turn. God is understood as love as well as power. Through the incarnation and the crucifixion, suffering love becomes central in the disclosure of God to man. Toynbee can thus regard Christianity as the supreme manifestation of the religious consciousness.

In the later stage of his thinking, however, this emphasis on the finality of the Christian religion gives place to relativism and ultimate syncretism. He develops his new view in a way strangely parallel to the later thought of Troeltsch. Because of the self-centeredness innate to human nature, every culture tends to regard its own characteristic expression of the religious consciousness as the only true religion.

In a chapter of the World's history in which the adherents of the living higher religions seem likely to enter into much more intimate relations with one another than ever before, the spirit of the Indian religions, blowing where it listeth, may perhaps winnow a traditional Pharisaism out of Muslim, Christian, and Jewish hearts.[58]

Hence Toynbee sees a critical period approaching in world history when there will be a spiritual struggle of the exclusive-minded Judaic half of the world to cure itself of its family infirmity.[59] He regards the practical test of the validity of any religion as "its success or failure in helping human souls to respond to the challenges of Suffering and Sin."[60] With the advent of the technological era, such suffering will become more acute and sin will be more devastating. Hence the testing time is approaching for all religions.

In all this movement, Toynbee sees God challenging man to move into the true universal religion and establish a universal and spiritual kingdom. He places Christianity alongside Islam, Buddhism, and, now, Hinduism as the forms of religion having most promise for the future, and he studiously avoids any postulation of Christianity as the form *par excellence*. Rather, the world will move toward a state of affairs in which men will move freely from one religion to another with deliberate choice. As the world grows closer together, such a free choice of religion in adult life will be more common.[61] Toynbee rejects, however, any idea of an artificial "syncretistic" religion, manufactured out of elements taken from all the existing religions.[62] He thinks that a coalescence of the historic religions is possible, but it may also be hoped that all the religions will become increasingly "open-minded toward one another as the World's different cultural and spiritual heritages become, in increasing measure, the common possession of all mankind."[63] He seems to be looking for a kind of mystical universalistic climax to man's religious quest, and makes much of a Jungian view of the subconscious as "the channel through which the Soul is in communion with God," "the organ through which Man lives his spiritual life."[64] This climax will result from a mystical intuition into the depths of the psyche, and it will embrace the best findings of all the religions.

The empiricist approach of Toynbee's earlier work would actually lead to this open-ended view with its hope that, beyond Christianity and on the horizon of the future, another religion will arise. So long as we adopt an immanentist and empiricist stance, the postulation of any religion as final and absolute is impossible. In his earlier view of religion, Toynbee cut across his empirical approach and his standards of scientific objectivity because of his Christian commitment. His attempt to justify the latter was more chronological and evolutionary than eschatological and transcendent. Hence his estimate of Christianity was more along the line that it was the latest and newest religious event than that it was unique and final. In the light of this, his later position is more logical and also understandable. There is a hidden naturalistic motif in his thought.[65] His basic immanentism and empiricism are parallel to those of Troeltsch. As a historian he looks for continuity, horizontal causality, analogy, just like the great German thinker. So long as he ignores the eschatological and finds little place for true transcendence, there can be no real justification for any idea of finality. Toynbee is bound to fall into the pitfall of relativism and regard religion as, in great measure, a cultural phenomenon. True in part as the latter is, religion is more, for it has in its consciousness the sense of the transcendent.

H. H. Farmer has presented us with a much more theological and Christ-centered approach to the issue of the world religions.[66] His general theological approach to the Christian faith is to emphasize the personal nature of the God-man relationship, on the pattern of Buber's "I-Thou." Exemplified in his other writings, it is central in his study of the religions. He believes that religion is always a personal relationship to a personal God and that the core of every revelation is its dimension of personal response to a divine disclosure. He frankly acknowledges that he is positing Christianity as the normative religion and that this is his basic value judgment. In the light of this, he declares that he is concerned with the essence of religion, "that in religion which is the source of its vitality, when it has vitality, and of its power to persist as a distinctive and irreplaceable factor in human affairs." [67]

Hence he assumes a common defining essence that underlies all genuine religious phenomena, as he assumes also that this is to be found at the point where ultimate reality impinges on the human consciousness. Thereby he dismisses the stance of those who regard religion as a cultural phenomenon, a man-made structure produced by intramundane material forces. He cogently remarks that

thinkers who offer interpretations of religion which in effect reduce it to an illusion . . . always start with the assumption, derived from their prior naturalistic viewpoint, that it *is* an illusion, there being no such spiritual reality accessible to the human mind.[68]

It is at this point that his Christocentric position becomes evident, for he declares that the idea of ultimate reality that underlies his thinking must be that disclosed in the incarnation. He is thinking as a Christian philosopher. Religion arises, he holds, where the disclosure of ultimate reality is personal. Living religion is a personal encounter between God and man.

Having placed Christianity among the religions, Farmer sees Christianity as the actualization of the essence of religion, the norm of all religion. Yet he faces the dilemma that besets all who study historical phenomena—the issue of relativism. If Christianity is the result of "God's unique personal entry into the world in the Word made flesh," it has a claim for uniqueness and stands in a class apart. Ought it then to be described as a religion among the religions?

He finds help in a distinction made by R. G. Collingwood.[69] The latter has shown that whereas the kinds of classes are mutually exclusive in the natural sciences, such traditional logic cannot be employed in the area of philosophical thought or of any of the "sciences of the spirit." In this area, classes may overlap, so that differences of degree within a class may be so great that members on the edge of a class may merge over into a difference of kind. Collingwood contends that the traditional logic shaped by the traditional sciences does not apply here, and points to two fallacies in it. The first is that where two defining concepts are

admittedly distinct, their instances are also necessarily distinct.
The second is that where instances cannot admittedly be separated, there cannot be any essential difference between their defining concept.

Employing the logical apparatus of Collingwood, Farmer shows
that both these fallacies may arise when we apply traditional
logic to the relation of Christianity to the religions. In the case of
the first fallacy, if we define Christianity by its distinctive essence,
then we conclude that Christianity is not a religion alongside the
rest or that, if it is a religion, the others are not. In the case of the
second fallacy, if we accept that all religions somehow belong
together, then they all share a common essence and there is no
essential distinction between them. In that case the uniqueness of
Christianity disappears.

Now, as Farmer points out, Christianity does make a distinctive claim at the point of historical incarnation. It offers a Christological and soteriological theism. But we can still include Christianity in the class of religions and yet retain its distinctive character, if we recognize that, in the case of spiritual and moral
phenomena, there may be differences of degree which merge into
differences of kind. "Difference of degree, when it reaches a certain point, may become difference in kind without ceasing to be a
difference of degree." [70]

This is clarified by a differentiation between a general defining
concept and a normative defining concept. Things may be regarded as in a single class, not because they are related to one
another as various instances of a general type, but because they
express or approximate to, in varying degrees, an ideal type. Such
entities would fall into an ascending ladder of forms, the higher
expressing the ideal or normative type more adequately.[71] Then,
if the ideal type were ever actualized, it would not fall outside the
class of which it is the norm, but it would yet be so remote from
the lower forms that it would also be in a class apart. Further, if
such an ideal or normative type was only actualized once, it
would be in a class by itself, while still being in the class of all
the related but inadequate forms. In the light of this differentia-

tion, Farmer contends that *"there is given to us through the Christian revelation the normative concept of religion."* [72]

Farmer then affirms that the personal disclosure of God to men in Christ constitutes the normative essence of all religions, and that there is a positive personal divine self-disclosure in all of them. He finds this normative concept defined in worship. While acknowledging distortions and perversions, he finds that an examination of the various modes of worship discloses seven points which are brought to a focus in the normative essence of Christian worship. These points are bound up with the religious response in the I-Thou relationship of man with God. We have, at the commencement of this chapter, expressed these points in other ways. According to Farmer, in Christian worship as normative there is an apprehension of a personal and transcendent presence, the realized perfection of all value, who comes as absolute demand and final succor, who is also immanently active in the deeps of the believer's being, and whose reality is felt in the *sui generis* numinous feeling. He finds these to varying degrees in the world's living religions and thus seeks to justify his claim that the Christian religion is final and normative.

The approach of Farmer is a valiant attempt to move beyond the relativism that, since Troeltsch, has beset those who would describe Christianity as a religion. The difficulty in this approach is that it seeks to express what is evidently a dynamic and personal understanding of religion in a somewhat abstract way. There is a tendency to obscure this thinker's concern with the personal approach of God to man and with the essentially dynamic responses by fitting the whole into a logical scheme in which little account is taken of the historical movement of the living religions.

Tillich, as we have already seen,[73] has a much more dynamic approach to the issue of finality. Furthermore, he does not, like Farmer, fall into the trap of seeking the absoluteness of Christianity in its religious expression, but in the Christ himself, the living truth of God. He sees, as does Farmer, that the Christian religion in its many expressions is full of man-made elements and subject to perversion. Hence the Christ is the final revelation who stands in judgment upon all religions, including the forms in which man's response to the historical Christ finds expression.

Tillich has a much greater sense of the historical movement. Within the limits of his characteristic and impressive ontological scheme, he is actually seeing the Christ as the eschaton, the end of history who also stands at the mid-point of history. In his last public lecture,[74] he would see a dynamic inner aim or *telos* in the history of religions in which there is taking place a movement toward the integration of the various elements contained in the experience of the holy—the sacramental, the mystical, and the ethical. He sees this movement as directed toward the realization of "the religion of the concrete spirit." This is not to be identified with even Christianity, but Tillich does believe "that there is no higher expression for what I call the synthesis of these three elements than in Paul's doctrine of the Spirit." [75] He sees the movement as "a fight of God against religion within religion," [76] of which the criterion is the cross. Here the eschatological aspect becomes evident, as he speaks of *Kairoi* in which fragmentary actualizations of this religion can occur and when he declares that "its fulfilment is eschatological, its end is expectation which goes beyond time to eternity." [77]

In the *Kairos* of the incarnation and the cross, the *Eschaton* has appeared at the mid-point of history. Thus Tillich is saying what Teilhard is indicating when he speaks of the presence of the Omega point in Jesus Christ so that the process of history is divinely directed to its fulfillment around the future Omega point in the hyperpersonal. It would seem that this emphasis on the Eschaton is more dynamic and historically oriented than the somewhat abstract and logical approach of Farmer, who is yet fundamentally concerned with the personal, the I-Thou dimension of the religious consciousness. He loses his personal emphasis by emphasizing a Christological and soteriological theism in abstract terms, rather than emphasizing the incarnate Christ as the disclosure of that Personal Truth who awaits the universe at the end and has already appeared in the midst of historical time.

What distinguishes the Christian religion is its relation to the Christ who is both the transcendent presence and power laying his claim upon the religious consciousness and also the immanent presence within driving on to that fulfillment in which he shall be all in all. To the implications of this, we must now turn. Philosophical categories cannot adequately contain what is essentially transcendent as well as immanent and thus expressible in theological categories.

# VII

## *The Christian Religion in a Revolutionary Age*

THE CHRISTIAN RELIGIOUS CONSCIOUSNESS is involved in the contemporary revolution that is taking place in the human consciousness. Moreover, it is intimately involved, since the revolution, the movement toward secularity, is a direct result of the influences released by that divine disclosure out of which the Christian religion itself takes its rise. We have contended that it does not thereby cease to be a religion nor can it arrogantly claim any finality for itself. The only finality that Christianity can claim is that of the Christ, to whom it is committed; in the light of whose divine disclosure it is moved to worship the transcendent presence; under the claim of whom it undertakes its mission in the world; and around whom it builds its understanding of man and the movement of human history. Every expression of the religious consciousness is the result of the active interaction between man's relation to the divine and his relation to his cultural environment. If the present stage of world history has a this-worldly concern and if the secular culture of our time addresses itself to man's life in this order of space and time, it must follow that the expression of the Christian religious consciousness will be transformed, but not its pivotal relationship to its incarnate Lord and his divine disclosure. But then, since the worldwide movement to secularity is itself bound up with that same disclosure and its consequences, there should be no difficulty in such readjustment.

The eschatological emphasis underlies the whole structure of the Biblical testimony. The presence of the eschaton in the midst of history incarnate in Jesus Christ was bound up with a future consummation. Throughout the history of the church, this note has been present but unfortunately not in the full dimensionality of the Biblical understanding. In the latter, this eschatological consummation has embraced the destiny of the individual, the fulfillment of history, and the completion of the divine purpose for the whole universe. The hope for the individual has been set within the framework of a historical and cosmic hope. The symbol of the Parousia with its accompanying mythical structures is an indication that, for the early church, more was involved than individual immortality. The sadly misunderstood and overliteralized myth of the millennium; the Pauline picture of the whole creation groaning and travailing, waiting for the unveiling of the sons of God; the vision of a new heaven and a new earth; the hope that all things, things in heaven and things on earth, will be reconciled and gathered up in Christ—all these are reminders that this historical scene and its cosmic setting were of significance in the ultimate outcome of the process. Even the New Testament eschatology has its this-worldly reference as most certainly had that of the Old Testament prophets. In some way, this earthly and historical order has its place in the future consummation. It is not just the stage of preparation across which pass the individual pilgrim souls on their way to their otherworldly destiny.

Unfortunately the latter point of view became so ingrained in Christian belief and practice, that the this-worldly dimension of the Christian religious consciousness seldom found adequate expression. Yet, as we have seen, so many of the implicates of the Christian understanding of the divine creation and the redemption wrought in Christ were directing the cultural life of the world to the very secularity with which now the church finds it difficult to deal. It is imperative that, to face our modern scene, the Christian religion develops a cosmic and historical hope in keeping with the current stage of human history. This does not, however, mean that it ceases to be a religion, that it has to lose its sense of a transcendent presence, or that it replaces worship by this-worldly involvement on the principle that *laborare est orare*. Nor does it mean that it loses its sense of real individual survival beyond death or its hold upon another dimension of being beyond that of space and time. One has the feeling that an incipient naturalism is making itself felt in much contemporary theologizing.

## Worship and the Transcendent Presence

Bonhoeffer's enigmatic statement that "we have to live in the world *etsi deus non daretur*" [1] has resulted in extreme and radical interpretations for which there seems little justification in his own prison life or in his statements during the prison period. In the same paragraph in which the above declaration is made, we are reminded that the God who ceases to be our working hypothesis is yet "the God before whom we stand continually." Elsewhere Bonhoeffer affirms that God desires us to be aware of his presence where our problems are solved and not just where we have failed to solve them. [2] Bonhoeffer can speak of our honoring God in our grateful acceptance of his gift of life with its blessings and in our sincere grief over our mishandling of the gift. [3] He can declare that we ought to love God eternally with our whole being and retain, in a kind of a heavenly polyphony, our earthly affections. [4] He writes of the piety of the home in which, in prayer, we learn "to fear and love God above everything, and to do the will of Jesus Christ." [5] He confidently affirms that an entirely new life is possible because we may always live close to the divine presence and that we are sustained by such fellowship. [6] All of which indicate that religion in the deep sense that we have defined it had a place in his life.

However preoccupied the religious man may become with the social concerns of the secular city and the technocratic culture, his spiritual resources for any real and lasting achievement reside in his vital awareness of and relationship to that transcendent presence who has become incarnate in the Christ. It is true that our understanding of our world has been so transformed by our scientific knowledge that we need to find new models in which to express such transcendence. What is immediately evident in the disclosure that centers in the incarnation is that we have to do with a personal depth in the universe and that the most acceptable models will be those derived from the personal level of creaturely existence. Just as the models for the electron vary between the wave picture and the particle picture, so we may well need more than one model in which to express what the divine disclosure conveys to the believer and the worshiper. The model of human self-transcendence may well need to be matched by a model of intrapersonal transcendence if the full richness of the divine otherness is to be understood.[7] Such models have the virtue of preserving the divine immanence as well as the divine transcendence. The divine disclosure in the incarnation points to a qualitative otherness which is also an involved nearness. Once such a sense of transcendence is lost, the pitfall of pantheism, usually in a naturalistic form, becomes the only viable religious outlet. With it disappears a true understanding of man in his creatureliness and finitude and of his estrangement, his alienated condition.

This sense of alienation is precisely the point at which Christian worship takes its rise. To hear some advocates of the secular city celebrate the coming-of-age of modern man is to listen to an almost pagan humanism or a non-Christian idealism. So often such of our contemporaries seem to ignore the demonic element in human society and the condition of estrangement or sin that is everywhere manifested in the lives of ourselves and our fellows. The loss of meaning in our time, the frantic search for identity, the mounting evidence of widespread neurosis—all these are reflected in our literature, both novels and plays, and evidenced in our news media. We may not want to celebrate "the good news of original sin" but we cannot evade the state of our humanity, despite our fine ideals and lofty aspirations. Granted that we are to think of man as a whole, a psychical-physical entity, and that overintrospection and preoccupation with our "sins" is unhealthy, yet it is precisely our integration as personal wholes that we face these days. Our fragmentation and lack of personal wholeness is very apparent. This is no boundary problem. It faces us in the midst of our common life, and we cannot escape it by taking refuge in some social crusade, since the reform of society can never progress beyond the personal condition of those who constitute that society. If it is true that modern man has come of age, then his maturity is a strangely perverted one at the spiritual level. His scientific knowledge and technological skill are not matched by a spiritual and moral competence. Now the heart of the Christian message is precisely concerned with this business of making men whole, of removing estrangement and giving meaning to life, of reconciling man to the personal "depth of the universe" who alone gives men an enduring purpose.

However we may describe such an experience of reconciliation in Christ, it is the ground of true worship. The healing and renewing Presence who has come to us in Christ evokes a responsive adoration and love. Furthermore, the symbol of the cross stands at the center of such a disclosure. The advocates of a secular and religionless Christianity who would make men fellow members of a team in which God is their teammate, have a strangely low-key understanding of the significance of the cross. Our strange mixture of maturity and immaturity is borne by God at a cost. If he is our fellow traveler, if he does guide our world by the persuasion of his love, he does so at infinite cost. Bonhoeffer suggests that we have crowded God out of our world on to the cross.[8] God's power in the world is the power of a restrained love that sustains us in our freedom with all its wrong choices and which bears our estrangement in redemptive suffering.[9] Again, we turn to Bonhoeffer with his declaration that "only a suffering God can help" and his conclusion that the decks are now cleared so that we may see the Biblical God as one who triumphs through weakness.[10] God comes into the world in the Christ, not in power, but in powerlessness. He is found in the suffering of the Christ, and thereby the cross becomes a disclosure of the nature of the transcendent presence and power at the heart of the universe—personal love with the power of suffering restraint. The cross becomes the revelation of a redemptive presence. Its symbol at the heart of Christian worship evokes a joyful response of thanksgiving and confession, adoration and commitment.

Yet that response is neither otherworldly nor selfishly individualistic. It is true that it may be perverted in these ways and has been so often. In Christian history men have been encouraged to turn their backs upon the world and concentrate upon their own blessedness. Many times Christian worship has been employed to direct men's eyes upon their destiny beyond death so that they may not be concerned with their present plight or with that of their fellows. Here the Marxist is right! Feuerbach's indictment, echoed by Bonhoeffer, has its validity. But when Christian worship has ever been truly practiced and communion with God in Christ has been rightly understood, there has been no attempt to escape from the world. For the object of Christian worship is he who has come into the world, shown himself as a transcendent presence who is yet involved in the very movement of history, suffered on a cross to redeem the world. The cross may become a center of sentimental adoration, but it is actually a grim and stark reminder of a God who loves and suffers, who bears the world redemptively and who triumphs over our human estrangement and every demonic power. When we see the cross as the disclosure that God so loved the world that he gave, we cannot, in our worship, turn our back upon the world.

Furthermore, such communion directs our attention on what God has done in Christ. Thereby it preserves the divine otherness, for it is concerned with the act of the transcendent Other who is yet very near to our humanity in his incarnate presence. The true worshiper can never fall into the trap of identifying God with man or of exalting the secular order and its human activity. He knows that he stands ever before the Christ who has proclaimed his Lordship over the world in the cross and in the resurrection. He knows too, that such Lordship is the way of kenosis, of self-emptying, and that the disciple is called likewise to follow the path of humiliation and suffering in the world. He, too, is called to love the world and make up what is lacking in the sufferings of Christ. Once again, we hear the voice of Bonhoeffer:

If we are to learn what God promises, and what he fulfils, we must persevere in quiet meditation on the life, sayings, deeds, sufferings, and death of Jesus. It is certain that we may always live close to God and in the light of his presence, and that such living is an entirely new life for us.[11]

Christ is the center of our worship, the Other who is also most near, the immanent presence with our humanity of the transcendent Reality.

This kind of religion has no place in it for the kind of pseudo Christianity that makes use of God. So often American Protestantism has had its popular preachers who have regarded religion as a useful accessory in self-help and have proclaimed a "God" whose chief value is that he helps his devotees to be successful businessmen, to make friends and influence people. The popular "folk-religion" of our time manifests, not only this structure, but what has been called "the suburban captivity of the churches." Religious structures can bolster up suburban mores or reinforce racial prejudice. Not without justification, it has been pointed out that the Christian congregation of worshipers on a Sunday morning is often the most segregated group in America. But if we truly worship the Christ as Lord of the world and respond to the claims of his cross, this kind of religion stands forever under his condemnation.

If worship is an integral part of religion, our Christian worship emphasizes its concern with this world, not only in the proclamation of the incarnation and the call to costly discipleship and grace, but also in its sacramental aspects. Here, perhaps most of all, we ought to meet the eschatological note at the practical level. The communion of the Lord's Supper is, in the tradition of the symbolic acts of the Old Testament prophets, a symbolic enactment of the gospel. As the prophet acted out in mime the divine intention—Jeremiah's shattering of the vessel or wearing the yoke (Jer. 19:1-13; 28:1-17); Isaiah's walking the streets of Jerusalem in the garb of a slave (Isa. 20:1-6); Ezekiel's knocking a hole in the wall of his house or joining two sticks together (Ezek. 12:1-16; 37:15 ff.)—God is thought of as initiating through such symbolic acts the fulfillment of this purpose. So, in the bread and the wine, the death of the Lord is acted out symbolically, and the worshipers are confronted with the reality of the gospel. The reality of our redemption is set before our eyes. As we eat, we do so under the shadow of the Lord's atoning act. Yet the Lord's Supper is also the medium of the living presence of the Risen Christ. It does more than point, it is a sacrament. The Anglican Book of Common Prayer defines sacrament as "an outward and visible sign of an inward and spiritual grace." There is no suggestion in the word that the bread and the wine are literally transformed into the body and blood of Christ. Rather they are signs that point to the presence of the living Lord, so that as we eat the bread and drink the wine, we may at the same time appropriate by faith the grace and forgiveness of the Christ to which these earthly elements point.

In many of the expressions of the human religious consciousness at all levels, sacraments using water and food are employed. Even among primitive peoples, water is a symbol of cleansing, and religious lustrations are universally associated with ceremonial and often moral purification. Furthermore, meals are not just for satisfying hunger, even under normal conditions, but opportunities for communal fellowship, social occasions. And, in religious practices, sacrificial rites have often been accompanied by the worshipers sharing in the flesh of the sacrificed beast and thereby communing with one another and the deity. The latter, in the case of the Hebrew people, was effected by the disposal of the blood at the foot of the altar, since the blood contained the life essence of the animal. We should not, therefore, be surprised if, in Christian worship, such symbols as bread, wine, and water are given peculiar significance in sacramental rites which point to the redemption effected through the sacrifice of Jesus Christ.

Yet, from our point of view, they are also effective reminders of the this-worldly aspect of the Christian religion. Such symbols take place within a sacramental universe. They make use of common symbols taken from man's earthly environment and pointing to spiritual reality. The living God has chosen to disclose himself to us in and through his created order—the activities of nature, the movement of history, the lives of finite persons in all the multiplicity of their relationships. Although hiding himself behind that order, he yet makes his presence known through it. Just as we know one another through the activities, gestures, and sounds that our psychosomatic structure and our natural environment make possible, so God makes himself known through his world. Again and again, this has been emphasized in the preceding pages. At the finite level, human self-conscious persons commune with and know one another through the somatic dimension of their personal wholeness, those aspects which can be seen, touched, and handled. The tangible, visible, and audible become symbols of the hidden "I" that embraces and yet transcends them. So words and acts become symbolic ways of imparting meaning and creating personal disclosures. Sensible signs convey the personal presence. Likewise with man's relation to the living God!

When we speak of a sacramental universe, we mean that there is no aspect of the natural order that may not, under the divine activity, become a sensible sign of and mediate to us his presence. Any aspect of nature can thus be a symbol in and through which men may receive a divine disclosure. As Paul Tillich has written: "Natural objects can become bearers of transcendent power and meaning, they can become sacramental elements. . . . This is the basis for a Protestant rediscovery of the sacramental sphere." [12] Then the peculiar symbols of water and food not only specifically point to the divine disclosure in the incarnation and the cross. They also typify the reality of God's presence throughout nature, so that, to quote Tillich again, even nature may be a "bearer and object of salvation."

When we consider our Christian Sacraments in this light, we are reminded that the salvation in Christ is concerned with this sensible world from which the common elements in our sacrificial rites are taken. In the Lord's Supper and Baptism we see the true end of all nature. We often see the world as material, instead of seeing it as the divinely ordained structure through which God in his hiddenness draws near to us. We misuse and mishandle nature for our own ends. But in the Christian Sacraments we see the goal of the natural process. As the water, the bread, and the wine are drawn up into the divine activity and set in a sacramental context, taken up into the life of God and energized by the presence of his Spirit, they "foreshadow the transfiguration of the cosmos and herald the new heaven and the new earth." [13] This world, this secular order is not rejected in Christianity but accepted into the redemptive setting. The only alternative to a secularized Christianity is a sacramental Christianity that sees God coming to man everywhere and anywhere in his creatures, that sees behind and through men in their joys and their failures, their kindly acts and their basic needs, the person of the Christ.

The eschatological note that we have just struck is only one aspect of the sense of the eschaton which has pervaded the Lord's Supper since its institution, for it is to be observed until the Lord come. Thereby we are reminded that Christianity is a religion of hope, and that Christian men live between the eschaton in the midst of history and that ultimate outcome when God shall be all in all. To this we must return later, for it says much about the nature of God as he comes to us in Christian disclosure.

Worship and the Sacraments have their place within the Christian community. Whitehead defined religion as what a man does with his solitariness, but the mark of the Christian religion is its communal dimension. Love for God is expressed in the love of our fellows, and Christianity can never be divorced from evangelical and social concern. Whitehead's definition applies to the mystical types of religion but it has no relevance when we look at ethical or teleological types of which the Christian faith is an example.

The Christian religion and its sacraments would be useless fabrications akin to symbolic magic, mere superstitions, unless celebrated in such a corporate body. They remind us that to be "in Christ" is never a solitary involvement with the risen Lord but it is to be "in the body of Christ." So they point to the involvement of the Christian with his fellows and again remind us that the Christian religion is no escape from the realities of the secular. In these days when our theological "angry young men" are often in rebellion against the theological and cultic establishment, they need to remember the historical continuity and fellowship within which they and we stand.

## The This-worldly Concern of Christianity

The saddest thing about the Christian religion and its communal manifestation, the church, is that so often they have been distorted by the all-too-human element in all religious life. Rather than being the *avant garde* of social progress, the church has often been the bulwark of an outmoded conservatism, not only theologically, but also socially and politically. Such distortions in the last century and a half have been influential in producing the bitter rejection of the Christian faith in men like Feuerbach and Marx. They have become the object of attacks by devout Christians like Bonhoeffer. Often the conservative stance of the church toward vital social issues has been made possible by over-concern with the otherworldly and by an evangelical zeal that is more concerned with getting people into heaven and saving them from hell than by a concern for vital Christian living within our intramundane relationships. Again, there has been a tendency to concentrate upon individual piety to such an extent that it has produced a kind of Pharisaism which has isolated the Christian from the world. The sacred and the secular, instead of being intimately bound together, as in the incarnation, have become radically bifurcated, and the way has been opened for our contemporary secularism. The church has lost, only too often, any vision of a sacramental universe.

Yet initially the New Testament men and our Lord himself were very concerned with life in the here and now. The eschatological note was always present, but the emphasis fell upon the appearance of the eschaton in the midst of history in Jesus Christ. The Holy Spirit was an "earnest" of the Christian's future inheritance, but as an "earnest" it was guaranteed to offer the same quality of life as in the consummated kingdom (Eph. 1:14; II Cor. 1:22). Eternal life, the life of the "age-to-come," had become a present possession in Christ. Belief meant to enjoy such life here and now. To be in Christ was to be already a new creation, to taste of the powers of the eschaton before the chronological outcome of the process of history, to have the "new being," in Paul Tillich's phrase. Just as the incarnation pointed to a total involvement of God with humanity and human history, so the church was the "body of Christ" and thus was to be as intimately involved with this world as its Lord. Christians were not to be conformed to this world in the sense of accepting its standards and norms and being completely merged into the secular. In some sense, they were amphibian, capable of living in the spiritual and secular orders and recognizing that the two were intimately bound together. In giving the cup of cold water to one of the least of the human family, they were giving it to the Christ himself. The ultimate test of a man's character lay, according to this parable (Matt. 25:31-46), in a man's concern for others. The love of Christ, his *agape*, self-giving love, flowed down through the cross into their lives and so out to the world. Christians were indeed to have concern for the world. Certainly they were not to turn their back on it, for was not the Son of Man described blasphemously as a gluttonous man and a wine bibber? Did he not eat with publicans and sinners? And so Paul admonishes his fellow Christians to make up in their own costly involvement, what is lacking in the sufferings of Christ.

Hans Jürgen Schultz [14] speaks about "conversion to the world," by which he means that Christianity needs to be converted from antiworldiness. As he sees it, the Christian needs to undergo a double conversion, a conversion to God and then, under God, a

conversion to the world. Schultz attacks religion, after the manner
of Bonhoeffer, and regards it as a man-made framework of doctrine, metaphysics, cultic observance, and institutionalized program in which the living Christ is held captive. He would have
us renounce such false piety and replace religion by faith. As we
have seen, "religion" has come to mean this so often in the modern scene, but we have sought to find an honest expression of religion, and this is exactly what Schultz seeks under the description of faith. He himself writes:

Whatever one's view of the current concept of the *end of religion,*
there is no getting away from the fact that the function and significance of religion is subject to inevitable and rapid change dictated by
the new nature of our relationship with the world, a relationship
transformed by technological influences.[15]

It seems here, as so often, to be largely a matter of semantics.
Schultz does not, in his description of "faith," see an end of worship or of true piety. What he rejects is the "holier than thou" attitude. He tells us that piety must go into the marketplace. Again,
worship must not attempt to preserve the sacred and surround it
by protecting walls. It must be worship with the doors open to the
world. But what are such but the marks of an honest Christian
religion?

Leaving this semantic issue on one side, let us look at the this-
worldly concern of the church. Schultz, from a continental perspective on a secularity which has been hastened by the Second
World War, is saying much to which we in America need to listen.
So often the prophets of secularity seem to finish in a nebulous
realm that seems as immaterial as the irrelevance of the contemporary church that they are condemning. We need to be reminded of two aspects of the incarnate presence of God in Christ.
The first is that it takes the form of a Servant. The second is that
at the heart of this divine disclosure there is a resurrection pattern that is bound up with the affirmation that this is an eschatological event. Let us look at the second aspect first. That a revolution is on in our thought and our life as Christian men and women

is almost a platitudinous statement. Schultz is right when he suggests that the church has shut itself up in a self-chosen ghetto and shut the world out. It has imprisoned the explosive power of the Eschaton, the redemptive and transforming presence of the Christ, in its theological dogmas, outmoded metaphysical systems, institutional programs, and cultic liturgies. Often the church has thereby ceased to be the church. But where the vital spark remains and the church has still some vision of itself as "the body of Christ," it must pass through the resurrection pattern. It needs to remember that God emptied himself and became involved with the world in the incarnation and that the church must do likewise. In the resurrection pattern it must die that it may live, die from under its distorting framework and be converted to the world, to use Schultz's phrase. Instead of escaping from the world, the Christians must turn to the world.

Such conversion to the world does not mean conforming to the world but identification, personal solidarity, with the world, loving men with the love of Christ. It is here the other aspect of the incarnation challenges us. In the Christ, God was present in the world *incognito*, and he calls us to do the same. The way of the incarnation is the way of humiliation. God rules and guides his world by the way of suffering love, and we are called to follow in his steps. We must be present in the world as brothers, expecting to meet God where men are and not in the introverted societies that often represent the church. From being mutual admiration societies, glorying in their holiness or concerned with their own salvation, Christians must move out to where the action is. Schultz quotes the dictum of Alfons Rosenberg that "instead of being 'a communion of saints' it [the church] needs to consist of the 'saints of the community.' " [16] This being in the world will follow the path of the Servant, the way of dialogue and service, not the way of Pharisaism.

We have found our own thought much in keeping with that of Schultz so far, but a criticism in keeping with our own position now needs to be made. He suggests that religion inhibits such a movement into solidarity with the world. Rather it dissociates and leads to disengagement.[17] He, like so many protagonists of complete secularity, often cites the life of our Lord, but he seems to forget that in the life of the incarnate Christ, there were also moments of disengagement, of retreat from the world to God. It is difficult to understand how the kind of thing that Christians should do in the solidarity of humanity, especially manifesting true love, could be possible without some renewing sense of the divine presence such as worship provides. Now Schultz may be concerned with monastic retreat or escapism in his criticism, but if so, he is not talking of religion in the deepest sense. There can be no renewal of man that does not flow from involvement with the Christ in moments of communion. So often the advocates of secular Christianity seem blind to this.

This might seem evident where Schultz frankly identifies being a Christian with being human.[18] We would agree that we need today a new Christian humanism, and we would agree that commitment to Christ, the "new being," makes a man truly human, a real person. Solidarity, Schultz tells us, means the loss of a privileged position, and that is true. To take the form of the servant is to be identified with our fellows. Yet the way of humiliation is also a judgment upon our perverted humanity. To be a Christian is not just to be human, but to be on the way to man as God intended man to be. We may be incognito in the world, but the way we love and serve will betray us. In some sense, as the writer of *Ad Diognetum* saw centuries ago, the Christian is the world's incarnate conscience. He can never completely merge with the secular, for his life in Christ is a judgment on the secular. Schultz acknowledges this when he notes that the church "hopelessly mixes up scandal and *skandalon;* in its attempt to avoid the former, it shirks its duty to *be* the latter, the conscience and therefore the constant irritant of society." [19] It is in sentences like these that he dialogically corrects what might seem to be too close an identification of the church with secularity. Our vocation is to be a Christian within our worldly profession and condition of life, sharing like any man in secular duties and tasks, and yet with a difference that will be manifested in the quality of our life and its activities.

Sometimes one has a feeling that overconcern with secularity blinds our eyes to the demonic aspects of social life and the alienated structures of human existence. Even so it is true that in dialogue with modern man, we must ourselves be modern men, and not make ourselves out to be otherwise. Says Schultz: "The modern man we are trying to get alongside strongly resents us in the role of pied piper." [20] Christians will enter into programs of social reconstruction and human betterment just as men, not as men with privileged status before God. The Christ will be commended through their incognito, for now the social and political order has taken over functions that are essentially Christian, but over which the church has dragged its heels. Yet the Christian will have an understanding of the forces that mar and distort such human efforts, for he knows the redeeming power of Christ's love and must manifest it, often at cost. The church must be the conscience of the secular order.

What all this may mean for the contemporary form of the church, it is not easy to say. The differentiation of the clergy and the laity will have to cease. Maybe, as Bonhoeffer daringly suggested,[21] the minister of Christ will have to be a working layman like his fellows. Maybe the future lies not with the church as we know it, institutionalized, powerful, wealthy, but with small groups of committed Christians who practice their religion in corporate worship apart from vast auditoriums or cultic edifices. Maybe, as social structures change, our mores of worship will change as to form, as to time, as to place. But worship and inner renewal there must be. And the body of Christ may take new forms, but it will not perish—beyond every seeming death there will be resurrection in a new body.

The church, so often aware of its own predicament, is equally often, not converted to the world, but conformed to it. It adopts the ways of secular man and tries to make itself relevant. But in so doing, it makes itself strangely irrelevant. For to be in the world as the servant church is yet to be so with the suffering that identification costs. It is certainly not to adopt the standards of success fixed by secular man. It is certainly not to offer to secular man no more than secular man already possesses. We may well have to alter our theological models in order to communicate the divine disclosure to our world, but we must never become so relevant that we become essentially irrelevant. We cannot reduce a redemptive gospel to the ethical, or Christology to Jesusology. Nor can we so emphasize immanence that we ignore the transcendent presence, however much we may need to alter our models for transcendence. Above all, religious we shall have to be, if we are to speak intelligibly to men of other religious faiths who also face the same dilemma as ourselves.

## A Religion of Hope in a Sacramental Universe

As we have noted several times, such an understanding of Christian religion has an eschatological dimension. Not only do the Sacraments point forward to an actual consummation, but equally a concern with man's life in this order, a concern with secularity, carries with it eschatological implications. If our Lord was concerned with man as a psychosomatic whole and if the church as his body must give concrete expression to its religious response in concern for man's intramundane relations and his total personal being, not just for his "soul," a certain teleological emphasis is at least implied. To be involved with secularity implies that this world, its social orders and its historical movements, its natural processes and actualization of human values are significant in the religious sense, that is to say, in relation to God. But the New Testament is very clear that there is an eschaton that is cosmic and not just individual.

We have indicated already that the incarnation, cross, and resurrection are the eschaton, but so often contemporary theologians have finished there. Bultmann and his group have been satisfied with an existentialist interpretation that celebrates "the presence of eternity" and speaks solely of "realized eschatology." Such an interpretation of the central disclosure of our faith gives full place to individual redemption and the personal commitment of faith. But it has little place for a forward movement in history as a whole, a development in the world process at the communal and even the natural levels, which is related to the divine purpose and moving to an ultimate consummation.

Three groups of thinkers have sought to rectify this one-sided emphasis of recent years. The so-called "process theologians" have seen the world process as open-ended and unfinished. It is a process in which, under the persuasion of the divine love, the universe moves forward in a cooperative effort between God and his creatures. The universe is knit together by a network of feeling-ful response at various levels of consciousness and unconsciousness, and, in the center, man is called upon to work with God for the completion of the whole. Furthermore, the process is within God's experience so that his own life is enriched as his creatures move forward creatively under the persuasion of his love. Such thinkers are basically panentheistic rather than theistic and think of the universe as an expression of the divine being. The whole process, with its elements of freedom and contingency is within God's life, and he himself is the all-embracing reality, so that the experiences of the creatures are also moments in the experience of God. He is thought of as the fellow traveler of the world, and because he is himself dipolar, both being and becoming, he stands fully disclosed only in the completion of the process that is continually enriching his own life. The divine being as love is accompanied by becoming. The divine perfection moves to fuller flowering as the process moves forward, but at every stage that perfection is a reality. God is always the norm of perfection at any such stage of the process, yet the full nature of God will stand unveiled only when the process is complete.

We would criticize the panentheistic presupposition and the rejection of creation *ex nihilo*. It vitiates any deep appraisal of evil and human estrangement and tends to produce a shallow understanding of the movement of history with its demonic aspects. Yet the view of history as open-ended and as moving to God as its ultimate fulfillment that he may be all in all is a valuable insight. So also are the understanding of the divine involvement and the suggestion that the processes of nature and history add something to the divine life. Often the understanding of the incarnation is treated in a shallow way, although this would not be true of the work of N. Norman Pittenger [22] and Daniel Day Williams.[23] We have here most certainly a contemporary concern with eschatology or teleology at the cosmic level, and the dimension of such hope becomes a vital aspect of any religious expression associated with such thought.

The second line of thought that reinforces a forward-looking dimension in religious thought is the contribution of Teilhard de Chardin.[24] This Catholic theologian, mystic, and anthropologist, has developed a philosophical understanding of the evolutionary process in which he sees the whole directed toward a consummation still in the future. He terms this consummation "point Omega," and strives to demonstrate that it is a present reality, transcendent to the process, itself both loving and lovable. This "point Omega" he identifies with God and, in much more traditional Christian thinking, sees Jesus Christ as the incarnation of point Omega within the process. Thus the end is already present and dynamically active within the process, moving the whole to its ultimate fulfillment around point Omega, the *eschaton*, the *Parousia*. Teilhard sees the evolutionary process becoming self-conscious with the emergence of man, and thus sees that human freedom may hinder and even mar the ultimate achievement. The organic and panentheistic view of the process thinkers is matched in his thought by a more genuine Christian theism with its emphasis on the personal. Hence he sees the ultimate consummation as the movement to the hyperpersonal. This stage is not the annihilation of the personal and the mergence of individuality into a larger whole. Rather, it is a state of being defined by love. Personal beings are bound around point Omega and to one another in bonds of love and mutual concern in which they become more truly personal and yet more truly one. In his mystic way, Teilhard sees the process as moving toward a consummation in which what is already manifested in the Christ will be fully unveiled and God will be all-in-all.

Here again human cooperation with God is emphasized. Men may refuse, despite the pressures of growing numbers and increasing social complexity, to move on to that last creative super saturation which will give birth to the hyperpersonal. Instead, they may choose to return to the totalitarian anthill. Yet one feels that Teilhard sees the process weighted on the divine side through the incarnation. He speaks of the Christification of the whole process and manages skillfully to hold together both an eschatological and an incarnational approach. The future again would appear to be an open-ended one in which the Christ travails with men at every level of their common life and guides the universe to its fulfillment in point Omega. Again the notes of hope and cosmic eschatology are struck.

Finally, we have the theologians of hope, especially represented by Jürgen Moltmann [25] and Wolfhart Pannenberg.[26] These thinkers emphasize the dimension of hope in Christian thought and find the creative point of such hope in the resurrection. They defend the historicity of the resurrection of Jesus and attack the Bultmannian attempt to confine it to *Geschichte* alone and banish it from *Historie*. If it be argued that such a historical event is a break in the continuity which characterizes history and on which Troeltsch placed such emphasis, this is countered by the emphasis on the resurrection as itself an eschatological event in which the hope of the ultimate eschaton is grounded. Moltmann, for example, holds that history is no closed system of cause and effect, but one in which the contingent and new may occur, although even the latter would not embrace the resurrection. Concerning this he declares that

the raising of Christ involves not the category of the accidentally new, but the expectational category of the eschatologically new. The eschatologically new event of the resurrection of Christ . . . proves to be a *novum ultimum* both as against the similarity in ever-recurring reality and also as against the comparative dissimilarity of new possibilities emerging in history.[27]

Moltmann's discussion makes it clear that such an eschatological hope can never be individual but embraces the personal within the whole process. Man's hope involves his relations to history and the cosmos. But such a hope, which involves the whole creation as Paul saw (Rom. 8:19), is only hope if it is unfulfilled, and so Moltmann sees the future as open. He will have nothing to do with a universe that is a self-contained system. The process of history is radically open to the future and the only clue we have is in the resurrection of Jesus. The resurrection of Christ signifies an absolutely new possibility for personal existence, for history, and for the cosmos. It points to a radical "eschatological process to which world history is subjected." [28] The resurrection, first of all, through the Easter appearances makes clear the identity of the risen Lord with the crucified Jesus.

Moltmann's emphasis on the resurrection unfortunately is not balanced by a concern with the incarnation. Indeed, his Christology is exceedingly defective, if one is explicitly stated at all. Pannenberg has compensated for this. It would, however, seem to this writer that a more balanced view of the process needs to hold together the two strands and to speak of Jesus Christ as the *incarnate Eschaton*.

The resurrection guarantees for Moltmann the Lordship of the crucified over all things. It opens the world toward the future. In the resurrection, the Christian recognizes "the future of God for the world and the future which man finds in this God and his acts." [29] It opens up to man "the inexhaustible future of Christ," and in this the Christian waits for his future and the future of history and the world. Before the world there is now opened up "an *eschaton* of the fulness of all things." [30] There is made possible a true human existence that is open to the world and to the future. The contradiction present in the unredeemed world with its concomitant suffering is "taken up into the confidence of hope, while on the other hand hope's confidence becomes earthly and universal." [31]

Such theologians see the Lord ahead and see the communal expression of the Christian religion, the church, as determined and controlled by the horizon of its expectation. It is always expecting the coming of the Lord. In its eschatological hope it looks for all things new in a future that is the future of Jesus Christ, even while it still lives. The Word of the gospel calls to faith and creates life, but always within the faith there is the prime dimensions of hope. This Word by which the church lives provides no final revelation, for it always points ahead and carries the eschatological promise of a universal future. It is, indeed, itself an eschatological gift. "In it the hidden future of God for the world is already present." [32] So the church waits for the Kingdom of God, and its life is determined by such expectation. Meantime its concern is reconciliation and salvation. Yet such salvation

does not mean merely salvation of the soul, individual rescue from the evil world, comfort for the troubled conscience, but also the realization of the eschatological *hope of justice*, the *humanizing* of man, the *socializing* of humanity, *peace* for all creation.[33]

As Moltmann sees it, the church in the light of the horizon of its eschatological expectation, should have a this-worldly concern at every level of intramundane relationship, a concern that it has so often left to fanatics and sects. There is an earthly and cosmic dimension in its eschatological anticipation, and this should control the Christian's religious concern. The hope of the coming Lordship of Christ must already set its stamp upon human society and lead to a historical transformation of life. The coming Kingdom casts, as it were, its shadow before and requires that the church "transform in opposition and creative expectation the face of the world in the midst of which one believes, hopes and loves." [34] Under the pressure of the eschatological expectation, the present situation is under judgment, and the church is called to seize on every chance for creatively transforming the present that it may correspond more nearly to the glorious future.

From these three parallel streams of thought, it is evident that a new religious dimension is attaining emphasis in Christianity. Troeltsch and others have seen every culture as having religious roots. We have noted that the new cultural situation of our time is a product of the Christian disclosure and of its impact on man's approach to and understanding of his world. Furthermore, this new secularity must not be viewed, in the tradition of Comte, as meaning that religion is *passé* and that an age of positivism has dawned. Nor, following Feuerbach, may we see religion as a projection, even though such a perversion can be discovered in all religious responses to divine disclosure. Rather we might expect that the Christian religion will itself be reshaped and attain a more genuine expression as it relates itself to a situation that it has itself produced.[35] In this new cultural milieu, the Christian believer must ask himself how best he can express in worship, conduct, and mission, the divine disclosure in Jesus Christ. The this-worldly emphasis that is required is undergirded and given foundation by this new concern with the eschatological dimension. The God who is sacramentally present throughout the historical process stands also at the end of the process. The *Eschaton* has become incarnate in Jesus Christ, and now that *eschaton* sacramentally overshadows all history and awaits it in the consummation. In our own understanding, the Kingdom has come, is now coming, and awaits the world at the end. This transcendent yet immanent presence of the Christ within the very movement of history is much more evident in the thought of Teilhard and in the concern of the process theologians when they speak the present reality of the divine persuasion. There is every reason to combine the eschatological hope with a sacramental universe. Moltmann and his fellow thinkers seem too much under the influence of Albert Schweitzer. They would seem to be anxious to avoid the element of "realized" eschatology in the New Testament records and often they seem lacking in any deep concern with the doctrine of the Spirit as the immanent presence of the Christ in his church and the world.

We may speak then of the incarnate *Eschaton*. By this phrase, we mean to convey the Christian conviction that in the Christ the *Eschaton* has already become incarnate in the process. We may not legitimately separate the resurrection from the life and death of Jesus of Nazareth. Together they constitute *one* redemptive moment in the divine life and activity. Furthermore, we cannot accept such a view without seeing the church as the body of Christ and without regarding the whole universe as in process of transformation or, to use Teilhard's phrase, Christification. It is moving to that day when all things shall be gathered up in Christ and God shall be all-in-all. The future is already dynamically active in the present, within and without the Christian community.

This surely is involved in any understanding of the New Testament concern with the Spirit.

The *Eschaton* has become incarnate, it is now, through the resurrection, in process of incarnating itself in the world, of gathering the cosmos into itself, and it stands at the end of the whole process. There is a "new being," a "new creation," taking place in Christ through his Spirit. This by no means does away with the presence of estrangement and the demonic distortion of the present situation. What we have in Christ now and by the work of his Spirit within us, we have in promise of that which shall be. We live in hope, but already the Christ is dealing with the "powers that be" in our world and calling us to cooperate with him in their ultimate overthrow. An incarnational emphasis in the great catholic tradition saves us from placing all our stress on the *Eschaton* as future.

Allowing for the position just stated, the transcendent presence of God gathers a new dimension. In the Christ he stands in our midst, but he also stands at the end. He is our future, and in him all things will be gathered up. In a real sense he is known in Jesus Christ, but he is also yet to come. Our future has begun already in Jesus Christ, yet its consummation is ahead of us, and we do not know its form. All we do know is that the Christ is with us and before us and that new possibilities are ever challenging us as we work with him and strive for point Omega. Furthermore, if our process matters to God and he is truly our future, then we can believe that his own life is being enriched thereby. He who is our future also has his future, even though we think of it in different terms from our own.

The Christian religion differs from other religions in its possession of Jesus Christ, the incarnate *Eschaton*. Only so can we claim both its uniqueness and its continuity with all religious history. Yet this does not mean arrogant pretensions. As in all else, the Christian believer must take the role of the servant. He is well aware that, in varying ways, the religions manifest the sense of a transcendent presence, the significance of love in the world process, the immanence of the divine in the life of man, the concern for man's estrangement. He must also be aware that the movement of the whole world toward secularity does not necessarily mean the end of mystical and world-denying religions such as Hinduism and Buddhism. He cannot assert that only the historical religions of Christianity, Judaism, and Islam are equipped to deal with a this-worldly concern because of their world-affirming nature. This may be true, but other religions, deeply bedded as they are in the life of a people, may adjust themselves to a new situation and manifest new dimensions. We must stand within our own faith and have our own religious reasons for such a stand,[36] but we cannot say that the Christ who lightens all men has not spoken and is not speaking elsewhere. We must share our riches, above all our understanding of the incarnate *Eschaton,* and be prepared humbly to listen to what they also have to give. And always we must do so with our eyes on the Christ in whose future our own future is determined. Our very openness to our future means that we can dare to believe that all genuine religious insights and all men honestly committed to the light that has come to them will be gathered into that final consummation which is the Christ.

Thus, in some sense, we need to see the place of our own faith within the general movement of religious history and to recognize that every religion must be understood within its own historical particularity. Phenomenological comparisons are invaluable as preparatory studies, but phenomenology implies a static view of religion. Religious expression changes with the movement of history, and it is with such historical concreteness that we must be concerned. As the created process moves toward its future in God, such expressions may change in all religious faiths, and to such changes dialogue between the religions will make its contribution. Now that we are seeing our world as one whole, we can believe that the Christ will triumphantly garner all things into the final *eschaton.* This does not mean syncretism but the final triumph of the Christ who has already appeared in the midst of historical time.

# NOTES

## Chapter I. *Religion and the Secular Order*

1. Dietrich Bonhoeffer, *Letters and Papers from Prison*, ed. by Eberhard Bethge, tr. by R. Fuller (The Macmillan Company, 1967), pp. 152 f.

2. *Ibid.*, p. 178.

3. *Ibid.*, p. 155.

4. Dietrich Bonhoeffer, *Act and Being*, tr. by Bernard Noble (Harper & Brothers, 1961), p. 46.

5. Reinhold Seeberg, *Dogmatik* I, p. 104. Cited in Bonhoeffer, *Act and Being*, p. 46, n. 2.

6. Bonhoeffer, *Act and Being*, vide, p. 47.

7. Cf. *ibid.*, pp. 81 ff.

8. Cf. Bonhoeffer, *Letters and Papers from Prison*, p. 156.

9. Eberhard Bethge, "The Challenge of Dietrich Bonhoeffer's Life and Theology," *The Chicago Theological Seminary Register*, Feb., 1961, p. 33.

10. Cf. Bethge, *ibid.*

11. Bonhoeffer, *Letters and Papers from Prison*, p. 174.

12. Cf. *Ibid.*, pp. 154 f., 174 f., 195 ff.

13. *Ibid.*, pp. 154 f.

14. *Vide* n. 2, above.

15. Bonhoeffer, *Letters and Papers from Prison*, p. 175.

16. *Ibid.*, p. 179; cf. pp. 188 f.

17. Cf. Gerhard Ebeling, *Word and Faith*, tr. by James W. Leitch (Fortress Press, 1963), pp. 148 ff.

18. Henry Fielding, *Tom Jones*, Book III, Ch. iii.

19. Bonhoeffer, *Letters and Papers from Prison*, p. 192.

20. Dietrich Bonhoeffer, *Ethics*, tr. by N. Horton Smith (The Macmillan Company, 1955), pp. 79–100.

21. *Ibid.*, p. 102.

22. Cf. Dietrich Bonhoeffer, *Gesammelte Schriften*, Vol. III (Munich: Chr. Kaiser Verlag, 1960), p. 76.

23. Cf. Bonhoeffer, *Act and Being*, p. 47.

24. *Vide* Bonhoeffer, *Ethics*, pp. 18 f.

25. Wilfred C. Smith, *Questions of Religious Truth* (Charles Scribner's Sons, 1967), p. 15.

26. Bonhoeffer, *Letters and Papers from Prison*, p. 122.

27. John A. Phillips, *Christ for Us in the Theology of Dietrich Bonhoeffer* (Harper & Row, Publishers, Inc., 1967), p. 226.

28. *Ibid.*, p. 227.

29. Cf. Bethge, *op. cit.*, p. 35.

30. Bonhoeffer, *Letters and Papers from Prison*, p. 162.

31. *Ibid.*, p. 209.

32. *Ibid.*, p. 152.

Chapter II. *From Absolute Dependence to Ultimate Concern*
Part 1: *Schleiermacher and the Cultured Despisers*

1. The title of Antony Collins' book.

2. Immanuel Kant, *Religion Within the Limits of Reason Alone*, tr. by T. M. Greene and H. H. Hudson (Harper & Brothers, 1960), p. 142.

3. For a fuller discussion of Hegel and his attitude toward Christianity, *vide* Eric C. Rust, *Evolutionary Philosophies and Contemporary Theology* (The Westminster Press, 1969), pp. 39–62.

4. Cf. Friedrich Schleiermacher, *On Religion: Speeches to Its Cultured Despisers*, tr. by John Oman (Harper & Brothers, 1958). (Hereafter cited as *Speeches on Religion*.)

5. *Ibid.*, p. 31.

6. *Ibid.*, p. 36.

7. *Ibid.*, p. 37.

8. Paul Tillich, *Perspectives on Nineteenth and Twentieth Century Protestant Theology* (Harper & Row, Publishers, Inc., 1967), p. 96.

9. Schleiermacher, *Speeches on Religion*, p. 43.

10. *Ibid.*, p. 39.

11. *Ibid.,* p. 43.
12. *Ibid.,* pp. 93 f.
13. *Ibid.,* p. 94.
14. *Ibid.,* p. 45.
15. *Ibid.,* p. 100.
16. *Ibid.,* p. 101.
17. Cf. *ibid.*
18. *Ibid.,* p. 95.
19. Cf. *ibid.,* p. 45.
20. Cf. *ibid.,* p. 46.
21. *Ibid.,* p. 105.
22. Cf. *ibid.,* p. 48.
23. *Ibid.,* p. 84.
24. There is an able exposition of the argument of the *Dialectic* in Gerhard Spiegler, *The Eternal Covenant* (Harper & Row, Publishers, Inc., 1967).
25. Cf. the excellent discussion in Richard Reinhold Niebuhr, *Schleiermacher on Christ and Religion* (Charles Scribner's Sons, 1964), pp. 116 ff.
26. For this section *vide* Friedrich Schleiermacher, *The Christian Faith,* tr. by H. R. Mackintosh and J. S. Stewart (Edinburgh: T. & T. Clark, 1948), pp. 12 ff. There is an informative and insightful discussion of this in R. R. Niebuhr, *op. cit.,* pp. 108–134, to which I am greatly indebted.
27. R. R. Niebuhr, *op. cit.,* pp. 182 f.
28. Cf. Schleiermacher, *The Christian Faith,* pp. 6 f. *Vide* also R. R. Niebuhr, *op. cit.,* p. 123.
29. Spiegler, *op. cit.,* p. 161.
30. Cf. Schleiermacher, *The Christian Faith,* p. 15.
31. H. R. Mackintosh, *Types of Modern Theology* (London: James Nisbet & Co., Ltd., 1937), p. 64.
32. Schleiermacher, *The Christian Faith,* p. 16.
33. *Ibid.,* p. 17.
34. Mackintosh, *op. cit.,* p. 65.
35. Schleiermacher, *The Christian Faith,* pp. 17 f.
36. Tillich, *Perspectives on Nineteenth and Twentieth Century Protestant Theology,* p. 109.
37. Spiegler, *op. cit.,* p. 165.
38. Schleiermacher, *The Christian Faith,* p. 21.
39. *Ibid.,* pp. 21 f.
40. *Ibid.,* p. 25.
41. Schleiermacher, *Speeches on Religion,* p. 93.
42. *Ibid.,* p. 89.
43. *Ibid.,* p. 90.

44. Schleiermacher, *The Christian Faith*, pp. 34 ff.
45. Mackintosh, *op. cit.*, p. 71.
46. Schleiermacher, *Speeches on Religion*, pp. 46 ff.
47. *Ibid.*, p. 54.
48. R. R. Niebuhr, *op. cit.*, p. 229.
49. *Ibid.*, p. 230.
50. Schleiermacher, *The Christian Faith*, pp. 39 ff.
51. Schleiermacher, *Speeches on Religion*, p. 54.
52. Cf. Schleiermacher, *The Christian Faith*, p. 52.
53. Schleiermacher, *Speeches on Religion*, p. 246.
54. Cf. Schleiermacher, *The Christian Faith*, pp. 54 f.
55. *Ibid.*, p. 58.
56. *Ibid.*, p. 64.
57. *Ibid.*, p. 213.
58. Mackintosh, *op. cit.*, p. 81.
59. Spiegler, *op. cit.*, p. 69.
60. *Ibid.*, p. 70.
61. *Ibid.*, p. 190.
62. Tillich, *Perspectives on Nineteenth and Twentieth Century Protestant Theology*, p. 107.

Chapter III. *From Absolute Dependence to Ultimate Concern*
Part 2: *Tillich on the Boundary Line*

1. Paul Tillich, *Systematic Theology*, Vol. I (The University of Chicago Press, 1951), p. 42. Cf. the comment of Robert Clyde Johnson, *Authority in Protestant Theology* (The Westminster Press, 1959), p. 69: "It is perhaps due mainly to a misreading of Schleiermacher that the close kinship that exists between these two theological systems has not been widely recognized."
2. Tillich, *Systematic Theology*, Vol. I, p. 9.
3. *Ibid.*
4. *Ibid.*, p. 41.
5. Johnson, *op. cit.*, p. 69.
6. *Vide* Paul Tillich, *Theology of Culture*, R. C. Kimball, ed. (Oxford University Press, Inc., 1959), pp. 10 ff.
7. *Ibid.*, p. 10.
8. *Ibid.*, p. 22.
9. Tillich, *Systematic Theology*, Vol. I, p. 163.
10. Cf. *ibid.*, p. 171.
11. *Ibid.*
12. *Ibid.*, pp. 168–180.
13. George F. Thomas, *Religious Philosophies of the West* (Charles Scribner's Sons, 1965), p. 400.

14. Tillich, *Systematic Theology,* Vol. I, p. 189.

15. *Ibid.*

16. Thomas, *op. cit.,* p. 401.

17. Tillich, *Systematic Theology,* Vol. I, p. 191, n. 7.

18. D. E. Roberts, "Tillich's Doctrine of Man," in *The Theology of Paul Tillich,* C. W. Kegley and R. W. Bretall, eds. (The Macmillan Company, 1952), p. 120.

19. Tillich, *Systematic Theology,* Vol. I, p. 199.

20. *Ibid.,* p. 200.

21. *Ibid.,* p. 206.

22. David H. Kelsey, *The Fabric of Paul Tillich's Theology* (Yale University Press, 1967), p. 60.

23. Tillich, *Theology of Culture,* p. 25.

24. Cf. *ibid.,* pp. 23 f.

25. Tillich, *Systematic Theology,* Vol. I, p. 205.

26. *Ibid.*

27. *Ibid.,* p. 206.

28. Alexander J. McKelway, *The Systematic Theology of Paul Tillich* (John Knox Press, 1964), p. 45.

29. *Ibid.,* p. 47.

30. Tillich, *Systematic Theology,* Vol. I, p. 22.

31. *Ibid.,* p. 14.

32. *Ibid.*

33. Paul Tillich, *Systematic Theology,* Vol. III (The University of Chicago Press, 1963), p. 103.

34. Paul Tillich, *The Dynamics of Faith* (Harper & Brothers, 1957), pp. 1 ff.

35. *Ibid.,* p. 4.

36. Cf. *ibid.,* pp. 6 f.

37. *Ibid.,* p. 11.

38. *Ibid.*

39. *Ibid.,* p. 12.

40. *Ibid.,* p. 6.

41. *Ibid.,* p. 8.

42. Tillich, *Theology of Culture,* pp. 27 f.

43. Tillich, *The Dynamics of Faith,* p. 52.

44. *Ibid.,* p. 22.

45. Cf. Tillich, *Systematic Theology,* Vol. I, p. 247.

46. *Ibid.,* pp. 188 f.

47. Tillich, *The Dynamics of Faith,* p. 16.

48. Paul Tillich, *The Courage to Be* (Yale University Press, 1952), p. 172.

49. Tillich, *Systematic Theology,* Vol. I, p. 207.

50. *Ibid.*, p. 118.
51. *Ibid.*, p. 120.
52. *Vide ibid.*, p. 121.
53. *Ibid.*, p. 128.
54. *Ibid.*, p. 133.
55. *Ibid.*
56. Tillich, *Perspectives on Nineteenth and Twentieth Century Protestant Theology*, p. 107.
57. Tillich, *Systematic Theology*, Vol. I, p. 42.
58. *Vide* Tillich, *The Dynamics of Faith*, pp. 55–73.
59. Cf. *ibid.*, pp. 60 ff.
60. *Ibid.*, p. 62.
61. Paul Tillich, *Christianity and the Encounter of the World Religions* (Columbia University Press, 1963), pp. 58 f.
62. Cf. *ibid.*, pp. 57 f.
63. Cf. *ibid.*, pp. 1–25.
64. Tillich, *The Dynamics of Faith*, pp. 72 f.
65. Tillich, *Systematic Theology*, Vol. III, p. 95.
66. *Ibid.*, p. 140. Tillich sees all religions as open to the Spiritual Presence and as anticipating to varying degrees the New Being in Christ (*ibid.*, pp. 141 ff.).
67. *Ibid.*, p. 144.
68. *Ibid.*, p. 147.
69. *Ibid.*, p. 144.
70. Cf. the discussion in Kenneth Hamilton, *The System and the Gospel* (London: SCM Press, Ltd., 1963), pp. 151 ff. "Although he denies that the created world is evil, he argues—consistently with his position—that evil is the necessary accompaniment of a created world as such." (P. 151.)
71. *Ibid., passim.*
72. *Ibid.*, pp. 118 ff.
73. Tillich, *Christianity and the Encounter of the World Religions*, pp. 93 f.
74. *Ibid.*, pp. 96 f.

## Chapter IV. *From Moral Value Judgments to a Religious* A Priori

1. Cf. Philip Hefner, *Faith and the Vitalities of History* (Harper & Row, Publishers, Inc., 1966), pp. 14 ff. For Baur, consult Peter C. Hodgson, *The Formation of Historical Theology* (Harper & Row, Publishers, Inc., 1966), *passim.*
2. Hefner, *op. cit.*, p. 56.
3. Cf. Albrecht Ritschl, *The Christian Doctrine of Justification and Reconciliation*, tr. by H. R. Mackintosh and A. B. Macaulay (Edin-

burgh: T. & T. Clark, 1900), pp. 156 f. Hereafter cited as *Justification and Reconciliation.*

4. *Ibid.,* p. 196.

5. *Ibid.,* p. 195.

6. *Ibid.,* p. 198.

7. *Vide* above, pp. 46 ff.

8. Ritschl, *Justification and Reconciliation,* p. 195.

9. *Ibid.,* pp. 203 ff.

10. Tillich, *Perspectives on Nineteenth and Twentieth Century Protestant Theology,* p. 216.

11. John Baillie, *The Interpretation of Religion* (Edinburgh: T. & T. Clark, 1929), p. 285.

12. Ritschl, *Justification and Reconciliation,* p. 204.

13. Note especially the thought of R. G. Collingwood and Michael Polanyi. This is dealt with at some length in Eric C. Rust, *Towards a Theological Understanding of History* (Oxford University Press, Inc., 1963), and Eric C. Rust, *Science and Faith: Towards a Theological Understanding of Nature* (Oxford University Press, 1967).

14. Baillie, *op. cit.,* p. 285.

15. Ritschl, *Justification and Reconciliation,* p. 222.

16. *Ibid.,* p. 205.

17. Baillie, *op. cit.,* p. 287.

18. Mackintosh, *op. cit.,* p. 154.

19. Ritschl, *Justification and Reconciliation,* p. 199.

20. *Ibid.,* p. 205.

21. *Ibid.,* p. 212.

22. *Ibid.,* p. 219.

23. Mackintosh, *op. cit.,* pp. 150 f.

24. Ritschl, *Justification and Reconciliation,* p. 202.

25. *Ibid.,* p. 201.

26. Cf. *ibid.,* p. 28.

27. *Ibid.,* p. 29 (italics mine).

28. Gösta Hök, *Die elliptische Theologie Albrecht Ritschls* (Uppsala: A.-B. Lundequistska Bokhandeln, 1942), pp. 234 ff.

29. *Ibid.,* p. 235.

30. Cf. *ibid.*

31. Cf. Ritschl, *Justification and Reconciliation,* p. 205.

32. Cf. Hök, *op. cit.,* p. 236.

33. Ritschl, *Justification and Reconciliation,* p. 195.

34. *Ibid.,* p. 206.

35. I am indebted to my friend and colleague Dr. David Mueller for referring me to Fabricius' study in which he shows that the influence of Kaftan had led Ritschl to modify descriptions of religion that

referred to "dependence on God" and to bring out his real emphasis on the free activity of both poles in the God and man relationship—*vide* Cajus Fabricius, *Die Entwicklung in Albrecht Ritschls Theologie von 1874 bis 1889* (Tübingen: J. C. B. Mohr, 1909).

36. Cf. Fabricius, *op. cit.*, p. 16.

37. Hök, *op. cit.*, p. 444.

38. Albrecht Ritschl, *Instruction in the Christian Religion*, tr. by Alice M. Swing in *The Theology of Albrecht Ritschl*, by Albert Swing (Longmans, Green & Co., Inc., 1901), p. 171.

39. Ritschl, *Justification and Reconciliation*, p. 197.

40. *Ibid.*, p. 13.

41. Cf. *ibid.*, pp. 11 f.

42. Hefner, *op. cit.*, especially pp. 88 ff.

43. Ritschl, *Justification and Reconciliation*, p. 398.

44. Cf. *ibid.*, p. 386.

45. *Ibid.*, p. 387.

46. *Ibid.*, p. 398.

47. *Ibid.*, p. xi (Ch. VI, §48).

48. *Ibid.*, p. 389.

49. *Ibid.*, p. 452.

50. Cf. *ibid.*, p. 469.

51. *Ibid.*, p. 280.

52. *Ibid.*, p. 381.

53. *Ibid.*, p. 293.

54. Rudolf Otto, *The Idea of the Holy*, tr. by J. W. Harvey (London: Oxford University Press, 1931), p. 112.

55. It is a matter of interpretation, as we have seen, whether this is fair to Schleiermacher. The description "absolute" would seem to imply a qualitative difference, not a merely quantitative.

56. Otto, *op. cit.*, p. 10.

57. Self-consciousness may also, as Augustine saw, involve the awareness of the Other. Otto does not find this in Schleiermacher, but we believe it to be present in Schleiermacher's thought as a kind of preconceptual cognition.

58. R. R. Marett, *The Threshold of Religion* (London: Methuen & Co., Ltd., 1914).

59. *Ibid.*, p. 13.

60. Otto, *op. cit.*, p. 31.

61. *Ibid.*, p. 119.

62. *Ibid.*, p. 148.

63. *Ibid.*, p. 149.

64. *Ibid.*, p. 151.

65. *Ibid.*

66. *Ibid.*, p. 140.

67. *Ibid.*, p. 117.

68. Herbert J. Paton, *The Modern Predicament* (London: George Allen & Unwin, Ltd., 1955), pp. 137–142.

69. *Ibid.*, p. 139.

70. *Ibid.*, pp. 140 f.

71. *Ibid.*, pp. 140 f.

72. H. D. Lewis, *Philosophy of Religion* (London: The English Universities Press, Ltd., 1968), pp. 218 ff.

73. *Ibid.*, p. 219.

74. Charles A. Campbell, *On Selfhood and Godhood* (London: George Allen & Unwin, Ltd., 1957), pp. 338 ff.

75. *Ibid.*, pp. 338 f.

76. *Ibid.*, p. 339.

77. Lewis, *op. cit.*, p. 220.

78. J. Oman, *Natural and Supernatural* (Cambridge: Cambridge University Press, 1931), pp. 58 ff.

79. *Ibid.*, p. 61.

80. *Ibid.*, p. 65.

81. Otto, *op. cit.*, p. 31.

82. Campbell, *op. cit.*, p. 343.

83. *Ibid.*, p. 343.

84. Oman, *op. cit.*, p. 61.

85. *Ibid.*, p. 72.

86. *Ibid.*, p. 69.

Chapter V. *Projection, Relativism, Rejection*

1. Ludwig Feuerbach, *The Essence of Christianity*, tr. by George Eliot (Harper & Brothers, 1957), p. xxxiii.

2. *Ibid.*, p. xxxv.

3. James D. Collins, *God in Modern Philosophy* (Henry Regnery Company, 1959), p. 241.

4. Ludwig Feuerbach, *Vorläufige Thesen zur Reform der Philosophie* (Kritiken, 244), quoted in Collins, *op. cit.*, p. 241.

5. Feuerbach, *The Essence of Christianity*, p. xxxv.

6. *Ibid.*, p. 5.

7. *Ibid.*, p. xxxviii.

8. *Ibid.*, p. 5.

9. *Ibid.*, p. 6.

10. *Ibid.*

11. *Ibid.*

12. *Ibid.*, p. xxxv.

13. *Ibid.*, p. 276.

14. *Ibid.*, p. 12.
15. *Ibid.*, p. 14.
16. *Ibid.*, p. 174.
17. *Ibid.*
18. *Ibid.*, p. 14.
19. *Ibid.*, p. 17.
20. *Ibid.*
21. *Ibid.*, pp. 19 f.
22. *Ibid.*, p. 20.
23. *Ibid.*, p. 26.
24. *Ibid.*, p. 29.
25. *Ibid.*, p. 48.
26. *Ibid.*, p. 53.
27. *Ibid.*, p. 268.
28. *Ibid.*, p. 271.
29. Cf. my discussion of this in Rust, *Science and Faith: Towards a Theological Understanding of Nature*, pp. 239 ff.
30. J. Baillie, *op. cit.*, p. 163.
31. *Vide* especially Adolf von Harnack, *What Is Christianity?*, tr. by T. B. Saunders (Harper & Brothers, 1957), *passim*.
32. Johannes Weiss, *Die Predigt Jesu vom Reiche Gottes* (Göttingen: 1909. 2d edition).
33. Albert Schweitzer, *The Quest of the Historical Jesus*, tr. by W. Montgomery (London: Adam and Charles Black, Ltd., 1945).
34. Hermann Günkel, *Die Wirkung des Heiligen Geistes nach den populären Anschauungen der apostolischen Zeit und nach der Lehre des Paulus* (3d edition, 1909).
35. Nathan Söderblom, *The Living God* (London: Oxford University Press, 1939).
36. Ernst Troeltsch, *Protestantism and Progress*, tr. by W. Montgomery (Beacon Press, Inc., 1958).
37. *Ibid.*, p. 41.
38. *Ibid.*, p. 85.
39. *Ibid.*, pp. 85 f.
40. Ernst Troeltsch, *Die Absolutheit des Christentums und die Religionsgeschichte* (Tübingen: J. C. B. Mohr, 1929). For an excellent discussion of Troeltsch's views on history, the reader should consult Thomas W. Ogletree, *Christian Faith and History* (Abingdon Press, 1965), pp. 32 ff.
41. Troeltsch discusses this at length in Troeltsch, *Die Absolutheit des Christentums und die Religionsgeschichte*.
42. From Troeltsch, *"Offenbarung,"* in *Die Religion in Geschichte und Gegenwart* (1st ed.), quoted in Mackintosh, *op. cit.*, p. 195.
43. William James, *Varieties of Religious Experience* (London:

Longmans, Green & Co., Inc., 1917).

44. There is a full consideration of Troeltsch's views on this in Baillie, *op. cit.*, pp. 238 ff. I have relied on it heavily.

45. Ernst Troeltsch, *Psychologie und Erkenntnistheorie in der Religionswissenschaft* (1905), p. 36. Quoted in Baillie, *op. cit.*, pp. 241 f.

46. *Vide* above, Ch. I, n. 5.

47. Ogletree, *Christian Faith and History*, p. 41.

48. James Luther Adams, "Ernst Troeltsch as Analyst of Religion," *Journal for the Scientific Study of Religion*, Vol. I, No. 1 (1961), p. 101, cited in Ogletree, *Christian Faith and History*, p. 41, n. 29.

49. Tillich, *Perspective on Nineteenth and Twentieth Century Protestant Theology*, p. 231.

50. Ogletree, *Christian Faith and History*, p. 41. The discussion on this issue is clear and incisive in pp. 41 f.

51. Ernst Troeltsch, *Gesammelte Schriften*, Vol. III (Tübingen: J. C. B. Mohr, 1922), p. 167.

52. *Vide ibid.*, p. 179.

53. *Vide ibid.*, p. 181.

54. *Ibid.*, p. 42.

55. Ernst Troeltsch, *Christian Thought: Its History and Application*, F. von Hügel, ed. (Living Age Books, 1957), p. 61. Hereafter cited as *Christian Thought*.

56. Troeltsch, *Die Absolutheit des Christentums und die Religionsgeschichte*.

57. Mackintosh, *op. cit.*, p. 213.

58. Troeltsch, *Christian Thought*, p. 50.

59. *Ibid.*, pp. 44 f.

60. *Ibid.*, p. 45.

61. *Ibid.*, p. 55.

62. *Ibid.*, p. 56.

63. *Ibid.*, p. 62.

64. Karl Barth, *Church Dogmatics* I, 2, tr. by G. T. Thomson and Harold Knight (Edinburgh: T. & T. Clark, 1956), p. 302.

65. *Ibid.*, p. 280.

66. *Ibid.*, p. 303.

67. *Ibid.*, p. 301.

68. Karl Barth, *The Knowledge of God and the Service of God*, tr. by J. L. M. Haire and Ian Henderson (London: Hodder & Stoughton, Ltd., 1938), p. 6.

69. Karl Barth, *Church Dogmatics* II, 1, tr. by T. H. Parker, *et al.* (Edinburgh: T. & T. Clark, 1957), p. 135.

70. *Ibid.*

71. Cf. *ibid.*, p. 86.

72. Barth, *Church Dogmatics* I, 2, p. 239.

73. Cf. *ibid.*, p. 243.
74. *Ibid.*
75. *Ibid.*, p. 258.
76. *Ibid.*, pp. 281 f.
77. *Ibid.*, p. 281.
78. *Ibid.*, p. 282.
79. See above, pp. 77 ff., 88 f.
80. Barth, *Church Dogmatics* I, 2, pp. 294 ff.
81. *Ibid.*, p. 297.
82. *Ibid.*, p. 299.
83. *Ibid.*, pp. 299 f.
84. *Ibid.*, p. 302.
85. *Ibid.*, p. 308.
86. *Ibid.*, p. 309.
87. *Ibid.*, p. 321.
88. *Ibid.*, p. 329.
89. *Ibid.*, p. 343.

90. John Calvin, *Institutes of the Christian Religion,* tr. by Henry Beveridge (London: James Clarke & Co., Ltd., 1949), p. 44 (Book I, Chap. III, para. 2).

91. *Ibid.*, p. 51 (Book I, Ch. V, para. 1).

92. Karl Barth, *The Humanity of God,* tr. by John Newton Thomas and Thomas Wieser (John Knox Press, 1960).

93. Emil Brunner, *The Christian Doctrine of God,* tr. by O. Wyon (The Westminster Press, 1950), pp. 346 ff.

94. Hendrik Kraemer, *The Christian Message in a Non-Christian World* (London: Edinburgh House Press, 1938), p. 122.

95. Hendrik Kraemer, *Religion and the Christian Faith* (London: Lutterworth Press, 1956), p. 334.

96. *Ibid.*, p. 349.
97. *Ibid.*, p. 193.
98. *Ibid.*, p. 359.
99. *Ibid.*, p. 350.
100. *Ibid.*, p. 359.

Chapter VI. *Christian Faith and Religion—*
*The Contemporary Crisis*

1. R. G. Collingwood, *Faith and Reason,* L. Rubenoff, ed. (Quadrangle Books, Inc., 1967), pp. 43–58.

2. *Ibid.*, p. 55.

3. Ninian Smart, "Revelation, Reason and Religions," in Ian Ramsey, ed., *Prospect for Metaphysics* (London: George Allen & Unwin, Ltd., 1961), p. 84.

4. Ninian Smart, *Reasons and Faiths* (London: Routledge & Kegan Paul, Ltd., 1958).

5. Essay cited in n. 3, above, in Ramsey, ed., *op. cit.*, p. 92.

6. Campbell, *op. cit.*, pp. 231 ff. gives a valuable analysis along such lines.

7. Smart, "Revelation, Reason and Religions," in Ramsey, ed., *op. cit.*, p. 83.

8. Bonhoeffer, *Letters and Papers from Prison*, p. 162.

9. *Ibid.*, p. 163.

10. Paul van Buren, *The Secular Meaning of the Gospel* (The Macmillan Company, 1963); William Hamilton, *The New Essence of Christianity* (Association Press, 1961); Thomas J. J. Altizer and William Hamilton, *Radical Theology and the Death of God* (The Bobbs-Merrill Company, Inc., 1966); Thomas J. J. Altizer, *The Gospel of Christian Atheism* (The Westminster Press, 1966).

11. From Nietzsche, "The Gay Science," 125, in *The Portable Nietzsche*, tr. by Walter Kaufmann (The Viking Press, Inc., 1954), p. 95.

12. From Nietzsche, "The Antichrist," 47, in *The Portable Nietzsche*, p. 627.

13. Van Buren, *op. cit.*

14. *Ibid.*, p. 128.

15. W. Hamilton, *The New Essence of Christianity*. Contributions to T. J. J. Altizer and W. Hamilton, *Radical Theology and the Death of God*.

16. W. Hamilton, *The New Essence of Christianity*, p. 69.

17. *Ibid.*, p. 59.

18. Altizer and W. Hamilton, *Radical Theology and the Death of God*, pp. 87 ff.

19. *Ibid.*, p. 88.

20. *Ibid.*

21. *Ibid.*, p. 92.

22. K. Hamilton, "Who Is the God That Can Die?" in *The Reformed Journal*, Vol. XVI (December, 1966), p. 12.

23. Ronald Gregor Smith, *Secular Christianity* (Harper & Row, Publishers, Inc., 1966), p. 167.

24. W. Hamilton, "The Shape of Radical Theology," in *Christian Century*, Vol. LXXXII (October 6, 1965), p. 1221.

25. Altizer and W. Hamilton, *Radical Theology and the Death of God*, pp. 48 f.

26. Thomas W. Ogletree, *The Death of God Controversy* (Abingdon Press, 1966), p. 43.

27. Bonhoeffer, *Letters and Papers from Prison*, pp. 219 f., 237 f.

28. Altizer, *The Gospel of Christian Atheism*, p. 103.

29. *Ibid.*

30. *Ibid.*, p. 104.

31. G. W. F. Hegel, *The Phenomenology of Mind*, tr. by J. Baillie (The Macmillan Company, 1931), p. 808. Cf. this author's discussion of Hegel in Rust, *Towards a Theological Understanding of History*, pp. 55 ff.

32. Altizer, *The Gospel of Christian Atheism*, p. 151.

33. *Vide* Altizer's "Word and History," in Altizer and W. Hamilton, *Radical Theology and the Death of God*, pp. 121 ff.

34. Altizer, *The Gospel of Christian Atheism*, p. 89.

35. W. C. Smith, *op. cit.*, p. 24.

36. *Ibid.*, pp. 20 f.

37. *Ibid.*, p. 22.

38. Arend Th. van Leeuwen, *Christianity in World History*, tr. by H. H. Hoskins (Charles Scribner's Sons, 1964), *passim*.

39. *Ibid.*, p. 173.

40. Friedrich Gogarten, *The Reality of Faith*, tr. by Carl Michalson, *et al.* (The Westminster Press, 1959), p. 54.

41. Lesslie Newbigin, *Honest Religion for Secular Man* (The Westminster Press, 1966), p. 9.

42. *Ibid.*, p. 10.

43. Van Leeuwen, *op. cit.*, p. 421.

44. *Ibid.*

45. Harvey Cox, *The Secular City* (The Macmillan Company, 1965), p. 262.

46. *Ibid.*, pp. 262 ff.

47. *Ibid.*, p. 265.

48. Van Leeuwen, *op. cit.*, p. 419.

49. John Macquarrie, *God and Secularity* (The Westminster Press, 1967), p. 58.

50. R. G. Smith, *op. cit.*, p. 209.

51. Arnold J. Toynbee, *An Historian's Approach to Religion* (Oxford University Press, Inc., 1956); A. J. Toynbee, *Christianity Among the Religions of the World* (Charles Scribner's Sons, 1957). I have discussed Toynbee's thought at some length in Rust, *Towards a Theological Understanding of History*, pp. 92 ff., and I have used much of this material in the present discussion.

52. Arnold J. Toynbee, *Civilization on Trial* (Meridian Books, Inc., 1958), p. 89.

53. *Vide* Arnold J. Toynbee, *Study of History*, Vol. I (London: Oxford University Press, 1935), pp. 271–299.

54. *Vide* Toynbee, *Civilization on Trial*, p. 206.

55. *Ibid.*, p. 205.

56. Toynbee summarizes his position in Arnold J. Toynbee, "The Christian Understanding of History," in D. M. MacKinnon, ed., *Christian Faith and Communist Faith* (London: Macmillan & Co., Ltd., 1953), pp. 194 ff.

57. *Ibid.,* p. 197.

58. Toynbee, *An Historian's Approach to Religion,* p. 284.

59. *Ibid.,* p. 285.

60. *Ibid.,* p. 298.

61. *Vide* Toynbee, *Christianity Among the Religions of the World.*

62. *Ibid.,* p. 103.

63. *Ibid.,* p. 104.

64. Arnold J. Toynbee, *A Study of History: Abridgment in One Volume,* D. C. Sommervell, ed. (Oxford University Press, Inc., 1960), p. 660.

65. *Vide* Rust, *Towards a Theological Understanding of History,* pp. 31 f.

66. H. H. Farmer, *Revelation and Religion* (Harper & Brothers, 1954).

67. *Ibid.,* p. 25.

68. *Ibid.,* p. 26.

69. R. G. Collingwood, *An Essay on Philosophical Method,* Sections II & III (Oxford: Clarendon Press, 1933).

70. Farmer, *op. cit.,* p. 33.

71. Cf. Collingwood, *An Essay on Philosophical Method,* p. 61.

72. Farmer, *op. cit.,* p. 35.

73. See Chapter III, pp. 73 ff., 83 f.

74. Paul Tillich, "The Significance of the History of Religions," in Jerald C. Brauer, ed., *The Future of Religions* (Harper & Row, Publishers, Inc., 1966), pp. 80–94.

75. *Ibid.,* p. 88.

76. *Ibid.*

77. *Ibid.,* p. 90.

Chapter VII. *The Christian Religion in a Revolutionary Age*

1. Bonhoeffer, *Letters and Papers from Prison,* p. 196.

2. *Ibid., vide* p. 174.

3. *Vide ibid.,* p. 119.

4. *Vide ibid.,* pp. 162 f.

5. *Ibid.,* p. 167.

6. *Ibid., vide* pp. 213 f.

7. *Vide* Rust, *Science and Faith: Towards a Theological Understanding of Nature,* pp. 133 ff.; Rust, *Evolutionary Philosophies and Contemporary Theology,* pp. 219 ff.

8. "God lets himself be pushed out of the world on to the cross."

Bonhoeffer, *Letters and Papers from Prison*, p. 196.

9. Cf. Rust, *Towards a Theological Understanding of History*, pp. 144 ff.

10. Bonhoeffer, *Letters and Papers from Prison, vide* p. 197.

11. *Ibid.*, pp. 213 f.

12. Paul Tillich, *The Protestant Era* (The University of Chicago Press, 1946), pp. 102 f.

13. Neville Clark, *An Approach to the Theology of the Sacraments* (Alec R. Allenson, Inc., 1956), p. 75.

14. Hans Jürgen Schultz, *Conversion to the World* (Charles Scribner's Sons, 1967).

15. *Ibid.*, p. 43.

16. *Ibid.*, p. 118.

17. *Ibid.*, p. 88.

18. *Ibid.*, p. 87.

19. *Ibid.*, p. 106.

20. *Ibid.*, p. 88.

21. Bonhoeffer, *Letters and Papers from Prison*, p. 211.

22. William N. Pittenger, *The Word Incarnate* (Harper & Brothers, 1959).

23. Daniel Day Williams, *God's Grace and Man's Hope* (Harper & Brothers, 1949).

24. This thinker has been discussed at length in Rust, *Evolutionary Philosophies and Contemporary Theology*, Ch. VI, where full bibliographical information on his own writings and on those of his interpreters will be found in the notes.

25. Jürgen Moltmann, *The Theology of Hope*, tr. by James Leitch (Harper & Row, Publishers, Inc., 1967).

26. Wolfhart Pannenberg, *Jesus—God and Man*, tr. by L. L. Wilkins and D. A. Priebe (The Westminster Press, 1968).

27. Moltmann, *op. cit.*, p. 179.

28. *Ibid.*, p. 180.

29. *Ibid.*, p. 194.

30. *Ibid.*, p. 196.

31. *Ibid.*

32. *Ibid.*, p. 326.

33. *Ibid.*, p. 329.

34. *Ibid.*, p. 330.

35. Cf. the stimulating discussion by Edward C. F. A. Schillebeeckx, *God: The Future of Man*, tr. by N. D. Smith (Sheed & Ward, Inc., 1968), especially pp. 167 ff.

36. Cf. Smart, *Reasons and Faiths, passim*.

# INDEX